hawker fare

hawker fare

STORIES & RECIPES FROM A REFUGEE CHEF'S ISAN THAI & LAO ROOTS

JAMES SYHABOUT

WITH JOHN BIRDSALL

FOREWORD BY ROY CHOI
PREFACE BY ANTHONY BOURDAIN
PHOTOGRAPHY BY ERIC WOLFINGER

AN ANTHONY BOURDAIN BOOK

ecco

An Imprint of HarperCollinsPublishers

FIRST EDITION

Designed by Suet Yee Chong
Photography by Eric Wolfinger

Library of Congress Cataloging-in-Publication Data has been applied for.

ISBN 978-0-06-265609-4

18 19 20 21 22   LSC   10 9 8 7 6 5 4 3 2 1

TO MY MOTHER,
FOR HER LOVE AND STRENGTH
IN RAISING ME WELL,
AND FOR GIVING IT HER ALL.

TO STACY, MY LOVING WIFE,
FOR HER UNCONDITIONAL
SUPPORT ON THIS ONGOING
JOURNEY TO FIND MYSELF.

TO EMMA AND MAGNUS,
MY TWO LOVELY CHILDREN,
WHO I HOPE WILL READ AND COOK
FROM THIS BOOK SOMEDAY.
EMBRACE IT, CHERISH IT,
CELEBRATE IT-LET IT BE YOURS.
LOVE YOU ALWAYS.

CONTENTS

FOREWORD BY ROY CHOI IX
PREFACE BY ANTHONY BOURDAIN XI
INTRODUCTION XV

ONE: MY STORY

1. WHAT'S LAO FOOD? 3
2. THE LAOTIAN GHETTO 11
3. THE PHAT THAI GRIND 25
4. A COOL, STRANGE PLACE CALLED HOME 35
5. HOMESICK IN ROSES 51
6. MY OWN PRIVATE TRIBE CALLED QUEST 63
7. STALKING UNICORNS IN THAILAND 73
8. SAME SAME BUT DIFFERENT 87
9. FAREWELL FUNK: AN EPILOGUE 101
10. HOW TO USE THE RECIPES IN THIS BOOK 105

TWO: RECIPES

11. SNACKS 111
12. TUM SOM 145
13. NOODLES AND SOUPS 155
14. LAAP AND GOI 197
15. MEATS 231
16. AWS AND MOKS 247
17. SAUCES AND CONDIMENTS 275
18. DESSERTS 309

ACKNOWLEDGMENTS 324
THE LAO AND ISAN PANTRY 328
CONVERSION SCALE 340
INDEX 343

FOREWORD

I started writing this just after midnight on that crease between the old and the new year, that time between twelve and six a.m. when it's not really one thing or another, not last year or fully the new one. It's a special time, a moment when it's everything and not what you think it is, all together at the same time. Fertile.

James reminds me of that time between the old and the new.

It was a dark and chilly night in New York City in 2010 when I first met James. We were both attending a dinner held by Dana Cowin and Kate Krader for *Food & Wine*'s Best New Chefs at Scott Conant's restaurant in Manhattan, right across from the *Village Voice* building.

It was an awkward time for me, coming straight from the streets, serving tacos, driving far away as I could from my past life as a chef, only to find myself right back in the middle of that world, closer to the sun than I had ever been. Because of that awkwardness, I was searching for someone who looked just as out of place as me, and it was James.

Maybe it was because he was Asian, maybe it was just a vibe, but I was like, *This dude right here imma be friends with*.

But this is where the complexity of James started to unfold for me. Of all of us, he actually was more in place than out. As a chef he'd done the trifecta of The Fat Duck, El Bulli, and Mugaritz, like a climber tackling the three major mountain peaks of the world. But when I said *Whattup*, he was like a homie I had known my whole life.

We spent the weekend together cooking at huge events, being the center of attention, taking pictures, feeling weird as shit, and cracking jokes the whole time, like we were kicking it on our bikes in a park.

I got to know him over the next couple years and every time I thought I got closer to knowing James, I found out so much more than I thought I knew.

To me he was a Thai kid who grew up in the 510 who was extremely meticulous, and stoic. But then I find out he's a Lao, a keen businessman who cooks really soulful food, and funny as heck.

He's also the dude that whenever you call him, he's always available. Multiple restaurants, Michelin stars, family man, always changing menus, yet always has time to pick you up in his pickup and just hang.

That's James.

I write this personal anecdote of my relationship with him because, as you read his book, I only hope you can become friends with him as I have. I hope you find a surprise and a smile and a revelation at every turn of a page, as I have in him as a person.

Because, like the crease between the old and the new year, James is a suspension bridge between form and flow, meticulous and laid back, Thailand and Laos, chef and friend, awkwardness and confidence, technique and soul. He's not one thing or another, and he's probably going to be someone completely different than you thought after you read this book.

He's a man of surprises.

And, like not writing the Commis cookbook first but going to find the food of his heritage, the title of this book should be: *Surprise!*

Ha.

Roy Choi

PREFACE

The Mekong is my favorite river on earth.

For most of its 2,700 miles, it's impossible to stand on its banks and not know that you're in Southeast Asia. Something I enjoy knowing very much indeed.

But up until about ten years ago, I had a shameful blank spot on my own map of the Mekong communities. And as someone who travels for a living, a blank spot was more than shameful; it was downright unprofessional.

So I went to Laos.

What I saw there was unsurpassingly beautiful—and strikingly painful. I won't and can't do justice here in this short preface to the history of America and Laos, but suffice it to say for now that there's a reason you'll see so many rusted bomb shells being put to creative use in the streets of the Laotian capital, Vientiane.

That is, if you ever go to Laos. Despite its recent reputation as an exotic destination well off the beaten path, few Americans will ever go. Few will ever even think about the place.

Which is why Hawker Fare is one of the most important restaurants I've ever had the pleasure of visiting. And, thanks to James Syhabout, it also serves some of the most delicious papaya salad and fried chicken I've ever had.

With *Hawker Fare,* Syhabout has done more than any other person in the world to get the word out about this unfairly, unnecessarily secret country and cuisine, and he's done so with the most perfect invitation ever invented by mankind: spicy, fishy, MSG-y bowls of goodness. And BBQ.

This book will make you a better person. That's before you even try any of the recipes.

Anthony Bourdain

INTRODUCTION

We all wear blue aprons in my kitchen because
we're all commis, we're all still learning.

MARCO PIERRE WHITE, *WHITE HEAT*

This is a book about forgetting everything you know,
about stepping into the void and trusting you'll land
in a better place than you started. I know it's possible,
because I did exactly that.

I'm a first-generation Asian American chef, a refugee
to the country that's long been my own. I was born in Isan,
Thailand's northeast region, in the village of my mother's
ancestors. My dad is from Paksé, Laos. When I was two
years old we came to the United States as Lao refugees.
We found ourselves in Oakland, California, with a bunch
of other refugee families. Lao and Isan food are closely
related—both developed in the Lan Xang Kingdom, a
collection of ethnic peoples who dominated Southeast Asia
long before the French colonists redrew the borders.

When I say I'm Lao Isan and came to the States as a
refugee in the spring of 1981, people who know me only as
the fine-dining chef of Commis look at me like I'm heaving
the deepest curveball. The truth is I never started out
being James Syhabout: I was born Somchith, a crying, two-
kilo lump of prematurity, all tangled up with IV tubes in a
hospital incubator in northeast Thailand.

Your name is the oldest and most basic thing about
you—it's weird when it just kind of falls away, and for a
reason as random as the Vietnam War. The ripples of war
can leave your whole family floating in the aftermath,

washed up on a block in a city that ends up making you who you are. But the place you were born never really leaves you—even when you try to forget it.

I heard somewhere that war is God's way of teaching Americans geography. For us, the newly minted Syhabouts, the end of the Vietnam War and the Secret War in Laos dumped more than a geography lesson on the United States: It delivered us, lugging memories of foods most Americans had never tasted—things people in my parents' generation figured most Americans would never want. But they were delicious. They were the foods that made me. After thirty-five years, I'm finally ready to unpack them.

I started writing a Lao Isan cookbook because I needed to learn something deeper about my own heritage. I wanted to honor my Asian culture and my immigrant parents, who raised me in a city that can be challenging for poor kids.

You could say I'm making up for lost time. When I left high school, I turned my back on the culture I grew up in. I went to culinary school, then worked and trained in Europe to become a fine-dining chef. I ran away from my past. Being Lao embarrassed me. I felt ashamed. I still loved the Isan and Lao food my mom cooked—loved it deeply—but I kicked it to the curb. This book is a sort of apology letter, an attempt at reconciling my past in many ways. Food is the main vehicle of this personal journey. I had to teach myself this cuisine, stitch it back together from memory, trips to the motherland, and many hours on the phone with my mom. I'll never stop learning. As Marco Pierre White once wrote, a chef is always a *commis*, a rookie, the cook at the lowest level in the kitchen.

The recipes in this book are not 100 percent Thai, Isan, or Lao, though the book has deep roots in those cuisines. Most are interpretations of my mother's ingenuity, based on ingredients she had to work with in California in the 1980s. Together, my story and the recipes from it are a retroactive log of my upbringing in California.

But I didn't write this book to be a personal snapshot album. I tried to make it a book that, in a really deep way, explores the idea of what it means to cook well. Not the textbook definition, where it's all about mechanics, but learning to cook by understanding nuance and trusting your own taste.

So yeah, these dishes are all pretty much

an homage to my past, and vehicles for reconnecting me to my ancestors' culture. But I also want them to be living and changing, responding to the reality of wherever you're cooking them. In that sense, this is the furthest thing from an authentically Thai or Lao book. It's an authentically American book, and my story is 100 percent American.

My larger goal for this book is to build an audience for Lao and Isan food. Some of it will be familiar (if you've ever eaten green papaya salad or *laap* at a Thai restaurant, you've had Lao food). You'll also meet some unfamiliar flavors. I haven't changed any of these recipes for Western palates, because that would only disrespect the food I'm trying to honor.

The biggest obstacle to cooking these dishes isn't technique (they're all simple), it's getting accustomed to new flavors and aromas. The palate isn't as sweet as the food in most American Thai restaurants. The Lao and Isan palate favors bitterness, heat, and the salty, savory influence of fermented fish pastes and sauces.

It also calls for eating with your hands—I mean, if sticky rice is going to be the basis of your diet, you're going to have to feel comfortable picking it up with your fingers. Otherwise it's like

going to an Ethiopian restaurant and trying to eat *injera* with a fork and knife.

Throughout this project I've been inspired by my chef peers, including Corey Lee, David Chang, and Roy Choi. They have their own stories of growing up in Asian households, and the challenge of pursuing cooking against the wishes of their parents. We've all heard something like it: "I didn't bring you to America to become a cook! You're going to become an accountant, a lawyer, a doctor, or a stockbroker."

Each of us lucky enough to have a choice has a duty to pursue work that's self-fulfilling. This is my way of saying thank you to my parents for coming to America and raising a cook, and bequeathing as a gift such an incredibly beautiful and delicious cuisine.

ONE

MY
STORY

WHAT'S LAO FOOD?

People ask me all the time. I answer, "It's laap, sticky rice, and papaya salad." Some say, "That sounds Thai!" and of course it does. The answer to what is Lao and what is Thai is simple, but also complicated—it has to do with colonialism, politics, war, and migration. In the States we feel like we know Thailand: It's part of the landscape of take-out menus we stuff in a drawer or click through on Yelp. But Laos . . . it's a mystery.

Geographically, Laos is a small, landlocked nation, put away from the eyes of the world. It's poor, it's communist, it's intensely Buddhist: three things that don't exactly play well in America. Unlike Thailand and Vietnam, its neighbors, Laos is rarely represented in American popular culture or mentioned on the news. Just like the U.S. campaign to drop a shitload of bombs on Laos during the Vietnam War was called the Secret War, Laos is kind of the secret country.

I think awareness of Lao culture also suffers from the lack of confidence of Lao Americans like me. Because for so long, when you tell people you're Lao they're like, "What?" When people ask that question, or they see your last name and try to pronounce it—honestly, you get embarrassed. Your self-esteem stumbles and you shy up, pulling your head back into your shell like a turtle.

It's just easier to say you're Thai.

Say you're a Lao refugee to America in 1981, the year my family and I arrived. Maybe, like my mom, you get a job in a Thai restaurant where all the other cooks are Lao, also refugees. And remember it's the '80s, when cool Americans in cities are starting to get excited about Thai food, get their first taste of curries and phat Thai and bright yellow chicken satay skewers, and start losing their shit over all of it.

Then say—again, like my mom—you finally save enough to open your own restaurant, and it's in a good spot out in the suburbs, way out from where most Lao people live. What do you do? Do you take a chance on Americans looking up Lao food in the Yellow Pages and finding you? Or do you call it Thai? Cook those sugary curries and orange phat Thais, and maybe mix in a few Lao dishes, tame versions of laap and papaya salad, and say it's all Thai?

Where it gets complicated, is that even though my mom is Lao by language and culture, she's technically Thai. I was born in the same tiny village in Thailand she was born into, in the northeast region known as Isan, just across the Mekong River from Laos.

And since way, way back, starting in the 1800s, Isan people have piled into Bangkok to find jobs as maids, taxi drivers, construction workers, cooks. It's like the movement of people from Mexico to the United States: Spanish is spoken everywhere here, and there's a ton of Mexican food, and all those tacos and enchiladas have crossed over to become American.

In Bangkok almost all service workers speak Lao, and the foods of Laos and Lao Isan are everywhere. They've crossed over. Naturalized as Thai. So yeah, you could say laap, sticky rice, papaya salad, and *gai yang* have become Thai but they're Lao by birth, conceived deep in the

Lan Xang Kingdom—Land of a Million Elephants—out of the Laotian landscape of river and jungle.

And while there are mirrors between Thai and Lao cuisines, there are also walls—as a popular Lao saying goes, "same same but different." The sweet-sour flavor combination is common all over Southeast Asia, but not in Laos. Lao cuisine favors umami. The flavors are salty, bitter, and herbaceous, fragrant with fresh dill and heavy with spice. A papaya salad in Luang Prabang tastes very different from one in Bangkok.

And Lao food tends to be focused inward; it's far less public than Thai food. You rarely eat in restaurants in Laos—if you're not eating at home, you're slurping noodles on the street. Restaurants are fairly new venues in Laos. It's a true farm-to-table culture.

Here in the States, the Laotian community isn't large enough to pique much interest from outside. Contrast that with the Korean community, which is large enough to spawn Koreatowns, each with multiple restaurants and bars. People beyond the community "discovered" Korean food. Diners started to educate themselves. The press took notice. The community of businesses expanded. A once isolated cuisine became mainstream.

But there are no neighborhoods in American cities called "Laotown," no commercial strips known as "Little Vientiane."

When a cuisine stays in its local expat community, its value stays depressed. Say a city has one, maybe two Lao restaurants. They exist to service the community, cook for mostly blue-collar

HOW LAO MORPHED INTO THAI

Vinya Sysamouth is one of the founders of the Center for Lao Studies in San Francisco. The nonprofit seeks to promote scholarship, and is engaged in an ambitious oral history project to record the stories of Lao refugees, displaced in the wake of the Vietnam War and the U.S. Secret War in Laos. One day in his crowded, book-lined office just south of San Francisco, he untangled Lao and Isan history, language, and culture for me.

James: I'm trying to get clear on the difference between *Lao*, *Laos*, and *Laotian*.

Vinya: Let's set a definition between *Lao* and *Laotian*. So *Laotian* came from the French, and U.S. speakers borrowed it. It means the citizens of Laos, no matter what ethnic group they're in. You're Laotian, that's your passport. But Lao is ethnicity specific. When you say you speak Laotian, that's not correct because you don't speak all sixty-four different groups of languages from Laos. There are all these various ethnic groups in the region and we all belong to the same stock—we're like brothers and sisters. Laos is ethnically diverse for a small country. What we call Laos was actually three different kingdoms, semiautonomous of each other. When the French came they consolidated those kingdoms—that's why they called them the Laos with an *s*: three different kingdoms, consolidated into one French colony.

J: And the people from northeast Thailand—the Isan region that I'm from—you call them Lao Isan?

V: I call them Lao Isan because they are ethnic Lao living in Thailand. The issue with Isan was it was always part of the Lan Xang Kingdom. When the French came in, they didn't want anything to do with Isan because there was

nothing there for them: It was just dry land, it didn't benefit them to conquer that part. And the Siamese (Thailand at that time was still called Siam) were claiming it anyway, so the French were like, "Just give it to them." At that point, in the early 1900s, Isan began its trajectory to be part of Thailand. When Thailand started to take control of the northeast they prohibited a lot of things: You couldn't play the *khene*, the traditional Lao bamboo instrument, you couldn't speak Lao, all that stuff. They had this policy called One Thai: Everybody inside the borders of Thailand had to be Thai.

J: How did so many Lao dishes come to be seen as Thai?

V: A lot of the Lao Isan began to migrate to Bangkok for work. At first they were mostly servants—this was the '70s and '80s, the Thai economy was doing well, growing 8 percent per year. All the R&Rs from the U.S. military in Vietnam were going to Thailand, all the tourists. For the Lao Isan in Bangkok, there was almost shame in being Lao. They didn't want to speak Lao in public, afraid people would know they were ethnic Lao. Even today the word *Lao* has a negative connotation in Thai society. Even today it's an insult: You're a country punk, uneducated, dark, unsophisticated. In Bangkok you have these class tiers, and the Lao from the northeast were looked down upon. A lot of them were maids, construction workers, things like that, taking care of babies, cooking, cleaning—really low jobs. And they didn't speak Thai well, and that's another thing: You don't speak my language, you automatically become stupid. It's like that for some people in the United States: If you don't speak English well, you must be stupid.

J: So Bangkok became an outpost of Lao food.

V: Lao Isan wanted to eat their own food from home. So they cooked and fed themselves, because there were so many workers there (still today, I'd say 90 percent of Bangkok's taxi drivers are from the northeast). They had to find ways to remind themselves of home, so they would eat Lao food, papaya salad and all that stuff. Later it became popular because other people liked it, Central Thais and people who traveled to Bangkok. They'd buy it off the street and it became popular. And they would market it to the tourists as Thai food because people didn't know, they wouldn't bother to tell you the history and where the food came from. And what was Laos anyway? It was a communist country that had just ended a war. Laos couldn't even stand on its own, let alone care about claiming anything.

J: And in the States, those Lao dishes were seen as Thai.

V: When Thai food got popular in the States—in the '80s, the '90s—papaya salad and laap were some of the most popular dishes, and they were marketed as Thai. Lao people were just beginning to come to the United States in the '80s, we were refugees, we couldn't open Lao restaurants and start advertising papaya salad as being Lao. Thai food already had its foot in the door. Americans already thought they knew what Thai food was. As a restaurant owner you wanted as many customers as possible. You didn't have time to start educating the public about Lao food. A lot of restaurants came from grocery stores where the owners would sell papaya salad in the back. A lot of people didn't know how to apply for a restaurant permit; it was easier with a grocery store. And, of course, many Lao Isan were so ashamed of their Lao heritage that some made an extra effort to hide it. It's like being ashamed of speaking Lao in the States because people would look at you: "You're immigrants, you're refugees!" We wanted to assimilate.

J: It's changing, though.

V: It wasn't until later on, in this decade, that more and more Lao restaurants started appearing in the States. Early on, I wrote a letter to Yelp asking them to include a Lao category. They still don't have one. But we both know, any time you go to a Thai restaurant there's a separate menu where you can order Lao food, and the other one for the "foreigners," offering phat Thai and all that stuff.

workers too busy to make Lao dishes at home: mechanics, service workers. As a restaurant owner you know your clientele, your people. And you're also doing a service by providing food for the community, but the price point has to stay low—it's what the community can afford, or is willing to pay. It sets the value of the cuisine, fixing a ceiling that becomes difficult to break.

That price point doesn't necessarily match the economics of a restaurant. At Wat Phou, the Thai restaurant my mom owned in the 1990s, a rice plate cost four and a quarter, maybe four-fifty. To make that work, she couldn't buy the best ingredients, although not that many customers cared about free-range, antibiotic- and hormone-free meats back then. Now they do, and at Hawker Fare—my Lao Isan restaurant in San Francisco—where we use good ingredients and try to charge a fair price, the pushback is hard from customers conditioned to think of Asian food as cheap. Sometimes I'm like, *Man, my ancestors really undersold themselves.*

Perfect example: The Oakland Friday farmers' market, where my mom used to shop, where I do now, and where a lot of the vendors are Asian. It's, like, a dollar a bunch for morning glories: They've been a dollar a bunch since 1986! Because that's what the community can afford, to feed their families. But I worry about the farmers and their families. Many times I refuse discounts for buying in bulk because I know how hard it is for them—we all need to support each other. I'm grateful to these farmers for growing the beautiful produce that keeps the heart of our culture beating.

Maybe when more and more restaurants call themselves Lao, things will change. It helps that second-generation Lao Americans are still interested in the traditional foods, proudly supporting Lao culture, Lao cuisine. There's strength in numbers.

Now it's time for the rest of America to discover Lao food. And the structure of Lao food is ridiculously easy to understand. It has two main

pillars: sticky rice, and the deep, chunky, mud-brown fermented fish sauce known as *padaek*.

Everything else—like laap and green papaya salad, the Lao dishes a lot of Americans already know, without recognizing them as Lao—is lifted up by sticky rice (page 277) and padaek (page 280).

THE LAOTIAN GHETTO

Since Pops was a citizen of Laos, it meant one thing for Uncle Sam after the country fell to the communists in 1975: giving us a chance to roll the dice on the American dream. You know us Asians—we love to gamble, test our fortunes. Kneeling in front of the Buddha as the candles and fragrant incense burn down, marking time like sand leaving an hourglass, hoping for luck.

Luck was a thing that had drained out of Laos. When the Vietnam War ended and the last American helicopter left Saigon, the new government of Laos dumped the king, a U.S. ally, forced him from the palace at Luang Prabang. The shit hit the fan. Lao people streamed over the border to Thailand, swam the Mekong, got out however they could. Northeast Thailand, the region called Isan, was where Pops, a kid from Paksé in Laos, met Moms. She's from a village too small to show on maps, Nong Jam Nak, outside the city of Ubon Ratchathani, on the muddy brown Mun River.

She's the sixth of ten children. My grandparents were rice farmers, raised chickens, ducks, pigs, and cattle. There was barely any electricity and the roads weren't paved. Water buffalo served as tractors. It was a timeless world surrounded by change: the U.S. military, who used Ubon as a base for their nine-year Secret War against Laos, were leaving. Bad luck was descending.

In 1980, the United States granted us green cards to get far away from the big bad communists: Pops, Moms,

and little two-year-old me, too young to recall much about the Ubon refugee camp where we waited. An immigration officer looked at my father's last name and for some reason thought we'd be better off with a new one. *Syhabout*—it must have sounded weird as hell to my parents. Still today, so many people say it wrong or can't begin to spell it, but I rarely correct them. I guess I've never really felt I owned it. The first step in our new life was walking away from our name.

Photos and 35-millimeter captures are all I now have as evidence of the refugee camp—my mom smiling, though she must have been scared, uncertain about this new life she'd carried me into. Not knowing how long we'd be in this cinder-block and chicken-wire limbo, waiting with other families just as scared as we were, all of us hoping for luck's touch.

Maybe our new name gave us good fortune.

Anyway, it was only a few weeks before the authorities allowed us to hop on the big bird that would swoop across the globe to a place my parents had never heard of: San Francisco. It was a city next to a shining bay as different from the Mun and the Mekong as anything they'd seen. The only thing my parents carried with them (besides me) was a suitcase each, plus two things Moms couldn't imagine leaving Nong Jam Nak without, her *khok* and *saak*, the clay mortar and hardwood pestle she used to pound *jaews* and muddle papaya salad. There was no going back.

But where were we? At home the sun washed out the river, the rice fields, and trees with the same intensity everywhere. Here, the glare hit you different depending on where you were: bouncing off the bay to blind you, blazing off the windows in the tall buildings as the sun went down, going west to the place we couldn't return to, the land of sticky rice and family fields.

They put us in a temporary apartment across the bay, on the island of Alameda, a navy town with barbershops and dive bars where almost everyone was white. Neither of my parents learned any English back home—Moms dropped out of school in the fourth grade to help my sick grandmother, learning to cook out of necessity. Alameda's Safeway supermarket must have seemed like the most bizarre place in the world, no smells, the fruits and vegetables dead in their bins or wrapped in plastic. Stacked up with boxes full of weird things, unreadable labels, a bland constellation of processed shit: Kraft singles, Wonder bread, Cap'n Crunch, bologna. Safeway was already an alien zone, since food stamps put limits on where Moms could shop. Grocery Outlet in Oakland was the spot. But that wasn't a place where you'd find jasmine rice, much less sticky rice, the thing that gives every person from Laos and Isan a sense of meaning.

My mother is a cook to the core, though. She used Uncle Ben's to make a delicious version of *khao pad*, fried rice with that frozen pea and carrot mix and diced Hillshire Farm Lit'l Smokies or Spam. She made sandwiches by heating sardines in tomato sauce in the tin can over the open flame of our tiny, low-pressure GE gas range and then dumping them on slices of baguette she'd toasted over the same flame. I still crave those.

Instinct helped Moms bring familiar meaning to our life in California, riding the 51 AC Transit bus, practically feeling her way to Chinatown in Oakland. The shops there made sense: open crates of Chinese broccoli and pomelos, smells of dried seafood, butchers hoisting pork carcasses on the sidewalk. It wasn't Talad Yai, the early morning fresh market in Ubon, but Moms knew what to do with this food. It eased her homesickness like a remedy.

Meanwhile our Lao social worker was working her magic to find us a new home. And after only a month in Alameda we were moving again, through the Webster Tunnel to Oakland, not far from Chinatown, to a big studio apartment in a complex on Twenty-Sixth Street between Telegraph and Northgate in Uptown. There were tall trees a block away on Twenty-Fifth that felt like they protected the whole zone. Moms said they sort of reminded her of the trees in Nong Jam Nak, which must have been partly wishful thinking since Oakland was about as unlike the village we came from as anywhere could be.

The building on Twenty-Sixth Street was big. You looked up at three stories of windows, curtains dancing in the lazy breeze to the sound of Thai soap operas and Molam music, socks and underpants on drying racks set up to catch that afternoon sun, moms snapping at their kids in Lao. The nest we were dropped in was full of refugees like us. They gave us a place on the third floor.

A year later we moved a block over to Twenty-Fifth and Northgate, a large Section 8 housing complex, subsidized by the government. Besides a couple of Cambodian families, it was probably 70 percent Lao. Later I found out everybody called it the Laotian ghetto.

The grid of our world was small. It ran from Twenty-Third to Twenty-Fifth Streets between

Harrison Street by Lake Merritt, sweeping west across Broadway over to Telegraph and ending at Northgate. This is the place that would shape me, the place I'd escape from, and the place I'd come back to.

Twenty-Fifth isn't like a regular street. It's more like a slot, an open tunnel between Telegraph and West Oakland, under the Interstate 980 overpass. Shimmering piles of shattered car glass looked like diamonds on the curbs, next to sidewalks with junkie shopping-cart pushers hauling recyclable goods, hustling for money. The underpass before you got to Martin Luther King Jr. Way, entering Sycamore Street, was a junkyard for stolen, stripped, and abandoned cars, stained and distressed mattresses, analog television sets, ironing boards, and La-Z-Boys. Used clothing was thrown here, a dumping spot for whatever and whomever. We were living in the Oakland version of *New Jack City*, littered with pookies, in the middle of the crack cocaine epidemic.

Nobody would ever just walk down Twenty-Fifth Street who didn't live there or have a deal to drop on the other side. Prostitutes and drug dealers worked the 980 off-ramp on Twenty-Seventh, hustling the white guys who swerved in from the rich suburbs over the hills. After my dad got a car, I remember looking down at the street from our third-floor apartment, seeing it up on milk crates with all the wheels gone: stolen. It was like, *Holy shit—where had we landed?*

Once a week we tiptoed through this urine-scented minefield of broken 40-ounce malt liquor bottles, crack cocaine vials, used syringes, and condoms, hauling our sacks and baskets of dirty clothes en route to the coin-operated laundromat. We only had enough money to wash, so we'd carry everything back to dry, heavier because it was wet. We didn't mind—we had the blazing Oakland sun and the dirt lot next to our building to hang clothes out. Sometimes it was so dry the dust would rise and get in everything. The clean clothes still smelled good, even if they were stiff like cardboard. And we had my parents' optimism for something that was impossible in Paksé or Nong Jam Nak: to make money and free me and my new little brother, David, from lives that never changed, versions of all the earlier generations in our family tending the rice fields.

Our spot on Twenty-Fifth Street nourished us, made us feel safe in a strange place, welcomed us with huge and open arms. Strangers became my instant aunts and uncles, suddenly I had a handful of cousins, all of us living on top of one another. The U-shaped complex had a narrow outdoor foyer, a brick courtyard out in front, formed by the wings. All of us new-formed cousins used to play tag there, trade baseball cards and Garbage Pail Kids, and shoot Styrofoam airplanes.

Moms, Pops, my brother, and me all shared a one-bedroom apartment small enough to feel like a studio. The food Moms and new aunts cooked beat on you like the hot sun over the Mun and the Mekong. The life around us felt like a movie set that mirrored village life back home, only with automobiles and asphalt replacing water buffalos and rice fields, and a dozen new aunties keeping their eyes on us.

There were refugee families who'd been living on Twenty-Fifth Street for years before us. They'd built up strong walls around the community and cushioned it with resources. For Moms and Pops, like everybody else in the ghetto of Oakland, chasing that American dream meant hustling, whichever way you could: lining up for food stamps and welfare checks when the first and fifteenth came around, then lining up again at the check-cashing place, the same spot you went to buy pagers, money orders, bus tickets, to chance your luck on the lottery, and to send money to family back home in Isan.

We had our own Lao internal network: where to shop for the cheapest household goods and everyday essentials, intel on the weekly arrivals at the Goodwill and Salvation Army on Telegraph so we could intercept the new stock and get first dibs. We knew which store had discount fabric so Moms could sew linens for our beds and pillowcases, got inside information about the dumpster behind the mattress store to know when to raid it for low-density foam. We tore it in little pieces to stuff our pillows, all of us sitting around, working our hands like we were breaking bread together.

We kept as much business as we could on the block, under the table. It was like a true village, with trading and barter. If we ran out of pickled fish, we'd make a deal with somebody in the building to exchange some of Moms's jaew—economics on the down low. My friend Bobby's mom was a seamstress. If my dad needed to get his jeans hemmed, we'd give her an equivalent amount of homemade beef jerky in exchange.

For twenty bucks a month, Pau Si drove all the kids to school every morning in his four-door sedan and picked us up again in the afternoon so we wouldn't have to walk through the crackheads. My parents got acquainted with a banker at a branch down the street so we could open an account and deposit their little bundle of cash, safer than Moms's old Ovaltine tin under the mattress on the floor.

Pau Tin was a mechanic Pops became partners with. They were the neighborhood handymen and auto repair guys, performing oil and fluid changes, transmission and engine swaps, hanging tarps on electrical conduit to construct painting booths—you name it, they did it, all in an empty lot. They worked seven days a week, taking occasional weekend mornings off to raid the auto salvage yards in East Oakland or roam the huge-ass Alameda or Laney College flea markets, building a library of tools from secondhand junk everybody knew was stolen. I grew up watching my parents figure out how to survive.

The white property manager of our complex lived a couple doors down, had a kid my age named Shomar. Their apartment smelled like cinnamon-apple pie, Shomar smelled like cinnamon-apple pie. When we didn't even know what Christmas was, they invited us over for the holiday, gave my brother and me presents, made us feel like we belonged.

Our neighbor Harold must have stood over six feet tall, a man like a muscular wall, with salt and pepper hair. I found out later he was an original Black Panther. He always dressed in black: black shoes, black pants, and a black T-shirt showing a fierce feline creature, posed looking like it was about to jump down from his chest and attack me. He drove this immaculate vintage matte-black Ford pickup truck with the loudest and deepest exhaust. You could hear him approach, a raging bull rocketing down Twenty-Fifth. When we heard the roar of his mufflers, we'd move our asses out of the street and get the hell out of his way.

Harold didn't care for the local police, but he was a gentle giant who loved food. He always seemed suspicious about what my mom was cooking, but he frequently barbecued out in the dirt lot we all shared, the smell of lighter fluid and charcoal briquettes wafting through our window. Harold gave me my first taste of American barbecue: hot links, ribs, chicken, baked beans, corn on the cob. His sauce was very sweet and smoky, lots of molasses and vinegar, spicy with cayenne and chili powder. I was into it.

Life would eventually bust all the way through the walls of the Laotian ghetto, letting in more smells of barbecue, cinnamon-apple pie, and other unknown things. But for now, we were preoccupied with what was happening inside.

Our kitchen was starting to smell more and more familiar: less like seared Ball Park hot dogs and Spam, more like comforting funks. Filling her pantry made Moms feel less lonely.

She dried *seen haank*, "beef jerky," on racks in front of the window or on the building's roof (every family had its corner of the roof for drying beef or fish—it was an important spot). Ketchup, mayo, and mustard were things I never knew as a kid. Instead, our refrigerator door was filled with chile dips and relishes. *Jaew bong* was our version of butter and ranch dressing, and *som pak*, "pickled fish," our sauerkraut. There was always som pak fermenting away in the darkest corner of the apartment, hiding from sunlight. When we used up a tub of Country Crock for the margarine and sugar sandwiches I ate for breakfast, it became a vessel for a new, ripe batch.

Moms's guerrilla Tupperware game was on lock. She repurposed yogurt containers and pickle jars from the building's recycling to hold her growing condiment collection. Veggies and meats were always marinating in floral-logo "Thank You" bags, recycled from Khanh Phong Supermarket in Chinatown. She built up a collection of bottled sauces: soy, oyster, fish. She stockpiled Thai chiles in the freezer, hoarded bags of sticky rice. She made the mother sauce of any Lao or Isan mom's kitchen: padaek.

Her first batch she made from local anchovies and small crabs we picked under the rocks on the west side of Crown Beach in Alameda, mixed with salt and rice bran. It aged patiently under the kitchen sink in a Rubbermaid bin, with bricks and cinder blocks pressing down on the fish, anchoring it. Moms's padaek slowly came to life in this new world like it was on a parallel ride with ours: ripped from the source, remade in California. Same same but different.

Even before I went to school I studied what was going on in our kitchen. I spent a lot of time at my mother's side. Instead of toys, a Melissa & Doug train set or a Fisher-Price puzzle to keep me distracted, Moms gave me little tasks. A head of garlic was my Rubik's Cube, my tiny fingers learning how to separate and peel. If she didn't let me throw my cloves into the mortar and let me pound away the best I could, without dropping the pestle on my Tic Tac–size toes, I threw tantrums. I was a petite little dude, and with that heavy pestle in my hands I must have looked like Bamm-Bamm from *The Flintstones*, smashing his club. I learned how to be a commis in Moms's kitchen, always up for taking on more and more, biting off more than I could chew.

Moms would catch me stealing warm rice out of the bamboo steaming basket, the Lao version of getting busted with your hand in the cookie jar. She would wad a ball of sticky rice for me and sprinkle it with granules of iodized salt, a ploy to buy time so she could get some real cooking done. Sticky rice was my jam. To this day, salted sticky rice is one of the most delicious snacks I know.

I think I enjoyed simple meals the best, sticky rice and whatever we had in the fridge, maybe some beef jerky, and a dip like *jaew mak len*, a sort of tomato jam with natural sugars, smoky from roasted shallots and garlic, and spiced with dry-roasted chile powder. That would be it, just those three things: a complete, wholesome meal.

As soon as I was old enough to eat it, I

ONE BOWL, MANY SALIVAS: THE ART OF COMMUNAL EATING

The whole infrastructure of Lao and Thai eating is built for groups, chasing the shared experience. It's part of the culture we brought with us across oceans.

For me, eating the way I was raised, in a big group dipping into shared dishes, is close to a holy experience. It's wholesome—relaxed conversation stirs appetites. In the Western way of eating, everybody with their own entrée, nothing in the middle of the table for you to reach out to grab a morsel of—it can make you self-conscious. When plates are shared, and you have to go for what you want, it al-

leviates worry about table manners, restores the innocence of eating. Sharing food and letting loose is purity in the act of eating. And I think touching food directly with the hands—having a tactile connection—helps make it more delicious.

Sharing is a way of living, families and friends coming together to tell the day's stories over food and drinks, to joke or talk seriously, dipping into the same dish with hands and spoons, totally balls-out family-style. Double-dipping makes everybody around the table or *saat* equally vulnerable—you need trust to eat so intimately. And inviting strangers around the saat is the ultimate civilized act. Food doesn't just fill the belly's void: It reinforces connection. It declares our shared humanness.

A couple of years ago in Isan, en route with friends to Khon Kaen from Ubon Ratchathani, I stopped for lunch at a restaurant on a highway by the river. The restaurant was laid out on wooden platforms floating on empty barrels. We ordered eight dishes to share, baskets of sticky rice for everyone, and a large bottle of Thai whiskey with soda water to hydrate in the humid September afternoon. I looked around and didn't see a single table for two—eating and drinking in groups is part of the culture here, the dishes coming out in random sequence. It's an acknowledgment that food and drinking is a celebration, not a solitary act, everyone bobbing on the planks over the river together. Nobody wants to eat alone.

loved *laap goong diep*, a raw shrimp laap. It looked like an ugly, brownish-gray blob: charred Thai eggplant and shallots, padaek, and raw shrimp, pounded and stirred together to form a paste, really unappetizing to look at but so good, with a kind of umami salinity. We dragged raw long beans through it . . . sometimes cucumber—everyone dipping into the big beige pile.

The Twenty-Fifth Street Lao world was one big family. Dinners floated from apartment to apartment, twenty or twenty-five of us sitting around the floor on *saats*, woven dining mats of plastic straw, the chairs pushed away against the walls. We chowed down family-style, hardcore sharing our meals, double-dipping and all, swapping the love. There were potlucks, each mom bringing a dish. Most times they were cooking parties, where my mom and all the aunts cooked communally, in one cramped kitchen.

Some nights we all just ate together—aunts, uncles, cousins, all of us related by proximity, not blood—the way we did in our villages back home, after long days in the rice fields under the burning sun, navigating water buffalos.

Other nights we celebrated somebody's good luck: so-and-so's new job, cousin Ped leaving the hospital after a car crash, an engagement—and there were so many birthdays, some of my aunts and uncles must have celebrated twice a year. The reasons to party seemed endless.

Moms would cook up some mean dishes for the neighborhood events, forbidding me to touch a thing. She had her game face on and brought it—you didn't want to mess with her when she was putting it on the court. I'd watch her, Auntie Mae Oun, and Auntie Mae Ae fussing over the dishes: a steamed fish curry in banana leaf parchment called *mok pla douk*; *mok gai,* chicken steamed in banana leaves; the spicy shrimp salad named *laap goong diep*; *soop naw mai*, a shredded bamboo-shoot ragout; *gang hed*, a sort of truffle soup; and the salty, spicy things you dip stuff into: *nam prik, nam jim, jaews*. Of course there was sticky rice—there were always baskets of sticky rice. It was almost a religious thing.

The messy prep would all be spread out on last week's free newspapers, in colorful plastic or enamel bowls and plates. The women cooked without recipes, using only their eyes, their tongues, and their hands, which always remembered.

When it was time to celebrate, it meant throwing down, even on work nights. A self-serve mini bar would be laid out on the saat, dotted by green bottles of Heineken (the beer of choice). Fifths of Cognac, O.G. Thai Red Bull, and Perrier were for mixing whiskey sodas (Thai whiskey was unavailable in the States so Cognac—always a favorite in Oakland—stood in).

Pops and my uncles smoked with red faces, grunting in Lao with mouths full of food. Stereo speakers bumped the bass, treble, and strings of Molam and Luk Tung tracks, sounds of the *pin* (a string instrument, sort of a banjo guitar) on cassette tapes brought from the homeland. Some weekend parties lasted for two days straight, marathons of cooking, eating, drinking, and gambling. Hours and hours of playing for dollars, in pop-up casinos on living room floors after the food was cleared away, Lao versions of craps and single-deck blackjack.

After the formal eating was over there'd always be a pot of stock on the stove and a basket of rice vermicelli with garnishes, for helping yourself to bowls of *khao poon*. The gambling would go on all night and still the aunties would be cooking, getting ready for morning. Dawn broke with bowls of *khao piak sen* or rice congee. If the aunties were really ambitious they'd make fresh rice noodles, using a fish sauce bottle as a rolling pin. They called it the hangover cure.

Some got carried away by all that gambling shit. I remember going to sleep and waking up nine hours later to see the exact same scene going strong—none of the adults had slept. Things could get crazy. Eventually they'd get insane.

The dirt lot next to our building was the unofficial neighborhood commons—it was where Pops and Pau Tin worked on cars. Moms grew mint and *rau ram*: just dug holes and planted. Every time she cleaned squid she'd save the purple saline liquid and use it for watering—the concentrated protein and nutrients made everything grow faster.

Other families raised shallots. Wood sorrel grew wild in spring, and nasturtiums. Behind the building were a couple of existing rose bushes and untamed shrubs we'd raid for tart red blackberries. There was a tree we'd climb for yellow-green apricots. We didn't care for ripe fruit. Firm and sour was the way we liked it.

Everything happened in that lot. My mother would buy live ducks and chickens, slaughter them, bleed them out, and save the blood for laap.

Weekends would be informal block parties, me and my adopted cousins playing kickball, waging water balloon fights, all of us ending up dirty, brown, and dusty. The liquor store on Telegraph took food stamps, so we were all good. I'd buy Slim Jims and potato chips, Lemonheads, Mr. Melons, Cherry Clans. We'd play marbles and candy was the wager: three Now and Laters, a purple and a green one mixed.

The lot was where we'd grill: Fill up the Weber with charcoal briquettes, dose it with lighter fluid, and watch it flame. *Moo yang* (barbecue pork) and *gai yang* (barbecue chicken) filled the grates. *Seen ping* (grilled beef brisket) was cooked medium-rare, then thrown on a chopping block where an uncle or aunt who stepped up would do the chopping on a slice of tree trunk, our butcher block. Not much of the juicy, fat-capped beef brisket would actually make it to plates—slices went straight into the bowl of jaew spiked with bile and on to salivating mouths.

Meanwhile Moms was starting to get her hustle on for real. She attended a few church-

sponsored English classes taught by a group of young Mormon missionaries during the week. The blond, blue-eyed boys who spoke pretty fluent Lao would come through the 'hood to try and spread their friendship and gospel, urge us to get on the free bus that drove up to the spaceship Mormon temple in the hills. But my parents, everybody in the building: we were dedicated Buddhists. Besides, school was never my mom's thing. She dropped out of English class as soon as she got a job as a cook at the fanciest Thai restaurant in Berkeley, Cha-Am on Shattuck Avenue, two doors down from Alice Waters's famous spot. They called Cha-Am the Chez Panisse of Thai food, not that anyone on Twenty-Fifth Street would have known what that was. Anyway, Moms's skill was cooking, not study, her passion making money to pad the grind in this cash-driven new world.

But before Moms started on the line at Cha-Am, one day when she was in English class, it was up to Pops to babysit. Between my mom's and my aunties' knives, mortars and pestles, and lard, and my dad's hand tools, motor oil, and chassis grease, I grew up around a lot of tempting tools and interesting fats. That day, like always, my job was not to touch anything at all, to do absolutely nothing but watch Pops and Pau Tin until Moms came home to cook dinner. It's always been impossible for me to keep still. When Pops was distracted, I carried a kitchen knife out to the yard behind our apartment and cut myself severely. I did not cry. I just stood there, transfixed by the sight of so much red fluid engulfing my palm until Pops found me.

When Moms got home she rubbed salt and iodine into the wound to stop the bleeding, an extremely painful remedy that felt partly like punishment. Maybe they weren't the first tears I cried in the kitchen, but they were the bitterest I recall. Looking back, I think maybe Moms was subconsciously trying to tell me to keep far away from the kitchen, a place of lurking hurts, where the things that stay with you are the scars.

3

THE PHAT THAI GRIND

989: Tuesday, October 17, 5:04 p.m. Pacific Standard Time. That's when the Laotian ghetto took its fatal hit—almost literally exploded—like it was rocked by a cluster bomb.

The Loma Prieta earthquake hit West Oakland hard. Everybody panicked—we didn't have quakes in Laos or Isan, didn't know what was up. I had just come home from school, fifth grade, my routine day, in the courtyard outside our complex, trading Garbage Pail Kids. The building shook once and then kept shaking for a long time. I saw the courtyard move like we were all in slo-mo, me and my cousins trying to run. When we made it to the street and looked back, I saw bricks on the front of our building come away. The grout seemed liquid, like rice congee.

Nobody was hurt, our luck held out, though the next few days of aftershocks were days of fear and misery. No electricity, no lights. We grabbed what we needed from our apartment and moved across Twenty-Fifth Street into the church parking lot, sheltered under the overhang out front of the recreation center. We all camped out, living off food recovered from aunties' kitchens: homemade beef jerky, dried noodles out of the package (we crunched them like potato chips), fermented cabbage and other preserves. In the sky we watched the dust of airborne rubble, the smoke from unseen fires.

Once in a while the gas came back on, but we camped outside for three or four days, until the city deemed it okay to go back home. The apartment building was safe, but some of the stucco was cracked. The façade was peeling. Nobody wanted to stay; almost everybody packed up and scattered. Richmond. East Oakland. Fairfield. Hercules. San Pablo. Some even moved out of state. Wherever they had family or friends and there was a Buddhist temple reasonably close.

The weird thing was, no one except a couple of families said goodbye, or even promised to stay in touch. It was like that thing after a big group dinner in a restaurant, where you can't say bye to everybody so you just nod on the way out. The Twenty-Fifth Street scene, so noisy, close, and vibrant, just . . . died. Within weeks the dirt lot where everybody played, grilled, gardened, and talked became this lonely place. After the winter rain it was overrun with weeds. No one tended it. There were no barbecues anymore. The community was broken.

We stayed in our apartment for a little while. Then Mae Won, who lived in an old two-story house on the corner, moved to Richmond and we took over her spot. It was actually a duplex but we pried open the door that separated the two units inside. Pops's side of the family had been settled in Rhode Island, so they came west and moved in. We occupied the whole house, three bedrooms for the eight of us. Luxury.

Moms was around less, since she was cooking at Cha-Am in Berkeley. It must have been a shocker to her at first, cooking in a high-volume setting on the line, for *farangs* (Thai for white people) who loved bland ingredients like bell peppers. I can hear her thinking: *A pepper with no heat? What the hell is this?*

Some days Pops would take me along to pick her up from work. I'd stand at the entryway to the kitchen, waiting for her to finish. Cha-Am was the first commercial kitchen I ever saw. It had huge stockpots I could have hidden in, a refrigerator chamber as big as our bedroom, wok burners roaring like jet engines. Everything about it was cool.

After a few years Moms and Pops finally rounded up enough savings from their respective grinds to open their own restaurant, with my uncles on my dad's side as

partners. Our Lao social workers were Mah Sounun and her husband, Pau Sieng. They'd found us our first Oakland apartment, got us set up, did all the paperwork for me and my brother to go to school. They lived in Concord, a sunny, low-key suburb twenty miles northeast of the Laotian ghetto, through the Caldecott Tunnel. They knew Moms was working at Cha-Am.

Mah was like, *There's no Thai food in Concord*—she smelled opportunity out in the 'burbs. There was a space not far from her house, a closed-up Vietnamese pho restaurant in the middle of a huge parking lot on Broadway, near the Park N Shop mall and a biker club. Mah and Pau Sieng helped us land the deal, handled the negotiations, all the legal stuff my parents couldn't swing without English. To make it to the next level in the game of the American Dream, sometimes you need a boost.

Moms, Pops, and my uncles opened Wat Phou, a Thai restaurant they named for a famous Buddhist temple in Laos. It was a way to hold on to their Lao-ness, with a name they chose as a kind of temple offering.

Pops worked the front of the house, Moms cooked versions of the Thai dishes she'd made for the farangs in Berkeley. Uncle Sam had worked at Benihana; he quit his job to come join the business. My older cousin Eric helped out as a server. Even I had a job. Not only did we all live together, we now all worked together. It was just like village life back home, only with the one big rule of life in America: Every day you gotta wake up and make that money.

Ever since the earthquake broke up the village on Twenty-Fifth Street, my parents had started to worry about keeping me off the streets. The Lao gossip mill was always churning, 24/7, spitting out stories about so-and-so's kid heading down the path of gangbanging and drugs. Their solution was to have me help out at the family business where they could watch me: after school, every weekend, and all through the long, hot Concord summers. I was a sixth-grade kid making five bucks a week! I could do whatever I wanted with it: buy hip-hop cassettes for my Walkman, save up six or seven months to buy a bicycle. *Shit*, I thought. *This is cake!* I did my homework in the little dry-storage room that doubled as the office, under towering stacks of jasmine and sticky rice bags with the ever-funky perfume of fish sauce. Sometimes I slept on the bags of rice.

At Wat Phou, I had my first taste of American Thai food. I didn't get it.

ME: What's this pepper in the phat kra pao? It has no flavor.

MOMS: There always have to be fresh peppers in phat kra pao and the Americans like bell peppers. If I use hot peppers all of a sudden they're complaining, sending it back, saying it's so spicy they can't taste anything! This is how we have to cook to make them happy so they come back and tell their friends about us.

Our phat Thai was syrupy sweet. Moms added red and yellow food coloring to make it orange, just like she added it to the marinades for moo yang and gai yang, grilled pork and grilled chicken. "To make it more attractive," she said.

ME: Why we use so much sugar in our food? [I was becoming a smartass.]

MOMS: The Americans like sweet flavors, it's delicious to them. Addictive—like donuts and Coca-Cola!

I still got to eat my mother's true cooking at staff meals many shades more vivid and interesting than the curries and noodles she made for the guests. It was amazing what Moms could produce from the trim of Wat Phou's menu: *soop naw mai* (bamboo-shoot stew), a bunch of different jaews, and of course, *som tum* and sticky rice, all just for us. We ate in the kitchen, Lao-style, just like at home. The stuff going out the swing doors to the paying customers didn't come close to the deliciousness of our private meals. Why wouldn't they want to eat what we ate?

At Wat Phou I did jobs I'd already learned on Twenty-Fifth Street—stemming chiles, peeling garlic and shallots—except there was way more, it never stopped. Moms gave me a little plastic stool with a cartoon character sticker on the top to sit on while I worked. I sat so long the heat from my ass made the cartoon character come off. I helped Moms skewer the chicken satay, portion them into sandwich bags, five skewers per bag, and freeze them. Restaurant life was just as brutal.

I hoisted stacked trays of iceberg salads (free at lunch with a rice plate) on top of the ice machine for the servers to grab. I helped fold the cloth napkins for dinner service. I scooped jasmine rice for the stir-fries, standing on a milk crate to be tall enough to reach the line. When I saw anything other than noodles being fired in the woks it was my cue to move: scoop the rice, using a ceramic bowl to mold it into a dome, place it at the right spot on the plate. I had to pack it just right: not so tight that I gave away too much (Moms stressed about food cost), not so loose that the pile would crumble.

I was proud of my rice skills like I was proud of being a human dish machine, washing soiled wares and pans back to an immaculate state. I squatted over the floor-mounted mop sink to clean woks and sauté pans—it was low enough to perform up to Moms's standards, working my 3M wire scrubby quickly and efficiently. Phat Thai woks were the worst: all that caramelized sugar and stuck noodles.

My school clothes had stains, because when you wash a wok the greasy water splashes everywhere (only cooks got aprons). At least I always had a pair of shoes I kept at the restaurant, like regular tennis shoes, no acid resistance. After a while the soles got bald and slippery. I burned myself many times. I'd get sloppy and my forearm would touch the searing pan edge. My mom's trick was toothpaste. It cooled burns and prevented blisters. We always had some in the staff bathroom.

I earned plenty of cuts. The iodine stung like hell but I got to the point where I was numb, like it was a challenge for me, a mental thing: how to embrace the sting without crying. When you're first generation, you learn to be tough. Maybe working in a restaurant wasn't cake like I thought. Maybe it was more like proving to myself and to my parents that just like them, I could survive anything.

Concord was so nice compared to Oakland: an orderly front-lawn world with no crack vials or condoms on the street. On weekends and all summer my brother, David, and I would skip out on the restaurant in the hour-and-a-half break between lunch and dinner. We'd link up with our social workers' kids, pay a buck-fifty to go to their community pool in the middle of a manicured recreational park. I was like, *Damn! It is greener on the other side of the tunnel.*

Everything in the suburbs was clean. Civilized. You didn't have to wake up to a drug addict on your porch or a homeless guy ransacking a dumpster. We asked our parents, "Why don't we move to Concord?" They said we couldn't afford it. "Don't waste time thinking about that," Pops said. "Focus on school and the restaurant."

David and I made friends with kids who lived across the street behind Wat Phou, in this apartment complex. There was a Vietnamese kid, a Portuguese kid, and a half-Japanese, half-white kid named Joseph. I'd steal money from the restaurant tip jar and we'd go play video games in the back of Dante's Pizza in the mall. We'd play baseball in the parking lot, ride bikes (we kept ours in the storeroom with the bags of rice). We tried to make our own summer camp, but it was hard sometimes not to be bored as hell. I was like, *What do other twelve-year-olds do in summer?* I knew, though. When Joseph and the other kids weren't playing with us, they were having fun at Little League and soccer camp, not folding napkins.

Days started early. Moms didn't have the luxury of calling up a fishmonger or butcher the

night before and having the goods dropped off at the delivery door, nor did she have the option of payment terms. It was strictly C.R.E.A.M.: cash rules everything at markets. So at seven a.m. she'd grab a wad of cash from the previous night's take and head to Oakland's Chinatown, then on to the wholesale produce terminal in Jack London Square, just like all the other Asian restaurant owners. She wanted to handpick everything: a case of bell peppers, broccoli, flats of mushrooms.

Fridays we hit up the Old Oakland farmers' market. That's where Moms did most of her

produce shopping, from stall after stall of Lao, Hmong, and Mien farmers from around Fresno, where the climate is perfect for Lao and Thai crops. Farmers in the community grew for their own consumption and sold the extras to pay the bills. (I still shop at the market for my own restaurants, buying from the kids of the farmers my mother bought from. You could say they're my distant cousins: We grew up together, every Friday.)

Moist stalks of lemongrass, sugarcane, tiny eggplants, bunches of morning glory, long beans, holy basil, cilantro with the roots attached, Thai chiles laid out on wooden planks—it made Moms feel like she was back in Ubon. I was her shopping assistant, meaning I held all the bags while she bargained with the farmers for discounts on bulk.

"Brother? Three bunches for the price of two?" She knew how to ask with just the right firmness and sweetness—I never once heard a farmer deny her plea for a break. She had the hustle down. We'd leave with Thai basil, herbs and what-not, chiles, pretty much everything in bulk to last us a week. Then we'd pack up the van full, to where you couldn't see out the back window, for the ride out to Concord.

We'd sometimes all caravan from Oakland, the uncles and us, usually get to the restaurant around nine a.m., ready for lunch at eleven thirty. On the way back home at night, my brother and I would fall asleep in the car for the half-hour drive. School nights, eleven o'clock or so, it was dark, quiet after the noise and hustle of the restaurant. We folded the back down, had blankets and pillows. The seats that had been loaded with crates of produce and boxes of dry goods that morning, on the way back they became my bed. I'd be passed out, no seat belt, flat in the back.

Sundays were what I hated most. They were half-days, dinner only. We had to leave Oakland around two thirty p.m. to get prepping, but when Sunday morning dawned my parents were so tired from the week. Too tired to go out, take us to the park, or drive us to another kid's birthday party. Everything was drained out of them.

We'd sit around until two thirty, then hear Pops yell. "Everyone get in the car, we all gotta go to work!" If I pushed back, my mother would use her Asian mom logic. "We're being charged for the rent anyway, so we might as well go make some money." Sundays were no fun.

By the time I was twelve I began looking around, exploring more, started to see Wat Phou through eyes that were more and more woke. I'd see commercials for Sizzler, and it was like, *Wow, so fancy: a salad bar and a big grilled steak, baked potatoes wrapped in shiny foil.* There was a Sizzler two blocks from the Laotian ghetto, Twenty-Seventh and Telegraph. I'd look at it through the windows as we drove by, heading to Concord.

Kids at school talked about weekends—I never had a weekend, I was always at the restaurant. My life stretched out in a narrow line, sitting on a stool, prepping chiles and garlic.

I wasn't able to go to birthday parties because they were always on weekends, unless it was a birthday for a son or daughter of one of Moms's friends, but they always turned into parties more for the adults than for kids. Whenever one of my school friends had a birthday it was like, "Forget about James, he's not gonna make it." I was notorious for that, all through high school. My weekend was nonexistent.

The first five years at Wat Phou were like the golden age. Every day at lunch we filled up with office workers, every night we were slammed with take-out orders. On a good day we could take in $1,700, pull down $50 or $60K a month—that, with rice plates priced at $4.50. Out the door, a customer might spend $9.00—that works out to almost two hundred covers a day. We worked our asses off. Nobody ever got to the American Dream sitting home watching Thai soap operas.

After three or four years the take at Wat Phou was enough to pay off the initial seed money, allowing my parents and uncles to get a salary, guaranteed, and save a little. We all had to work hard, seven days a week, count every phat Thai shrimp, grain of rice, and complimentary orange wedge that went out to the customers to make sure food cost was on point. It was a grind, every day the same, over and over.

It looked like we were going to make it. Then business started to taper off a little bit. I started noticing FOR LEASE signs in the office windows I'd ride past on my bike. Finally, the drop-off took hold for real.

When a family business is rolling, it's all good. When it slows down, everybody gets sucked into the gears. Minds get active, everyone starts looking at everybody else's pile. Once the suspicion genie comes out of the bottle, there's no stuffing it back.

I heard family accusations, raised voices from the storeroom office.

"I've been here for twelve hours, I only came in to work three!"

"How come *I'm* taking a pay cut. Are *you* taking a pay cut?"

"Where's all the money going?"

Fingers were pointed. Blame sat like an uninvited guest at our staff meals, a heavy silence that drowned out the talking and laughing that used to happen. Going into business with family lifts everybody up in the good times. When things turn, distrust and resentment pin you to the floor.

Everybody had invested everything in the restaurant—emotionally, financially. Moms and my uncles left steady-paying jobs to take a risk, but sacrifice and total commitment eventually take a toll, especially when you have very little to start with. This is part of the Dream nobody tells you about. But there was something else going on.

I noticed it when I turned fourteen—more pressure than usual to pay the bills, conversations I heard late at night when I pretended to be asleep. "Why can't we buy a house? Where's the money going?" There started to be more shouting matches, a lot of drinking, mostly by my dad: Cognac and soda water, sometimes Red Bull in it. Soon nobody could ignore it: Pops had a gambling problem. It became the family's problem.

When the restaurant was doing well and everybody was getting paid, nobody talked about it, but when things got tight everything ruptured. Pops gambled away his portion of the take and then some, embezzling money to pay his debts. My uncles confronted him, accused him of having affairs. Then they turned on each other.

I tried to stay out of it, but you can't—my uncle would say something bad about my dad to me. That's when things got more and more fragmented. They started to fall apart, at home and in the restaurant.

People talked. At parties, gossip filled the corners of the room. It would come back home with us and escalate. One night it got physical—the shouting match that broke the camel's back.

My brother and I woke up to shouting. I saw Pops shove our mom, then put his hands on her neck, choking. I intervened, throwing myself between them. My mom's face was red. She was crying, threatening to call the cops. "Go ahead!" my dad roared. My uncle was upstairs. He heard the walls banging and rushed down. I grabbed my brother and shoved him behind me on the couch—he was in shock, white-faced, no emotion.

My two uncles ended up moving out of the house, one to Rhode Island, the other to San Diego. It was the second time a rupture on Twenty-Fifth Street caused everyone to scatter.

4

A COOL, STRANGE PLACE CALLED HOME

On the outskirts of Ubon Ratchathani in Isan—northeast Thailand—the Mun River winds like a grass snake around rice fields, forest temples, and wooden farmhouses, but the land is dry. It's where I was born, but I didn't really see it until I was twelve.

My parents hadn't been back home in ten years. It was just before things got bad at Wat Phou. My brother and I were old enough to travel, and my parents had saved up enough money for the plane tickets, plus my uncles said they would cover for us at the restaurant for three weeks. I think my mom needed to go—badly. The minute we landed in Bangkok and she saw her youngest sister, Saun, she was in tears. Everybody was. I didn't know what was going on.

I'd grown up with stories told by my parents about where I was from and who I was. This was supposed to be me, this country, but as we traveled north from Bangkok in a box van, which my uncle drove, I felt like we were going on safari in the most foreign place in the world. I stayed awake the whole time so I wouldn't miss a thing.

After many hours we got to Isan, Surin province, a waypoint. It was raining, and all of a sudden the road looked like it was heaving: hundreds and hundreds of frogs were hopping across the tarmac! My uncle had to drive slowly so our wheels wouldn't slip on smashed frogs and

35

make us slide off the road. Moms said we'd eat frogs once we got to the village. She said they tasted like chicken. This place was strange.

We got pulled over for speeding (everybody speeds on country highways in Thailand), and I watched my uncle bribe a Thai cop to let us go. He folded bills into his hand and slid them along the top of the rolled-down window, toward the cop's hand. I was like, *Ah, dirty cops, it's just a hustle—same as Oakland*. Maybe it wasn't so strange here after all.

We approached Moms's village under a blazing sun, on unpaved roads in a land of clay-like orange dirt. There were fewer cars, and herds of water buffalos coming back from the fields. I saw burning mounds of dirt and pointed. Charcoal, my uncle said: People were making charcoal. Maybe Moms needed to be with family. For me, this visit was definitely going to be a tripped-out emotional journey.

At home I was used to going to sleep with the sound of the late BART trains zipping by, but here there was only the sound of crickets and critters in the pitch-black night, a nonstop hypnotic trance. The house my mom grew up in, and where we stayed, was a shophouse on stilts. In front was this big platform elevated off the ground. We took naps and hung out there. That was the communal table, covered with *saats* (dining mats) where we ate multiple times a day, two dozen of my actual blood relatives sharing simple meals built around the work of procuring them.

One day my cousin took me out to Nong Jam Nak, the little lake the village took its name from, to watch him shoot fish with a rifle. The next time I watched him slaughter chickens on the

farm for my aunts to make laap. I went out with my cousins to forage bamboo shoots—I had never seen fresh bamboo shoots before. Same thing with fresh jackfruit, longans, and lychees, fruits I knew only canned and packed in syrup, just like Dole fruit cocktail.

We went shrimping in the Mun River. My uncles went down with nets, dragged them through the water, and all these beautiful writhing shrimp appeared. That's when I had my first bite of *goong dten*, live "dancing" shrimp. The distance between what we ate and the place we ate it was often as short as a morning's walk in the heat.

Thick stands of bamboo surrounded the farm. My uncle cut down a stalk and packed the hollow with sticky rice that had soaked in coconut milk, sweetened with a little palm sugar. He stuck it in the ground and built a fire. It smoldered, charring the stalk and cooking the rice. When it was done he took his machete, split the stalk, and offered my brother and me what was inside: coconut rice pudding, salty, sweet, chewy, custardy, and gummy, held together by the rice paper–like membrane lining the bamboo. It was called *khao laam*; it was delicious, like nothing I'd ever tasted.

It was the rainy season, so my aunts and uncles were planting rice. We went out to the fields with the water buffalos, my mom helping. I stood knee-deep in water rippled by the fragrant beetles called *maeng da*. We caught grasshoppers and crickets with our hands. My cousins gave me a cage that looked like a rice basket; on top there was an opening like a one-way valve, with woven prongs so you could drop insects in but they couldn't climb out. We'd circle the rice fields at the end of the day—sundown—when it wasn't too hot, catch them, bring them home alive, fry, and eat them like French fries with salt, sometimes with lemongrass or

other aromatics: crispy and caramelized. I was like, *Am I really gonna eat these?* I did. I thought it was cool.

My uncle—the cool one who took me fishing—took me to an underground cockfight. Later I found out he was the organizer of fights in a few neighboring villages. All my cousins were really into Muay Thai. My fourteen-year-old cousin Thu had been training since he was ten. He took me to fights. That's what Isan is famous for: training fighters.

There was an unguarded feeling I never knew in Oakland, a sense of trust. The honor system ruled at shophouses—you ordered and ate, then paid later. No one in the village locked their doors, everything sat out in the open. Everybody knew each other's name, knew each other's ancestors.

My uncle ran a ride service from Nong Jam Nak to the city, his truck was the village taxi. People packed twenty deep in the back of his red Isuzu diesel pickup, paying five baht to go to the market in Ubon. They had two or three hours to do their shopping, before they had to hop back on to return to the village. It was my first time riding in the back of a pickup, no seat belts, nothing, just kids sitting on the rail of the bed—it was all okay. The village was a true community, a place where everybody took shared risks, lived shared lives, prayed for shared good fortune.

You bartered with your neighbors. Someone in the village was growing papaya—"Can you take him some mangoes from our tree," my aunt yelled, "so we can have papaya salad instead?" We needed cassia leaves—"Go ask so-and-so can you pick from their tree." It was a closed loop, Twenty-Fifth Street lifted up and dropped down in the middle of nowhere.

All the houses had corrugated metal roofs, and coconut trees were everywhere. I was napping in the middle of the day in my aunt's house and all of a sudden I heard this *boom*, like I was home and it was gunshot. I tore out—it was only a coconut that had fallen on the house. I was scared shitless. I didn't need to be.

My mom was a different person here. I could see she felt more relaxed: wanted to go shopping early every morning, wanted to have a big party every night. She felt like she knew everything here. It made me think about how alienated she probably felt in Oakland. She was a social butterfly here in a big family, with siblings who now had kids, and she had kids, plus cousins and the whole community. I realized that's what she was trying to build on Twenty-Fifth Street, that Lao community held together by food, the reason I had to call someone "auntie" even though we weren't blood-related. It was like, all this shopping and foraging and cooking: It wasn't really about getting fed. It was about tying ourselves to a world that had existed for a long, long time.

Early mornings we piled into my uncle's pickup and went to Talad Yai, the fresh market in Ubon, looking out on the Mun River below. The first time I saw it, I was like, *Ah, I get it*—I understood Oakland Chinatown, why everything was out on the sidewalk. The open-air butcheries and fish counters at Talad Yai, and no refrigeration: It didn't gross me out, it was stimulating. This is how we presented ourselves, everything out in the open to judge.

POUND. CRUSH. GRIND.

Food is digestible culture, and the tools that make that food create a very strong sense of place. In Italy you have the chitarra and the gnocchi paddle. In Japan it's the katsuobushi shaver, in Morocco the tagine. It's the tandoor oven in India, and in Laos and Thailand you have the *khok* and *saak*, the mortar and pestle.

The hypnotic sound of a working mortar and pestle is seared into my identity. Ever since I was a kid it was pretty much our household's wake-up call coming from the kitchen. It was the first thing I heard in the morning, and the sound in the background as I got ready for school: the bass of the thump mixed with the treble scratch or scrape of a spoon. It vibrated the wood floor of our apartment, as my mother cooked lunch or breakfast or worked at stocking the larder. She'd be making some jaew or other, or stocking up on red curry paste for the weeks to come. Something was always cooking, for sure. You didn't need to smell it to know what was happening.

Besides sticky rice, no other dish is made more often in the Lao Isan kitchen than *tum som* (Lao) or *som tum* (Isan). Every home kitchen in Isan or Laos is equipped with a mortar and pestle—it's even more important than knives. Everything centers around this simple, humble tool that does multiple tasks well, better than any kitchen appliance the Industrial Revolution ever dreamed up. Unlike the blender, which merely chops, the mortar and pestle grinds, crushes, and pulverizes; it breaks down fibers; it bruises to release and extract essential oils; it juices. A food processor does these things, too, but the results just aren't the same.

You can source mortar and pestle sets in pretty much any market selling Southeast Asian products, and some online shops selling specialty cookware. Two types are useful for Lao and Thai food:

GRANITE

Use an all-granite mortar and pestle on heavier, tougher, and more rigid ingredients, for instance dried spices, lemongrass, galangal, and ginger. It's the one to choose for producing fibrous pastes, jaews, and marinades, such as Red Curry Paste (page 301) and Dry-Fried Fish Chile Relish (page 293).

CLAY AND WOOD

This is the most-used mortar and pestle in this book, also at Hawker Fare and in my home kitchen. The walls of the mortar are taller, tapering to a cone shape at the bottom, giving it a higher capacity compared to granite mortars. It's for light use, when the goal is to help tender ingredients like papaya and cucumber soften and release their natural juices. Use it for gentle bruising and macerating in tum som, also to make softer dipping sauces and relishes such as Charred Tomato and Chile Relish with Fermented Fish (page 289).

HOW TO USE A MORTAR AND PESTLE

It's easy, fun—even meditative, once you fall into the rhythm. Using a mortar and pestle always makes me feel like I'm really cooking, putting in real effort. It's rewarding.

Start with the ingredient. To achieve a smooth paste with tougher, fibrous ingredients, you'll need to cut them down into smaller pieces before you start pounding away. (If hard pieces are too large they'll slip and slide and eventually jump out of the mortar.)

On a flat surface—a table, the kitchen counter, even directly on the floor—set the mortar on a folded towel. This prevents the mortar from sliding around, and helps absorb vibration, muffling the noise of pounding. If you are using the mortar on a tabletop, please make sure the surface is heavily supported to prevent any damage to furniture.

Always start with the toughest, most rigid ingredients, such as lemongrass, dried chiles, and galangal. Gradually you'll add less rigid things like cilantro root. Finally, the wetter ingredients: fresh chiles, shallots, garlic (both raw and roasted), and seasonings such as shrimp paste or padaek. Add the pieces of the first ingredient to the center of the mortar and lightly crush them to flatten, then continue pounding to achieve a fine paste.

For powders such as Toasted Rice Powder (page 283) and *prik phong* (ground toasted chile; see page 329), you'll need to firmly pound and then grind the smaller bits, moving the pestle in a circular motion against the curved sides of a granite mortar. Pound the ingredients in small amounts at a time to the desired texture before adding more. As ingredients become wet and sticky it'll take more time to add new ones. As you pound away you'll need to do some scraping with a spoon—things start

to build up on the walls of the mortar. You want to keep moving ingredients toward the center, the eye of the mortar.

Pounding shouldn't require much muscle. Let the weight of the pestle do the work, especially when using a granite pestle. Keep a fairly loose wrist and let the pestle drop from its own weight, your hand and wrist guiding the pestle toward the target.

When making tum som in a mortar, use both hands: One to work the pestle and the other to stir with a spoon. Avoid pounding softer ingredients at the center of the mortar—the goal is not to smash or make a puree. Don't pound straight up and down, but approach it at a slight angle, banging the pestle against the conical wall. This allows the pestle to gravitate on its own toward the center, creating a thump. While you pound from above use the spoon to scoop the ingredients from the bottom and back up the sides, alternating back and forth between the spoon and pestle in a tumbling motion. Do not overdo it or you'll make your tum som too watery and limp.

At the butcher stalls I smelled the freshly slaughtered meats, the bile, the gaminess of skin, and the saline fragrance of blood, like an ocean breeze but without any nuance of sea. I smelled the smoke from hawkers grilling beef balls, of toasted water buffalo skin for *jaew bong*, someone always grilling—all the time—over homemade charcoal. The noise, everyone speaking Lao (I didn't hear any Thai at all, except in Bangkok). It felt like a different place.

I started to get it: why we cooked for ourselves the way we did at our restaurant, the way we ate here, and why we couldn't serve the same food to the American customers. It was different worlds, so far apart. Here it was sitting on the floor and not using utensils other than a spoon. There was no phat Thai. I didn't have a single curry dish. Food here was so much simpler than that, like it flowed naturally out

of the daily activities of my uncles and aunts in this landscape: take bones, make soup; steam vegetables; fry something, grill something; pound chile pastes and dips in the mortar that was always ready. That was the meal, three times a day, sticky rice every time. At the restaurant, we didn't even serve sticky rice, much less any dishes that went with it.

When it rained here, the puddles in the orange dirt looked like Thai iced tea. It stayed in your clothes. Working in the family restaurant at home, grease from the woks stained my shoes. Here, the land itself turned them orange. I swear this place was trying to mark me. I got it, but it just wasn't for me.

Back in Oakland, I thought a lot of the things that happened in the village were cool, but I thanked God I wasn't growing up there. My life in Oakland was all structure: get up, run around for fifteen minutes getting ready, peel out the door to be at school by eight thirty a.m., get on with my stuff. We had a flushing toilet and didn't have to take baths outside with a cold hose. In Ubon we would wake up early to the sound of roosters, and every day went on forever, held together not by the rigid structure of events but by a stretchier one of community. I wasn't in a hurry to go back. I felt like an outsider, even though everybody talked about the village like it was supposed to be my home.

I did understand Moms better. Going home filled a big void in her, and for a long time. I always thought she and my dad had come to California to better *their* lives. After that trip I started thinking she'd come to make things better for my brother and me. I wore the responsibility of that, like I wore the orange dirt stains in my sneakers.

The last straw of my dad's gambling and drinking had dropped onto the camel's back of my parents' marriage. But they didn't get a divorce: They kept on, working at the restaurant, struggling to pay the bills. I realized later that my mom was holding on for my brother and me to become adults before she made the split. She still won't admit that (she wouldn't want to put any kind of burden on her kids). But I know that for sure. As soon as I turned twenty-one, when my brother was eighteen, they filed for divorce.

Fights over money and the restaurant didn't stop. I was more protective of my mom, and wanted to help out more. Running a business, there's always the money factor.

Money bored deeper into my own thoughts. My Wat Phou wages suddenly weren't enough—not enough to get those black Air Jordan 6s and all the CDs I wanted: A Tribe Called Quest, *Midnight Marauders*; Dr. Dre's *The Chronic*; Snoop Dogg; Ice Cube. The cool kids had Russell Athletic hoodies, the hat with the weed leaf on it, pagers for no reason. I needed to hustle harder.

Eighth grade, ninth grade: I noticed things started to get more segregated. Fourth grade, fifth grade, you just play with anybody, doesn't matter their skin color. Sixth grade you start to gravitate toward the Asian kids, and everything sectors out between the math club Asian kids and the gangbanger Asian kids. I started to resent that I didn't have a social life, being at the restaurant all the time, under my mom's watchful eye.

There was a remnant of the old Laotian ghetto on Waverly Street across Broadway from Twenty-Fifth Street, closer to Lake Merritt. It was a lot safer over there—you didn't get as many homeless people or drug addicts. There was a 7-Eleven, a Cadillac dealership. There were Lao people there we'd never met. The old neighborhood sprang back up again. It was Oakland's new Lao hub.

Some of the Lao people there came to work with my mom at the restaurant in Concord, others worked at other Thai restaurants. It was the same closed-loop system that used to exist on Twenty-Fifth Street: You make this, I'll make that, let's barter. We went to potlucks there, birthday parties, and there was more gambling.

There were slightly older kids (sixteen, seventeen) who lived there. Gangbangers—the Lao Crips, they were called. Technically OTC: the Oak Town Crips, always hanging out in the parking lot with their tattoos, their Dickies pants and wife-beaters.

One day on Twenty-Fifth Street a car hit me. All I remember was looking up and seeing this yellow thing coming at me and waking up in the street. I opened my eyes again and I was in an ambulance. I opened them one more time and I was at home. My face was all scratched up, I had a cut on my head, stitches. Moms said she knew something bad happened. She was inside with my brother, all she heard was tires screeching and a scream, she knew it was me. I was home for a week.

After I got better we had a *Baci* in my aunt's backyard on Waverly Street. A Baci is a Lao celebration ceremony (technically I had a *sou khuan*, a blessing for health). The Buddhist monk came, did the ritual, tied white yarn around my arms for healing. After that it was one big dinner party: gambling on blackjack, dice games. The Heineken was flowing, along with the Rémy Martin mixed with soda water, 7UP, or Red Bull. We grilled chicken, ribs, brisket, intestines. Everybody came, even the Lao Crips, drinking forties instead of Heineken, eating sticky rice. I thought they were cool.

My mom kept her eye on them. She heard the gossip. There was a lot of it.

"That one got shot."

"That one's going to jail, does his mom know?"

"That one sells weed to my son."

"I couldn't sleep last week, looked out, and saw that one in the parking lot at two a.m. What does he do out there so late?"

The one time I was really afraid for my life I was walking home from school through the block where the OTC hung out, their headquarters. I was wearing the wrong color or something. I turned the corner and these guys rolled up, a rival Latino gang in a brown Mustang. The car was full, driving up slow next to me and two other Lao kids I was walking with; one had a brother affiliated with the OTC. One of the Latino guys said something; I spotted a shotgun in the car. Just then my friend screamed, *"Run!"* I had this heavy-ass backpack, weighed down with *Elements of Literature Volume Three* or some shit like that, my heart pounding out of my chest. Like a scene out of *Boyz n the Hood*, we hauled ass around the block to a house with an opening under the stairs, a crawlspace. We hid. They drove away. Maybe the Baci was still protecting me.

I didn't tell my mom. I had my eye on a different world.

Saturday morning, I clicked through the channels and saw it: a white chef in an immaculate chef's coat, in a kitchen that looked like the *Starship Enterprise*. It was my first time seeing *Great Chefs.* The guy working with a wood-handled knife that looked thinner and more pointed than the Chinatown knives at Wat Phou was slicing a carrot, crushing garlic, chopping feathery green herbs. It was Michel Troisgros. I was mesmerized.

All I knew about kitchens was that they were hot and cramped. Compared to burning charcoal in a shophouse, or the blast of heat on the line at Wat Phou, the TV kitchen looked cool. My mom and aunts all sat down to perform a task, snipping green beans, even butchery. Moms would set up her milk crate with a towel and a cutting board and a little plastic stool and just sit there, doing butchery. This foreign TV world was calm. It was elegant.

I went to De Lauer's newsstand downtown and found the food magazines. I looked at every page of *Food & Wine* and *Gourmet*, even the ads. I pored over *Art Culinaire* so long the man told me to get out. I saw a story about The French Laundry and it

was like—shit! Everything was so clean and refined. I remember the thought that came into my mind: *I need to do this*.

I looked at my mom's food at the restaurant, her kitchen at Wat Phou. I knew it could never be like The French Laundry, but for the first time I judged it, judged her. Why were we doing things this way? It wasn't how it was supposed to be.

My mom's like a hoarder—she hates throwing things away, or giving them away, because she worked so hard to get them. It annoyed me.

"Mom, why are you saving this? It's just an empty bottle."

Tenth grade, sophomore year—that's when I decided I wanted to go to culinary school. The restaurant was in decline, my parents had kind of given up on it, had definitely given up on each other, even though they still went through the motions, day after day. I told my high school counselor at Oakland Tech I wanted to be a cook, spend my energies elsewhere besides trying to go to college. So I just took classes, the required ones, to graduate, as few classes as I could. I had a goal in mind. I took my PSATs but not my SATs. I wasn't going to pay for a test I didn't need.

I researched culinary schools. I looked at the Culinary Institute of America. Man—it was dumb expensive, plus I was scared to go to New York after high school. California Culinary Academy in San Francisco was still expensive but I could live at home, and the program was only eighteen months.

That's when I told my mom I totally wanted to get into cooking. She didn't try to discourage me, it was more of a warning.

She said, "We're making a lot of sacrifices to have this restaurant. It's a lot of hard work, and there's very little good outcome on the other side. There's a lot of stress." I wanted to do it anyway.

She asked me again, later. "Are you sure you want to go into the restaurant business? It's not torture, but it's draining. Emotionally. You'll be very poor."

"Poor?" I said. I was thinking about the magazines.

"Not necessarily poor in money, but you won't have time for yourself, for your friends," she said. "You'll be tired all the time. Grumpy all the time. It's very demanding on everyone."

I was like, *Okay, okay*. She knew I wasn't listening.

At the restaurant, I counted down the days till high school was over and I could start culinary school. My interest in cooking deepened week by week. Moms allowed me to do more.

I tried to use the knives like I'd seen on *Great Chefs*. Did you ever notice how Asian cooks peel or slice things only going forward with the knife? Mangoes and stuff like that. That's how I grew up, peeling mangoes and apples and pears, going forward. On TV I saw the European chefs peeling backward, peeling potatoes by drawing the knife toward themselves. That was a new motion for me—I tried, but it was awkward. It didn't feel natural. I switched back to Moms's way. It made more sense going forward.

5

HOMESICK IN ROSES

I slipped into my first white chef's jacket and checkered pants, tied my neckerchief on, and adjusted the stiff toque on my head. Last week I was graduating from Oakland Technical High; this week I was starting my eighteen-month associate's degree program at the California Culinary Academy (CCA) in San Francisco. I bought my first decent knife, and took my first step away from the family business. I distanced myself from all the fish funk, bile, blood, and spice that—honestly—I'd come to feel embarrassed about, even though I still secretly loved all of it. I was turning a page.

In 1997, the program cost $30,000. I took out a student loan for part of it; Moms helped with the rest. I don't think she sweated the money—she just wanted me to be on track, do something positive with my life. She'd watched her friends' kids pushing dope, never even making it through high school. Around us, going to any kind of school after twelfth grade was rare. At eighteen, some people I grew up with already had two kids.

CCA was my intro to first-world cuisine. I may have been brown, scrawny, and small, but at least I was dressed like the elegant European chefs I'd seen on TV. Like an anthropology student excited about Mayan pottery shards, I geeked out on everything related to French cuisine. Marie-Antoine Carême, Auguste Escoffier, Fernand Point: I butchered the pronunciation. I'd learn.

I was the youngest student in my class, with a résumé

that listed only Wat Phou. Some students had already been cooking in serious restaurants, others were career changers who'd made it big in the dot-com game and had a secret passion to cook. A few were ex-military. The rest were the lost ones. They'd seen the culinary school infomercials while drunk or stoned and drank the Kool-Aid, believing the promise of a high-paying placement after graduation. I was an outsider.

I ignored the conversations in the basement changing rooms about getting hammered after class, where to score dope, and who wanted to bang who. I had goals. I had a timeline. Poor kids don't have the luxury of fucking around. I knew my parents didn't have much and I didn't want to be a burden, so I still helped out. Class was 7:00 a.m. to 2:00 p.m. I'd get home by 3:00, put my stuff away, go to the restaurant, and work till closing. I'd known long days since I was a kid. It didn't faze me.

Classes were in two-week blocks, each devoted to a specific curriculum. Safety and sanitation was first, then basic knife skills. I mastered the French cuts (julienne, bâton, concassé) while the other students struggled to tourné a potato. I was so far ahead of the game—I'd had a knife in my hand since I was ten. Butchery class was my favorite. I grew up watching my mom and aunts butcher carcasses. I knew what to do.

The concept of roux blew my mind. The science of mayonnaise was a revelation. Classic mother sauces? Shit, ours had always been soy sauce and fish sauce. Gelatin? I never knew it came unflavored (it was always cherry or grape). Butter? Never cooked with it—all I'd seen at home was margarine. Brown butter changed my life.

I was curious enough to cook after class. I made crème brûlée in our restaurant kitchen, just to dick around. My mom was like, "Oh, this is just like our steamed pumpkin with coconut custard inside. I could have taught you this." But I needed to be in a professional kitchen, even if it was only a school setting, with stacks of shiny third pans and sheet trays, and where the walk-in wasn't full of food in recycled Chinatown shopping bags. I needed to be in a kitchen that wasn't just a hodgepodge of cheap equipment, everybody cooking in street clothes.

For all its revelations, culinary school moved too slowly. I wanted to learn fast, on my own terms. I didn't enjoy it, but I got through all the bullshit and made it to the finish line. I was ready to take on the world, chasing the dream of working in a fine-dining kitchen and becoming an accomplished chef. I had a degree. I should be able to get an interview or a *stage* and eventually get hired, if only as a prep cook. Right?

One of my chef instructors told me Chez Panisse was the finest restaurant in the East Bay. He said I'd be able to continue my education there, climb to the next level. I'd never heard of the place. Mention Alice Waters and I wouldn't have known her from Julia Child. I put on my best pair of pants, blue Dickies lifted from my father's closet. I threw on a collared shirt, a tie, and a pair of dress shoes that were uncomfortable to walk in. I got on the 51 AC Transit Bus to make my way to Berkeley with my résumé. I knew this block! Chez Panisse was two doors up from Cha-Am, the Thai restaurant where Moms used to work. I relaxed a little. I almost felt at home.

I walked through the gate, up the steps, and through the main door, right before lunch service.

The host stopped me immediately. "Can I help you?" Suddenly I felt like the brown kid from Oakland I was, dressed in stiff shoes and borrowed baggy pants.

I asked to speak to the chef, but Chef was busy. The host offered to take my résumé. I handed it to her and walked out the door, back to the bus. Months went by: no call from Chef, no e-mail to say thanks but no thanks.

When it was clear the silence coming from Chez Panisse was permanent, I felt defeated. I needed to try to figure out this game of life that was playing with me. Just showing up with the degree the system told me I needed wasn't enough, especially since I still had only Wat Phou on my résumé. I needed to be on the hustle again, only this time the corner was totally different.

I started helping at the family restaurant again, now at a new spot in Oakland, just a few blocks from where I grew up. Manyda was the name; it was my mother's place alone. The tension between my parents had reached a climax. I knew it was coming. Part of me wished it had come sooner. As part of the divorce, they had to sell Wat Phou. Moms was getting a new start. She bought a little house just south of Oakland. I was living there, putting in time at Manyda.

I was nineteen, thirsty for knowledge, and broke, still in search of a job. I looked for line cook positions in the classifieds (Craigslist wasn't a thing yet). I focused on casual places, since nicer restaurants like Chez Panisse seemed far out of my league. I looked for more upscale Asian

restaurants—they might look at my Thai restaurant experience and not stick my résumé at the bottom of the pile. Maybe I'd have a chance.

I saw an ad for a new restaurant in Berkeley: Xanadu. It said the food was "pan-Asian with Western influences." This is what I needed: a kitchen with modern systems to ease me into Western cooking. I got an interview right away with the chef, Alex Ong. I made my way down to the restaurant. I thought, *Screw dressing up*.

Alex has a Malaysian background and knowledge of American and European cooking. He was at Stars, Le Colonial. His food was more intuitive, refined without being too polished, or having all the nuances stripped away. He hired me on the spot to start the next day. I was nervous as hell. It was my first job outside of Wat Phou!

Xanadu's food was fantastic, Asian with subtle Western touches—Alex's food. It got really busy right away, and after good reviews things exploded. We were doing at least 250 covers on weekends and only slightly less on weekdays.

I felt a sense of fulfillment, cooking differently than I'd ever known, plating differently. After a few months I started to cross-train, moving around the kitchen pretty rapidly: from grill to wok, and from there to garde manger and desserts. In less than a year I became sous-chef: I was at the right place at the right time, no lie. I was able to start paying back my stupid student loan to the CCA and had some leftover dough to save up for a turbocharged Mitsubishi Eclipse.

I saved for months to eat George Morrone's food at the Fifth Floor in San Francisco. I was pumped, got dressed up, and walked across the zebra-print dining room floor, sat in an oversized plush chair at a table with pressed linen. I ordered the tasting menu with wines to pair. They didn't even card me! (I had a really good fake ID on me anyway so I wasn't tripping.) *Amuse-bouche* with caviar; pumpkin risotto with lobster, stuffed in a baby pumpkin; and Morrone's signature seared tuna with foie gras tower. I remembered the kids I grew up with in the Laotian ghetto and thought, *I gots my foie gras, bitches!* It was a feast to remember.

After a busy weekend I had a Monday off, but the days I wasn't at Xanadu I helped out my mom at Manyda. Tuesday morning I decided to sleep in. The night before I was hanging out with the boys—we found out the street races down at the Port of Oakland got moved to Mondays because there were less cops on the beat that day. We'd stayed out till three a.m. I finally got up, showered, was eating cereal,

and decided to turn on the TV to kill time before I had to leave for Xanadu. I flipped through the channels. I thought, weird—they were all playing the same movie. I'd blazed a J last night but I wasn't still *that* high. I turned up the volume and heard it: *Two planes crashed into the Twin Towers of the World Trade Center in New York this morning . . .*

Everything came to a freeze that day. Business at Xanadu declined immediately—by the end of 2001 it shut down permanently. I cried. Happiness fades. What now?

Alex had already left Xanadu before it closed. He was now executive chef in San Francisco at Betelnut, another modern pan-Asian spot with an emphasis on street food. Alex called and asked me to be his second in command: executive sous-chef. Not bad for a Lao kid just a couple of years out of culinary school. I made a one-year commitment.

Betelnut was beyond busy. Seven hundred covers on a Saturday! It was mind-boggling. This place was a meat grinder, no doubt. I did all the scheduling, learned how to read a profit-and-loss statement. The clipboard was almost never out of my hands—I got more paper cuts than knife cuts. The burn of a high-labor cost hurt worse than splatter from a wok. Toward the end of my year I began to get bored and burnt out. I missed cooking.

I had met Bruce Hill, chef at Bix. He helped out here and there at Betelnut. Bruce got me through the kitchen door of Masa's. On my days off, chef Ron Siegel let me *stage*. I didn't get to touch much but I was able to see firsthand how a high-caliber brigade functioned. I was amazed by the cleanliness, the professionalism, and the discipline, the opposite of my mom's commando kitchen. I wanted to work at Masa's badly, but I had to wait for a position to open up. I was twenty-two and running out of time. I didn't want to relocate to New York, even though opportunities were better there. I couldn't leave my mother and brother behind.

Bruce mentioned a restaurant by a chef I'd never heard of, in a town I had no clue existed. "David Kinch just opened a new restaurant in Los Gatos called Manresa," Bruce said. "From what I've read he's doing awesome work and he probably needs cooks down there in the South Bay. Look it up." I went home, turned on my computer, and summoned the gods of Google to give me information and driving directions. Next day I jumped in my Mitsubishi rice rocket and jetted down to Los Gatos without an appointment.

I saw the Manresa delivery door. I was sweating: I'd removed the air-conditioning unit to make my car lighter for drag racing, but mostly my nerves were out of control. I saw a guy in a pristine starched white chef's coat putting trash in the dumpster. It was Josef Centeno, Manresa's original chef de cuisine. He looked intimidating as hell. "Hey!" I said nervously. He eyed my scrawny body. "Can I help you?"

"I'd like to *stage*, just in case you were hiring."

"Where are you working now?"

I told him about my *stage* with Ron Siegel at Masa's. I failed to mention my real experience on purpose—Betelnut and Xanadu might disqualify me from even getting a chance, because they were casual and Asian.

"Are you available tomorrow?"

"Yes I am, Chef."

"See you here at noon. White chef's coat, black shoes, black pants."

"Thank you, Chef!"

I got there too early. I put on my chef's coat and it was like walking onto the *Starship Enterprise*: Everything was immaculate and crisp. It had bright, clean lines, glistening stainless steel and no open flames anywhere. Josef was at the pass, in front of the Bonnet cooking suite in an island configuration custom-made in France. The kitchen floor had carpeted mats instead of the perforated rubber ones studded with hunks of onion and tofu I was used to. David Kinch came up and greeted me with a simple introduction and shook my hand. I was pretty much reeling.

My first call of duty was to use the meat slicer to cut frozen logs of rice blackened by squid ink. They got dried out and fried at high temperature to puff up, a small snack. I tasted gazpacho made with strawberries, a madeleine made with black-olive caramel. How did someone even think up these things, and then put them together so they harmonized?

The amount of discipline was astonishing. There wasn't a single water drop or grain of salt to be seen on any stainless surface. We had to label the *mise en place* with masking tape cut at a ninety-degree angle, never torn. Work towels were placed at stations with the stripe on the right and the folds facing away from you. I wanted to work here.

That night I stayed through the end of dinner service and helped break down the kitchen. I helped scrub the French tops back to new form. I polished the copper pots and pans with a slurry of distilled vinegar and water with flour and salt. This was my boot camp. It's what I wanted. This is what I put my time in for, all those nights, weekends, and summers as a kid, getting burned and stained with grease at Wat Phou. I hopped in my pumped-up Eclipse and sped off back to Oakland and the street races, even though it was after midnight. My

Manresa *stage* already felt like a dream. I waited for that 408 area code to show up on my caller ID.

In the meantime I went back to help my mother at the restaurant, kicking it with the guys, working on cars, and talking shop. Exactly a week later I got the phone call. It was David himself. "When can you start?" I pressed "end" on my Nokia before I could even exhale. *You better not fuck this up,* I kept telling myself. I wasn't

a rookie but I was an amateur, with large kitchen clogs to fill. Everyone was watching this new kid on the block.

Months passed, I started working my way through the stations, adding more disciplines and knowledge to my skill set. I was butchering whole ducks, suckling pigs, and spring lambs. I broke down fish I had never heard of, much less eaten. David gave me the freedom to explore my curiosities. He let us learn on our own, make mistakes on our own.

Days at Manresa were long. I went in early and left late, voluntarily, on my own time. I didn't mind. I loved every minute. Being there kept me out of trouble, the jarhead level of discipline kept me focused. I learned how to respect ingredients. I learned refinement and consistency, how to bring concision to a dish.

My vegetable puree game was strong. I learned how to leave the blender on for minutes to get that silky texture, then strain through a *chinois* to catch any unwanted textures. Not quite like pounding away in the mortar and pestle.

For close to five years I commuted an hour each way to work, returning home late at night to Moms's leftovers from staff meal at Manyda. It was always a treat. Manresa became a home for me, a second refuge, since my main place of love and comfort would always be Oakland. I had a secret

wish to return one day to do something for myself and the city where I'd learned how to eat, a long time ago on Twenty-Fifth Street.

Manresa wasn't just the place I learned how to cook, it was where I got closer than ever to Europe. David introduced me indirectly to the cooking of Michel Bras and Alain Passard, because that's where his inspiration came from.

I got tired of reading about these and other chefs. I wanted to see their restaurants.

What really sparked the fire was when David brought in his copy of *El Bulli* in 2003. The book was absolutely nuts, the food looked extraterrestrial. This was next-level shit I needed to see directly, with my own eyes. I also wanted to run away for a bit and see the world. I'd been in Oakland essentially my whole life. I needed a refresh.

As 2005 dawned, I sold my car and bought a one-way ticket for a yearlong European cooking and eating tour, without even a return date in mind. Europe was going to be my grad school—I secured *stagiaire* positions at The Fat Duck in Bray, England, and Mugaritz, outside San Sebastián in Spain, with a detour to Barcelona to work a bit at Alkimia. I dreamed about finishing off with a season at El Bulli, though that seemed a distant possibility. I left with David's blessing.

In Europe, my three *stages* came to an end. I decided to take the train from Barcelona to Paris to link up with my friend from back home, Pim Techamuanvivit, who happened to be in town. She knew Paris well. Who better to be with than someone familiar with the city and its food?

I was feeling a bit homesick—I'd never been away and on my own, punching bigger and bigger holes in my credit cards from all the Michelin-starred restaurants I was dining at. I bought a ticket for my flight home the following week. The next day I got an e-mail from Albert Raurich, El Bulli's co–chef de cuisine. A stagiaire hadn't worked out. They had room in the kitchen, plus a place to stay, for the remainder of the season. I was thrilled, but the homesick bug had bitten me hard. I was craving my mom's food.

I told Pim, called home to talk to my mother, and asked Jeremy Fox, my best friend at Manresa at the time and now my brother, what I should do. All I heard in the background from the kitchen in Los Gatos was "GO!" *Fuck it*, I thought. My family would always be waiting for me. I got on the next EasyJet plane to Barcelona and caught a train to Roses on the Costa Brava.

El Bulli was the UN of cooks. I cooked next to Jimmy (Denmark), Soon Jin (Korea), Takeo (Japan), Giovanni (Mexico), and Lucca (Italy). There was a guy from Greece and two fellow Americans, one of them my roommate, Anthony "Tony" Secviar. The American *stages* had secret numbers. Tony was 11, I was 12. I asked what number Grant Achatz had been (number 4, apparently). The world traveled to El Bulli.

Oriol Castro, one of two chefs de cuisine (he was the one in charge of creativity), gave the stagiaires our morning assignments. We'd start at ten a.m., after finishing at one the night before, followed by partying at the local discotheque (as stagiaires we never had to pay a cover). We'd leave the club as the sun came up and the bakeries were pulling the day's first batch of baguettes from the oven. The smells were unforgettable.

One morning Oriol's assignment was to make a soup from home, something we ate as kids and that we now craved. It was a rough morning—I was feeling a bit woozy from the previous night, still slightly drunk. We all sucked it up and went to work.

The seafood here on the Costa Brava was prime. And in my state, I needed something warmly aromatic, acidic, and spicy. I made what came naturally to me: *dtom saap* with prawns from the sea. El Bulli had a well-stocked international pantry. I found coconut milk, fish sauce, tamarind, lemongrass, lime leaves, and galangal. I was cooking in a modernist kitchen. I thought, *How do I refine this? Turn it into a jelly or a foam?*

"Make it like you're making it for yourself," Oriol said. I forgot about trying to make it fancy.

I pounded away at the aromatics to the rhythm of my pounding headache, my ears still ringing with house music. I closed my eyes: The vibration of the pestle against the mortar was hypnotic. The soup was delicious. It comforted me on multiple levels and gave me encouragement for the long day ahead. I tasted it so many times only half the pot was left for Oriol. All the stagiaires presented their soups—it wasn't technically a competition, just one of the many clever ways El Bulli did research for new dishes. All these Spanish and French chefs could do global research without actually traveling.

This was nothing new. How many chefs have learned about a cuisine from a prep cook or a dishwasher's staff meal? This was the same idea, only better organized. I realized then how it worked: high-caliber kitchens look to rustic food as starting points for creation. There's a shadowing of cooking that harbors innocence, food that's not overthought, that's grounded and honest: delicious food not striving to be more than it is.

The taste of that soup banished my homesickness. I was cured. Later, close to midnight, when we were almost done scrubbing down the kitchen, Tony and the rest of the gang were ready to hit the clubs again. I decided not to go. I thought of the discipline I'd learned in fine dining, how I looked to it to help cure the shit of being a poor, invisible kid with parents who only wanted me to succeed. I'd matured a lot, but still had a long way to go as a cook, and as a person. I'd always be a commis, striving to be better, never getting all the way there.

When the season was up, I got a certificate signed by Ferran and Albert Adrià. I had $30,000 in credit card charges. It was the best experience of my life.

On the flight home I kept thinking how hardcore my mom's experience of being a chef was, given the tools she had to work with. No fancy three-hundred-dollar Masamoto knives, no carbon blue steel of any type, period. Her kitchen tools included thin and warped aluminum pots; a shitty peeler; Kiwi knives you can buy for less than ten bucks, the blades as thin as sheet metal; a roll of foil; some skewers; and a mortar and pestle. And yet her cooking had innocence, ambition, and soul.

Real cooking was cooking with instinct, the thing I'd made that dtom saap with. Oriol Castro had loved it—he recognized the fire in it. I'd gone to Europe hungry for refinement. In a weird way, the chefs there were hungry for the rough purity of food like my mom's. I'd learned refinement for its own sake wasn't the answer. I was still struggling to form the question.

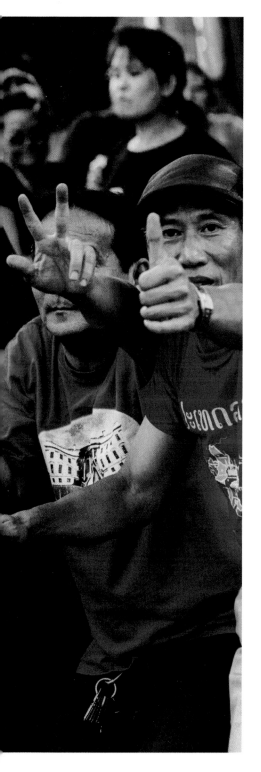

6

MY OWN PRIVATE TRIBE CALLED QUEST

My mother always preached the gospel of immigrants chasing the dream: Work for yourself. I was back in Oakland, twenty-six, full of what I'd seen, tasted, and cooked in Europe. I was tired of commuting to Manresa, even though I still considered David Kinch my chef. I dug up the business plan for my own place that I'd put on hold two years before. I wanted to open a fine-dining spot in Oakland, a city without one.

Commis opened its doors in June 2009, more than a year into the Great Recession and the global financial crisis. More and more people were jobless, their homes in foreclosure. Maybe it wasn't the smartest move to open a fine-dining restaurant with a rigid menu format, especially in Oakland, which didn't have a single prix fixe place. I was in unmapped territory.

But every big decision requires some level of gut call. I always knew I wanted to establish my career in my hometown—I wanted to be close to Moms and my brother. I thought, *What the hell? I'm all in.* I'd gotten some friends to invest. I maxed out eight or ten credit cards. I was single, living at home. I figured if I failed and filed for bankruptcy, so what? I started out basically cooking Kinch's food in Oakland, the foundation I learned at Manresa. I knew I'd find my way. I was on my own culinary path.

At the same time my mom's restaurant, Manyda, was in steady decline, not only from the economy but because Moms was burned out.

Manyda opened in 2002 (the same year I started at Manresa) on the corner of Twenty-Third Street and Webster, in an old Vietnamese pho place a few blocks from where I grew up. My parents sold Wat Phou when they divorced; my dad moved to Rhode Island and Moms married again. Manyda was a partnership between my mom and a friend. It was a busy Thai restaurant with the same formula as the one in Concord, slamming out plate after plate of phat Thai and tofu coconut curries. The place was jamming.

But by 2006 Manyda's jam had slowed to a trickle. And at the end of 2009, just as Commis was racking up some good national press, shit started really hitting the fan. Owning and operating a restaurant for more than twenty years had taken its toll on Moms. Her passion was gone. She was living paycheck to paycheck, stripped of a social life. Her partner left—it was just her and my stepfather shouldering a 48-seat restaurant. They did it all: shopping, cooking, serving, cleaning. I used to drop in to eat my mom's staff meals. They'd shrunk radically since the old Wat Phou days. Manyda wasn't doing great. It wasn't even doing good, actually.

One night she broke down at the table, a very uncharacteristic thing for my mom to do. She sobbed, exhausted and in despair about the future. I could feel her pain. For twenty-five years she'd worked on her feet in crappy kitchens, dealing with the emotional stress of strained finances and raising two boys right. Her wrists were hurting, her back was hurting, her shoulders: all those years of raising pans and lifting boxes. And I could tell by the way she was cooking, she'd almost stopped caring. Except for short visits now and then she'd been away from her family for almost three decades. Her life had gone by in a flash. I needed to do something.

"What's keeping you here?" I said. "You always wanted to go back home, why don't you leave all this?" The main reason she and Pops came here as refugees was to try and give me and my brother a better life. She worked every day for the money to raise us, worried every day about keeping us off the streets. That was her personal American Dream—getting us set up to make something of ourselves. She'd done it. There was nothing much left for her here now. Definitely not the Thai food she was cooking for customers who'd stopped coming.

"I have a lease," she said. "You know I want to sell this place but I'm not going to get anything for it."

I wanted to say her assets weren't worth anything, this broken-down kitchen with thin pans and woks, the mish-mash of cheap utensils and milk crates, but it would have been disrespectful. All of it had sentimental value for her. How could I tell her everything she'd amassed was now useless?

She still had another five years on her lease. "Don't worry about it," I said. "I'll put it on the market. I'll get a broker. Everything will be fine."

We shopped the lease around: nothing. Months went by. The broker got a couple of interested parties to walk through, but the place required some pretty big investment. The hood had to be replaced. The kitchen floor was shot. My mother's physical and emotional distress continued. It was tough to watch. I couldn't bear to see her suffer. I knew what she'd put up with.

And then one night, when I dropped in on Manyda to eat after another long, slow service, something clicked. I cried and held her. I told her it was taken care of. "I'll take this off your hands," I said. "You're free. Go back home to Ubon. I'll handle it." I told her we'd transfer the lease to my name.

I spoke from my heart—it had never crossed my mind to take Manyda off her hands. As her eyes got misty with relief and love for me, a thought seeped into my mind: *What the fuck am I going to do with a broke-down Thai restaurant on a dead corner?*

At that point Commis had a Michelin star. Maybe I should turn Manyda into a little bistro: steak frites, mussels—Commis lite. It made business sense, but something didn't sit right. Taking the burden of the restaurant off my mother's back had been pure reflex. What was I going to miss most about Manyda, broken down as it was?

It hit me like a baseball bat to the back of my dome. The thing I was suddenly freaked out about missing was my mom's cooking.

The dishes I was raised on—everything I loved most—I had no idea how to cook. My training in fine dining hadn't even given me a clue about where to start. Freaking out turned into ice-cold panic: How come I never realized that the food I was raised on, the laaps and papaya salads and jaews, were a mirror reflection of my true self? It spun me into an identity crisis. I really didn't know

MSG IS THE SECRET OF SOUL

Like a lot of other Asians, I was raised on it. It's the taste of home-cooked meals, the flavor of restaurant cooking, the thing that made all those after-school bowls of Mee Mama ramen go down so good. I'm talking about MSG—monosodium glutamate—the soul of "authentic" Asian cooking. Fairy dust, I like to call it.

Granted, MSG has a bad rap. Some say heavy amounts cause headaches and other feelings of discomfort. But then, heavy amounts of anything will make you feel like shit. Science says consuming MSG produces no ill effects, but the headache myths persist.

I hate to be the bearer of reality, but if you've ever traveled to Asia (especially Southeast Asia) and gone crazy over the food, ninety-nine times out of a hundred you slurped down MSG: that tasty bowl of noodles from the hawker stall, the delicious Hainanese chicken from that mom-and-pop shop. MSG is a major part of the culinary fabric of Asia. In Laos and Thailand, you couldn't avoid it if you tried.

MSG exists naturally in foods we eat every day: nori, kombu, and all the sea vegetables; soy sauce; tomatoes and Parmesan (is it a coincidence how much we all crave margherita pizzas and spaghetti with red sauce?). Our tongues register the natural compounds in MSG as the sixth flavor.

There are some health upsides to MSG. Since it amplifies flavor, seasoning with MSG lets you cut down on salt and still produce something delicious. At home I've tried reducing the salt in a dish and adding a sprinkling of MSG. I found it's possible to reduce salt by almost half without sacrificing flavor. MSG creates a bridge on the palate between the various taste buds, harmonizing saline and acidic flavors, heightening nuance. It's the zoom on your digital camera, a 10x magnifying glass.

Like any tool, MSG has its limits. It will not magically make bad food taste better—if what you're cooking doesn't taste good to start with, MSG will not save it. MSG will not tolerate abuse. Too much leaves an undesirable flavor. MSG is like salt, meaning you can add a sprinkle to whatever you're cooking, anytime.

You'll notice I've included MSG in many of the recipes in this book. You can leave it out (we don't cook with it at Hawker Fare, to accommodate guests with aversions, though I wish we could). I encourage you to do your own tests: Make a dish with no MSG, then make the same dish with. I guarantee you'll want to start cooking like an Asian mom. When you do, look for the Ajinomoto brand. It comes in bags of different sizes.

myself. I'd carelessly discarded the mirror of my food and culture, left it for salvage. Never once since culinary school had I studied my own reflection, or faced who I really was.

In my teens I learned to speak in a voice I thought everyone would like, reaching after haute cuisine, trying to grab that status and respectability, show everyone I wasn't just a poor kid from a beat-up block. I spent so many years as my mom's kitchen assistant and I hadn't even shown her the respect of learning how to cook her food. I took it for granted, turned away from it when I found it embarrassing, shunned the culture that *is* me. I fucked up.

My mother's departure from cooking was going to be the end of something I'd never be able to get back. This space where Manyda was, these blocks, had deep personal history. What if I did something like the food I grew up with here, simple, like rice bowls?

And that's how the restaurant I'd name Hawker Fare was conceived, in a shotgun start of a journey into crisis and self-discovery.

Where would I begin? I didn't have much to rely on—I didn't even know where to shop for all the ingredients I'd need. I couldn't learn from my mom, she didn't have time to teach me the recipes. As soon as I took over the lease she was gone, moved back to Thailand with my stepdad. Anyway it was too soon for her. She was broken, mentally and emotionally. She didn't want to stick

around. The healthiest thing for her was to leave, abandon the place for a while and come back when everything was new again.

Unfortunately all the recipes were in her head. She never wrote anything down, it was all by taste and feel for her. The closest places I knew to taste food anywhere near my mom's were a few Lao restaurants in East Oakland. Friends of my mother's—essentially my aunties—ran them. But I wanted to learn the exact Lao and Isan dishes my mom made, the way she made them. I'd have to teach myself, relying on memories of taste and smell, going back in my mind over all the events in my life this food was essential to.

I knew the dishes I wanted to learn—they were the ones of my mother's I missed most. Thank God haute cuisine taught me how to analyze flavors and understand the chemistry of taste. Memory would be the compass to get me close, but fine dining would serve as the map to get me there.

When Manyda was officially gone, after Moms had packed up and left for home, carrying the same mortar and pestle she'd brought with her to California, I took a look around the empty space. The ventilation was poor, and Moms never opened the windows in the dining room (the ceiling fans were always on). The stale air smelled like water you've used to soak rice, mixed with a residue of grease from the grill.

Moms hadn't changed much from the pho restaurant it was when she took over. There were water stains on the ceiling from leaks that never got repaired. The previous owners must have liked roses—the wallpaper was pink ones on a light blue pattern, roses everywhere you looked.

The floor was covered in off-white linoleum tiles. You could tell they replaced the squares as they chipped: Some were newer than others, a checkerboard effect of old and new. It was

a metaphor for my heart: the old me of the Laotian ghetto alternating with the new me of a Michelin star, nostalgia clashing with the effort to forget my past. I always said a restaurant should be the extension of a chef's personality. No reason this new rice-bowl place of mine shouldn't have complicated textures. But what should I call it?

I had many memories of Manyda's block—I used to hang out in the back parking lot with my friends because the Lao Crips hung out there; it was a cool spot. I knew the Crips but I never associated with them (it was my mom's biggest fear). They'd be smoking all the time, hanging out late, blasting music, girls everywhere. Yeah, I remembered that block. They used to push dope from the corner. It got me thinking about selling food on the street, how it wasn't all that different than hawking drugs. "Hawker fare" floated into my brain.

I looked up the definition of *hawker*. I saw the phrase "One who offers goods for sale by outcry in the street." The Lao gangs were out there crying in the street, that's for sure. Hawker stalls in Southeast Asia hustled bowls of noodles and curry rice plates. In Oakland we hustled, lifted, and hawked everything from stolen goods to dime bags. Hawker Fare stuck. It was a private joke that merged my two worlds, old and new, the checkerboard of who I was. The menu was going to be a personal apology for going astray. I wanted to reclaim my youth, make it right again.

I had a ridiculously small budget to turn Manyda into Hawker Fare. We did the things we needed to do to clean it up first; the kitchen needed a big overhaul. The only thing left over from my mother's day was a three-door freezer, the walk-in, and a dishwasher we leased.

I wanted to keep it simple. I wanted it to have this mom-and-pop restaurant feel, not overly done. We ripped the linoleum tiles off the floors but we couldn't get all the adhesive off. It looked cool though, this natural-looking patina over the concrete. We stained it to look like the floors of the shophouses in my mom's village, the orange-brown dirt that once stained me as a kid.

A graffiti artist who went by one name—Rich—lived across the street. I asked him to do a mural on the back wall of the dining room. I compensated him Oakland barter style, with a bunch of forties and trade at the restaurant. The art posters, the music posters: Music was always a big part of my youth, hip-hop was always a presence on that block. So I wanted to bring something nostalgic, a sensibility. I started looking online, went to swap meets in Alameda, began looking for old posters from Oakland venues. I got one from the Clash, the Prince show at the Oakland Coliseum, Blackalicious.

We started recipe testing at Commis—four months of staff meals were experiments for Hawker Fare. We ate a lot of rice. It was ground zero for understanding all the building blocks of Lao Isan food, the foundation of Moms's cooking. In Western cooking you make your mother sauces from scratch. Thai and other Asian cuisines rely on bottled sauces: fish, oyster, and different types of soy.

It took salty tastes of many different brands of sauces to pierce my cloudy photographic memory of the ones my mother cooked with. I closed my eyes and tried to picture the labels in our kitchen on Twenty-Fifth Street. I amassed a huge pantry at Commis. The dry storage room and walk-in cooler were filling up with strange ingredients from Asian markets. Shrimp paste sat next to salt-packed capers; fish sauce coexisted with Gravenstein cider. It was a snapshot of who I was.

The first weeks were frustrating. Where was point A? I needed a starting place. I tasted sauce after sauce, keeping notes on salinity, aroma, and sweetness. I was reconstructing the past as a mosaic of brown, salty, and funky flavors.

I planned the menu with Justin Yu, the chef de partie at Commis who'd moved over to Hawker Fare. I came up with the recipes, Justin came up with the systems (he'd worked with Dave Chang at Momofuku; I was picking his brain). We wanted to start off laid-back and approachable with a menu of rice bowls, mostly grilled meats over rice. Our rudimentary 8-foot line was equipped with a grill, a steamer, and a fryer, and—funny enough for a rice-bowl shop—a French top. That was it. We didn't even have a wok station. Hawker Fare opened in May 2011 with 49 seats, busy right off the bat.

I knew from the get-go I wasn't going to be happy with the dishes, but it was a starting point—we needed to open because we were paying rent. I thought everything was delicious, it just didn't match what I had in my head. We used to eat rice bowls at home for lunch. We called it *ahan kap khao,* "food with rice," so I felt there was some link to my past. It was fine when we were doing lunches only, but as soon as we opened for dinner, my dissatisfaction boiled over.

I struggled against public expectations. People knew me from Commis, so they thought Hawker Fare was going to be this polished thing. Some were surprised we played loud music and had graffiti on the wall. People were asking for chopsticks, and we didn't have chopsticks. We only used chopsticks for noodles, something we didn't serve. Customers were bringing wine, requesting stemware—we didn't even have a corkage policy, we didn't want to serve wine. I was like, *Whoa, hold on, this is a rice bowl shop! We don't course anything out here—it's rice bowls.*

I wanted to build more of a communal style of eating. We didn't even serve sticky rice when we opened. If we really wanted to do the food I ate as a child, we'd have to go all the way.

The food was missing something, a soulfulness, grit. I was using an expensive Japanese knife and nice, heavy-bottomed pots and pans—my mom and aunts never had those things. I was picking cilantro leaf by leaf—Moms threw cilantro stems into dishes and froze the roots for marinades and curry pastes. I always assumed it was because we were broke and she couldn't afford to throw anything usable in the bin. I started to realize it was for flavor.

I put the blender and food processor away as often as I could and gave my forearms and biceps a good workout by pulverizing lemongrass and galangal in the mortar. I stopped skimming my chicken stock—the total opposite of what I'd been taught to do for the last decade—because the impurities lent protein and flavor. I switched up my eating habits and table manners. I started to eat my portion of staff meal on the floor at Commis.

My chefs de parties gave me that "what the fuck" look. I said, "I'm taking this shit back, Chef. This is how we used to do it." They stopped laying out silverware for me.

I needed to go deeper than even my memories of my mom's cooking. I needed to go back to the source: the place where, twenty years before, I'd experienced food as the seamless expression of rice fields, rivers, and jungles. I was ready to find my place there.

7

STALKING UNICORNS IN THAILAND

The pilot announced we were descending on Bangkok, told the flight crew to prepare for landing, and it started: the chills, a pulsating shiver through my body.

Last time here I was a teen traveling with the family, passing through to get to Ubon Ratchathani. It was weird as hell to be coming back as a chef. Organizers of the World Gourmet Festival had invited me to cook a Commis dinner at the Four Seasons. I was honored they asked, though I had other reasons for being here. I wanted to reconcile the past with the present.

Since Hawker Fare, I'd been trying to reclaim my heritage in the food I was learning to cook. Something was missing. My point of reference was memories of my mom's cooking in Oakland, circa 1980s, but there was a film on the mirror I couldn't wipe away, no matter how well my cooking reflected memory. What was it? After the World Gourmet event I'd be heading north, back to Ubon and my mom's village to see the uncles, aunts, and cousins I'd left behind twenty years ago. I was excited to go back "home." It felt very close but also distant. First I'd have to survive Bangkok.

I was embarrassed to think of trying to speak Thai in the capital—the language had evaporated off my tongue. I'm still fluent in Lao. Talking to my mom over the phone and shooting the breeze with aunties and uncles in Oakland had kept it alive. My mother told me not to worry.

"Most of the cab drivers in Krungthep are from Isan," she said, using the locals' name for Bangkok. "Just speak Lao to them." Even in Thailand, the country I was born, I was feeling like an outsider. Maybe, as a refugee, you never really stop feeling that way.

Those chills I was experiencing on the plane weren't anxiety about landing or fear of messing up the vocabulary. They were the feeling of not knowing what the hell to expect, and at the same time knowing exactly how it was going to play out: the anticipation of going somewhere familiar and the self-inflicted guilt for being away so long. As a young buck I rejected my heritage. Now the American kid was coming back to confront an abandoned past.

I stepped off the plane and the wind of the Thai language blew over me like an air curtain in a doorway. I was ready for the awakening. I had arrived at the source.

My cousin Eric from California met up with me in Bangkok. I'd also brought along my chef de cuisine from Hawker Fare, Manuel Bonilla. Manny had been a chef de partie at Commis— he could help cook dinner at the Four Seasons and join me on the Isan research trip. We both needed to find that point of reference.

Walking the bustling streets of Bangkok, we felt like mites dodging giant ants on a sugar hill. There was so much going on in every corner, everywhere. We strolled Sukhumvit, stopping every few steps to watch the food carts, how they conducted service, their setups for mise en place. It was all strangely familiar. The street cooks arranged their carts the way my mother set up her kitchens at Manyda and Wat Phou: same quality of tools, same movements when they cooked.

Wandering one day, we started at Yaowarat Road in the Samphanthawong district, home to Chinatown. What an amazing place: alleyways like dark, damp corridors filled with people, cars, and food stalls, the owners grinding away, feeding hungry locals.

I picked an alley and just walked it, guided by my nose and eyes. We breezed by vendors selling children's toys, dried seafood, and housewares, down lanes dotted with fruit and food stalls. It was lunchtime and I was starving and thirsty. The warm, humid day wasn't helping. It had rained earlier in the morning and now the sun was out full blast; the wet asphalt was steaming, evaporating quickly. I turned a corner and found myself posting up at a sugarcane juice stall.

The owner kept sugarcane on ice, so none was needed after she juiced the cane to order. I was interrupting Auntie from her lunch; I quickly apologized. She was slurping a bowl of *kway jup* that looked so good I had to ask where she got it. "A few meters down, past the shop with the stuffed animals, and on your left, on the corner."

We arrived at this corner in the middle of this maze of alleyways. I looked around: Everyone seated at the thirty or so stools was slurping kway jup. This was the spot.

The energy of the place was magnetic, the aromas of the simmering broth intoxicating. It was obviously a family operation: what looked like two sons and a daughter greeting, seating, bussing, taking orders, running food, and collecting the money. The mother—Auntie—was cooking all by herself. We got the best seats in the house, right next to Auntie.

She was decked out in full makeup, jewelry, a beautiful blouse, and an apron. She turned out bowl after bowl of deliciousness efficiently and with ease, without fancy pots or fine-mesh strainers. Half the time she was talking on her phone as she worked. Her mise en place was immaculate. She worked clean and steady, not rushed, never stressed. She made me feel unworthy as a cook.

I watched her grab a deep plastic bowl. In went the flat rice noodles (blanched by pouring hot water over them in a wooden basin, then straining); crisp pork belly; ground pork; sliced pork kidneys and pork cake; ham hock; chunks of blood; herbs; fried garlic; and a ladle of rich, aromatic broth heavily laced with white pepper. Boom! From start to finish, it took twenty seconds. Auntie's movements were precise, never missing a beat, never doubling back; she smiled the whole time. It was a happy bowl of kway jup.

Over the next week we stopped at any food stall that was bustling, a healthy mix of well-dressed businessmen, cab drivers, policemen, university students. We walked and ate at the same time: fried drumsticks of *gai thawt* in one hand, fresh-squeezed orange juice in the other, everything made to order in front of us, hot, delicious, and wholesome. I was amazed. *"Fuug!"* My nervous sweats evaporated in the heat of Thai chiles in *phat kra pao moo saab*. Tears of joy replaced them.

In the Four Seasons kitchen there was a diverse staff, all regions of Thailand represented. I heard everything spoken, from Lao to formal Thai. I had to be careful not to mix them up in my own sentences or risk sounding like a fool, at least to myself. The dinner we did went off without a hitch. Afterward some of the cooks took Manny and me out eating and drinking till the early hours in Bangkok Chinatown, with the sun coming up in the city that *truly* never sleeps.

The truth is, I was on a mission to find authenticity in Thailand. The food I knew as a child was a product of adaptation and adoption, just like everything in a family that migrates to the States.

My mother wanted to cook as she had back in Isan, but her hands were tied by the limitations of ingredients in California. Her food was a delicious stepchild.

Was I America's stepchild? I didn't feel that way—I was 100 percent Oakland. That didn't stop people from suggesting I was less than that, tell me with a look or a dropped comment, the way they asked where I was from or told me my English was good. I learned haute cuisine in part to prove I belonged. Now I was looking to the authentic roots behind my mom's cooking to do the same, seeking to learn the level of intuition I'd need to cook this food convincingly, without struggle.

Late Sunday afternoon, our last day in Bangkok: I wanted to walk around the city a final time and catch the vibes. I started at Talat Noi, one of the older markets (mostly locals) on the perimeter of Chinatown. I found myself at a shophouse where the specialties were *khao moo krob* (crisp pork belly over rice) and *nam suki* (hot pot). I snuck in my order before they broke down the kitchen for the day. The owner, Mae Krua ("Mom Chef" or "Kitchen Mom"), put her own spin on the dish—she sauced the Chinese-style pork with a slightly sweet but very savory sauce that had a hint of curry powder, different and delicious. Mae Krua saw I liked it. Once she found out I cooked for a living and spoke some Thai she sat me down like a son, smiling, giving me a tap on the hand each time she started to speak.

MAE KRUA: How did you like the food? Was it delicious?

ME: Yes, very much so. The sauce is quite different from what I usually have with khao moo krob. I like it.

MAE KRUA: I'm glad to hear that. This is a family recipe, it hasn't changed in eighty years, since my ancestors opened the shophouse. I have neither a wish nor the right to change it. I am just carrying along the tradition, the family's namesake.

ME: This is a true family business.

MAE KRUA: You can call it a labor of love.

ME: It has to be. Mother [the polite way to address her], your khao moo krob is 30 baht [then about $1 U.S.]. You are definitely undercharging. At 50 baht, no one would complain. It would still be fair.

MAE KRUA: I know, but it's okay. I'm doing well at this rate. I really have no complaints.

ME: Do any of your children have an interest in taking over the shophouse and carrying on the tradition when you retire?

MAE KRUA: I can't worry about that, it's never even crossed my mind. It's their choice, not mine. I want to take it one day at a time and cherish today, not live for tomorrow, not

FEED THE ROOTS, GROW THE LEAVES: A MUSICAL INTERLUDE

I grew up listening to Molam and Luk Tung, music genres from Isan that sound to me like a fusion of bluegrass, jazz, and spoken word. The instruments are winds and strings made of bamboo. The sound is hypnotic. I listened to it on cassette tapes and from uncles singing covers at backyard barbecues. I wanted to hear it again, closer to the source.

I found a vintage vinyl shop in Bangkok: Zudaranga on Sukhumvit Soi 51. It's an amazing source of hard-to-find old-school Thai funk, Molam, and Luk Tung along with an international selection of reggae, soul, Afro jazz, and dub. Zudaranga doubles as a recording label, turning out new and remixed Molam and Luk Tung with modern sensibilities. I was skeptical at first. Then I asked the shopkeep to throw a 45 on the turntable and drop the needle on a track called "Pu Tai Dub" by Bangkok Paradise International Band. Holy shit! The music blasting from the vintage audiophile speaker monitors and subwoofers was raw, a return to roots but new. It was fucking fresh to death. It blasted wind into my sails.

Bangkok Paradise International Band has been around for a few years; they've toured in Europe and Australia. It's made up of older and younger members playing traditional instruments fused with a turntable and modern drums. They turn out great rhythms, making a Molam sound of their own.

I get it: There's room to wiggle, to make music or food your own while paying homage to tradition. The owners of Zudaranga are about the same age as me—we share a generational experience, going back to basics, exploring and celebrating our origins before moving them forward so they're never lost or forgotten.

Food, like music, should be able to evolve. I love it when I hear a great cover of a classic song. Is it better than the original? I don't care—the intention of a cover artist is to create a tribute out of personal emotion, little touches to make it theirs for that moment. I feel the same about cuisine. There's nothing wrong with being inspired, taking something original and remixing, using the tools in front of you. It makes you realize how good the original was, feeding the roots so the tree sprouts new leaves and branches.

worry about twenty years from now. I've been approached with opportunities to open more locations, or sell my recipes. I told them all no, I'm very comfortable with where and how I live, I love my daily routine. I have enough. There are successful restaurants in malls trying to copy the food I make here and they're busy. They charge anywhere from 150 to 250 baht for a single dish and customers are willing to pay. My recipes are easy to replicate but there's always something missing in their versions. Modernizing this style of cooking doesn't make it better. Wait right here.

She ran off behind the kitchen station and started slicing meats, making a sample platter for me: bites of crisp pork belly her brother makes; Chinese sausage from another old-school artisan in the neighborhood; char sui; and a piece of roast chicken thigh, light on the curry, that she'd cooked. She was fucking right! Updating traditional food doesn't make it better! An obvious revelation, but sitting here, it hit me like a two-handed swing of a hammer; it was going to leave a permanent mark. Mae Krua returned with the platter, explained every morsel it held. I ate it all.

> **MAE KRUA**: Have you had *nahm suki* before? I
> make it different than anywhere else in Bangkok.
> Let me go make you a small bowl to taste.

Out came the nahm suki, a two-part dish. First: clear bean thread noodles with pork, fish balls, napa cabbage, and morning glory leaves and stems in a flavorful clear broth flaked with tiny pixels of scrambled egg much finer than in standard Chinese egg drop soup. Second: a shallow ramekin of suki sauce (fermented red tofu, vinegar, fresh chiles, sugar, garlic). The broth was like consommé in terms of flavor and clarity. The bomb!

MAE KRUA: Take some of the noodles, a slice of pork, cabbage, and some broth to create a single bite. Put some of the suki sauce on top. Be careful, not too much! It's spicy.

ME: I like the heat.

MAE KRUA: That's right! You're from Isan, so you can eat very spicy food. Am I correct?

I took the first bite: My body had the tingles, the hair on my neck stood up. I looked up at Mae Krua with wide-open eyes and nodded. I'd had these flavors before but never like this. There was nothing refined about it, but it was beautiful. Magical.

MAE KRUA: How does it make you feel?

I was lost for words—even if I could have expressed myself it would have been muddled in translation. A great chef didn't ask if I thought her food was delicious, she wanted to know about my emotions. All my time in fine dining and nobody ever asked me that—the language of haute cuisine was always cerebral, technical, analytical. I didn't know it till now, but this is what I came to Thailand for, more than finding authentic som tum: food that worked on my feelings the way my mother's did. I was smiling ear to ear, as if I'd just landed my first flawless 360 on a skateboard in a half-pipe. I didn't need to say it. Mae Krua knew. Soulfulness isn't locked into a recipe. It's what comes when you cook in a particular mindset, with freedom, generosity, and self-acceptance. Being open to the world.

We talked playfully, about nothing important, until it was time for me to go.

For the next three weeks Manny, Eric, and I traveled across the northern third of Thailand. Everything we ate was good; some of it made a deeper connection. A bowl of *khao soi* in Chiang Mai, and in Ubon, at a restaurant built on platforms on the river, a dish of grilled, chewy beef brisket that was at least half yellow fat. It was humbling, especially watching the street vendors, a different discipline for a different art. They worked with what they had and did it in high volume, like the lady in pearls making amazingly delicious kway jup at a thirty-seat stall, doing 10-minute turns, on the phone while her kids ran around.

COOKING WITH INSTINCT, OR REFINEMENT, ISN'T ALWAYS BETTER

In 2011, once I got into fast-forwarding Hawker Fare and learning how to cook my mom's food, I struggled. I had all this cooking muscle memory from fine dining, which is all about refining raw materials. In the Lao Isan style I was trying to grasp, it's all about preserving the rustic quality of ingredients—a completely opposite approach. It was really hard to switch.

It sounds easy to cook rustic dishes—you just throw things together, right? But rustic and sloppy are different things. Some dishes were not meant to be refined just because you can.

At Hawker Fare, the food went through an evolution that matched my own change of consciousness that refinement is not always the highest expression in cooking. When you refine a dish that's meant to be rustic, you strip out part of its flavor and texture. It took me a while to realize that my Lao Isan dishes weren't as good as my mom's because I was trying to be too refined.

At the moment I thought I was just cooking according to the rules as I'd learned them. But I had to learn new rules based on the truth that detail in cooking doesn't have to be about fine lines and perfect ninety-degree angles, everything all in a row. The Japanese esthetic concept of *wabi-sabi* finds perfection in imperfect things. That's what I had to learn to get my mom's dishes right. It was a hard lesson to absorb. Cooking rustic food is pretty damn hard. Mostly it takes confidence.

As a cook you have to be able to trust yourself. This is essential for cooking with instinct. When I started to do rustic cooking like my mom's, I was incompetent because I didn't trust my instincts. It didn't feel natural, it wasn't in my muscle memory to cook this way. Learning to execute technique with less telescopic mindfulness made me a better cook. And it taught me to trust myself.

One day, walking in Bangkok near the Old City, I heard pounding—it was coming from the courtyard of a Buddhist temple. I've always liked temples; I've been going since I was a child. I walked through the gates, moving toward the noise. I spotted two gentlemen in shorts and open-toe sandals swinging large and heavy wooden mallets. They lifted them way above their heads and brought them down on a wooden block—I was too far away to make out what it was they were crushing with so much force. When I got closer I smelled peanut brittle. They were making praline.

The way they made it was astonishing. It was definitely not how I learned to work with sugar: It defied food science. Here I was, chef of a Michelin-starred restaurant who regularly screwed up caramel using high-tech equipment. There was a third man, Uncle, rocking flip-flops, working with a wok set over charcoal and zero fucks for theory, crushing it over and over again making peanut brittle. It was a humbling moment. I smiled.

I stood and watched for a long time. Uncle had two knee-high charcoal burners, each with a

wok. Large buckets of sugar, glucose syrup, water, and peanuts sat under a covered shed in the humid air. He took a pan he used for the previous batch without cleaning it first—there were still a few peanuts stuck to the pan. He added glucose and sugar to the wok and used a blow dryer on the charcoal to make it burn red-hot.

The sugar melted and started to caramelize around the edges. Uncle had no wet brush to wash the sugar crystals down the pan, and no thermometer either. He monitored the temperature by eyeball. He added a handful of peanuts, picked up the wok, and stirred the caramel with a large broken-off wok ladle to incorporate everything and poured the mixture out onto a large chopping block.

After a few minutes for the mixture to cool slightly and crystallize, the two mallet guys stood on either side of the wood block and began rhythmically hammering away. I watched the entire process on repeat, about ten times. Every batch of Uncle's praline was perfect. Damn.

It defied theory. We rely so much on technology, the guidance of measuring devices, and the best tools and we can still fuck up. We scale our sugars and peanuts to the absolute gram and make our caramel in nice, heavy-bottomed pans on induction burners with a candy thermometer and still sometimes burn it. Goes to show how valuable instinct is, even when you cook something guided by science. It always boils down to technique.

Technique is a particular way of receiving information about a process enacted in real time. With gauges and other instruments, cooks seek to simplify information gathering by relying on abstract data. The thermometer outputs a number. How much does that number really matter? It represents something—a partial summation of the state of the caramel in the pan. It's assigning a "number" to the color of the sugar, but you still have room to fuck it up. You can't totally trust it; it's not tactile so you can't sense it. A number is an incomplete understanding of what is going on at the molecular level.

In that temple courtyard, Uncle was the thermometer—a well-calibrated one, in fact. What he saw, felt, smelled, and heard was all information, much more varied and nuanced than the things a mechanical thermometer could ever express. Uncle was unencumbered by the tunneling significance of the gauge. That's why his praline was perfect every time, despite the imperfect conditions. I learned a lesson that day: You have to rely primarily on instinct. As long as the cook is calibrated, he or she never has to worry if the tools are.

I ate *som tum,* green papaya salad, at least once a day—I was on the hunt for that authentic version. I tried more than twenty: from street vendors, at truck stops, in private homes, and restaurants in Bangkok, Ubon, Udon, Khon Kean, Chiang Mai, Chiang Rai. I found nothing to hang consistency on, much less authenticity. Some were with peanuts, some without; some with salted crabs, some without; some with *plaa raa*, some with none. I tasted sweeter ones and funkier ones. They were all som tum, none more correct than the others. Authenticity turned out to be a unicorn: cool to think about but just try tracking one down. What makes food delicious is a whole range of nuances, adjusted to each cook's taste. They're all just as good. That's the trippy part.

At my family's village, my aunts and cousins cooked for us. In a funny twist of fate, my mom wasn't even there—she was back in California for a big party for one of her friends (I'd see her when I got home). Being in Isan again brought back what I knew when I was a kid: that cooking is about working with whatever you have, whether it's frogs you catch in a rice field near your farmhouse or supermarket bacon you buy with food stamps. Instead of thinking about my mom's cooking in Oakland being make-do, based on what she could find, I saw she was in the tradition of cooks everywhere.

Once I was home, I couldn't wait to go back. Only next trip I'd go deeper.

8

SAME SAME BUT DIFFERENT

Less than two years later I was landing in Bangkok again, but only for a layover. This time I was traveling north to Ubon Ratchathani to see Moms and the rest of my family before moving on to the country my dad's from, and the origin of so many things in my life: Laos. I was heading there to check out the old capital of the Lan Xang Kingdom, Luang Prabang. It was April, so I'd be there for *Pi Mai Lao*—Lao New Year—a time to wash off the old year and get ready for the one to come. I was ready.

Hawker Fare was finding its voice. The food was closer than ever to family-style Lao cooking. I had expanded, opening a second restaurant in San Francisco, in the heart of the Mission, on Valencia Street. We struggled there with expectations. Customers read the opening press that we were a Thai restaurant and showed up expecting coconut-milk curries and phat Thai. There was still confusion over the line between Thai, Isan, and Lao. In a weird way, I was facing the same dilemma my mother had almost thirty years before, only she made the calculation to cook those curries the customers wanted. The world had changed since then, but some of the same challenges of running an Asian restaurant remained. Like it says on T-shirts for tourists in Laos, SAME SAME BUT DIFFERENT.

Moms's village had changed in small, noticeable ways. The roads now were all paved, and Ubon was getting bigger, sprawling farther and farther out. Everything else felt the same, though it was now the hot season. The fallow fields looked brittle except for rows of Thai chile plants showing red fruit in the dry foliage. The rice fields weren't so green as in September. Moms said they were experiencing a drought, just like California was. The lake was low.

It was humbling to be here, in the new farmhouse Moms had built after she moved back. It was mostly a hang-out space with a big TV and a kitchen in the corner, a gathering place and communal cooking spot for all the aunts, uncles, and cousins. My brother, David, and his wife, Linda, flew out from California. We all hung out in the warm night while my aunts cooked. It was what Moms always wanted Twenty-Fifth Street to be, and what it was for a time, until the earthquake made everybody scatter.

Moms shipped a lot of our furniture from Oakland here: the sofa and coffee table, a dining room table and chairs that were mostly for show, since the extended family generally ate on saats on the raised platform outdoors. It didn't make sense to ship it, but I know how my mother thinks. She worked hard, spending almost thirty years in a foreign place. She'd earned them. They were part of her now.

I tried to help Moms in the kitchen. I think she'll always talk to me like I don't know how to cook. I made breakfast one morning, like French toast only coated with egg and ground pork, which essentially takes the place of butter.

Moms kept an eye on me. "Make sure the flame is not too high! Just because it's browned doesn't mean it's cooked." I'm like, *Yes, mom.*

The thing about my mom's cooking—about Isan and Lao food—is the simplicity of it. Simple food can look less exacting, but it's actually less forgiving. When I can't figure out a fine-dining dish, when I mess up a modernist technique—a foam or a gel or a consommé—I don't feel so bad, but when I fuck up one of my mom's dishes I feel terrible. The techniques are so simple, but you've got to watch everything. Maybe I cut the herbs too fine, or overpounded the rice powder. Usually with Western food it's like the finer the better. Here it's the opposite, but there's still detail

involved. That's the beauty of this cuisine: You have to pay attention, but not control too much.

You know what they say: Simple things aren't easy. As I'd learned on my last trip to Thailand, learning to cook food isn't about capturing authenticity. It's about mastering nuance.

Shopping with Moms at the fresh markets in Ubon made me think all over again about how weird it must have been to leave this to move to California. Things spill into sidewalks here, there's a density of people and food and vehicles, there's color and flowers. Oakland must have seemed comparatively empty, people living life indoors. It must have been hard to stay positive, to not feel completely depressed as a refugee.

That must be the original driving force behind a lot of food in America: the need to adapt, to keep alive a shred of who you were before you left your home village, and raise your kids in a way that makes sense to you. We sat in a noodle shop near the university in Ubon, my mom, my brother and his wife, and me. The man making the coffees and pouring the juices had a headset plugged into the loudspeaker, and in Thai he called out reminders about how to be a good, stand-up person, to the mostly student clientele: listen to your parents, go to school, stuff like that. It must have been hard for Moms to raise us right, without the support of uncles and aunts and grandparents, but also of the bigger community.

Having us work at the restaurant was a way to teach us the value of hard work and being resourceful, but also to keep us under her eye, like we would have been if we'd grown up in her village. Mom-and-pop family restaurants in the States are ways for people like my parents to try and control their own destiny. It was trying to take charge of the disconnect, the rupture, between the old world and the new one.

My own life has these complicated layers. In this book, I'm trying to capture my mom's experience, the dishes she had to adapt to Oakland realities. At the same time, I'm trying to find my own meaning in my parents' experience.

I think that's the universal experience of kids whose parents came from Asia: making sense of that rupture, that sense of disconnect and adaptation, and finding our own identity there. Not in its so-called purest sense, in Isan or Laos for me. It's finding my place in the rupture of my family's experience. It's not about trying to reconcile two worlds that can't easily merge, like fine dining and rustic food, Commis and Hawker Fare. It's about keeping the rupture open.

I got off the plane in Luang Prabang in the season of burning, farmers setting fire to the jungle to clear space for planting, before the rains start. The sky was a strange amber, a strong smokiness was in the air, raining down black wisps of ash. Man, it felt like stepping back to the time of the Vietnam War, the tragic years of secret bombing.

Laos is a poor country with a communist government, lots of unpaved roads, and essentially zero commercialization. On the road from the airport to the heart of the city, on the peninsula

THE ANARCHY OF AW LAM

An iconic stew from the mountainous northern part of central Laos, *aw lam* (also *ow lam*, or *om* in Thai) is a dish of humble village life even Lao royalty had a taste for in all its variations. "There is no one definite recipe for ow lam," wrote Phia Sing, chef to the royal kings of Laos until 1967, "because there are no fixed rules about how to make it." Aw lam changes from village to village and from cook to cook, lawless as the Wild West.

A good aw lam is both simple and complex. It's a mildly spicy stew layered with flavors and textures, and, even though there's a lot going on, a subtle harmony prevails. There's meatiness, the sweetness of vegetables opposing the bitterness of greens, everything surrendering to the aroma of fresh dill or lemon basil. The best feedback I ever got after serving aw lam is that it tasted like the jungle. That brought a smile to my face. Aw lam takes you there.

The stew's base is a mild peppery broth prepared by slowly simmering lemongrass, fresh or dried chiles, and pieces of pepper wood (*Piper ribesioides, sakhaan* in Lao), an Asian climbing shrub with thick, woody stems. It has a strong peppery flavor and a hint of bitterness. It gives aw lam its unmistakable warming heat and has a numbing effect on the lips, same as Sichuan peppercorns.

Preparing aw lam follows the chill and resourceful base law of village cooking: Make do with what grows around you and what you can get your hands on. The aw lam recipes in this book combine various meats, vegetables, and herbs in ways that reflect different versions I've eaten. Then again, once you're past the basics the rules just fall away. Make it your own.

formed where the Mekong and Nam Khan rivers come together, you don't see supermarkets or a single fast-food chain. I figured if I wanted a time travel for Lao food, a place where the cuisine is preserved really well, this would be the place. It's a UNESCO World Heritage Centre, an ancient city of Buddhist temples and the remnants of French colonialism.

The whole vibe of Luang Prabang is forgetting time. For the next two weeks I never once looked at my phone to see what time it was. You kind of get lost in the whole setting, being on the Mekong River in a clearing of jungle. It transformed me, showed me what you can do with very little and still be happy. Walking through villages on the outskirts, you see a home on a plot of land growing rice and herbs. No electricity, they probably have to go a couple kilometers to pump water. Definitely makes you feel like an asshole for complaining about your bad days in Oakland.

Doing almsgiving in the mornings, kneeling in quiet streets with a basket of sticky rice, dropping clumps in the monks' begging bowls—what a different way to start your day. Kind of sets you up right, slows you down, makes you pay your respects. It made me grateful for what I had, nudged me to make the most of being alive. Daily almsgiving is something you look forward to waking up early for. You really don't look forward to waking up at six o'clock to answer e-mails.

I found so much innocence in Luang Prabang. There's some slow gentrification going on over the past decade, more guesthouses opening, more moto-taxis on the streets. But tasting my first bowl of *khao piak* on my first morning, down the street from the hotel, I noticed the owner had plastered the walls of his shop with photos of the places around the world he'd been: Paris and Switzerland, China, Japan. And there he was, happy as a clam, selling khao piak every morning from seven a.m. till it ran out at one or two. He'd be done for the day. No stress.

Luang Prabang is a city with no visible guns. The red hammer and sickle flag flies in front of businesses, I was expecting to see guards with rifles at the airport, military vehicles everywhere. There was none of that. Police officers on the street didn't even carry batons. I got a good kick out of, like, going to a noodle stall, sitting next to a bunch of police officers, enjoying the same bowl of *khao soi*. That was their routine. During New Year's water fights rage in the streets for days, a ritual of purification that feels a little like spring break. People on the street would come up and pour water on a cop, everybody, including the cop, grinning, it's fine. You're not worried about getting shot. It's just very different from home.

I stopped at roadside farms on the way out of town, up to the mountains: neatly rectangular raised beds in patches, dotted with a couple of shelters, made of wood and old corrugated metal, overhanging roofs to shelter from the sun and heat, open on three sides, large platforms for napping and sitting around to eat. Food is built into the culture.

I met a Hmong family whose ancestors had lived for generations up in the mountains; they'd moved to the city to find office work. They invited me for a meal that was a total curveball: no sticky rice, no fish sauce. "Hmong people," my host said, "we don't like to be by the river, most of us can't swim, so there's no fish sauce. There's no padaek. We live in the mountains. There's lots of herbs, and livestock. Gourds."

We ate an unsalted soup of boiled squash—you spooned the broth into jasmine rice and made a kind of porridge. The chile dip was just green peppers with

cilantro and salt, very spicy. There was grilled pork and boiled vegetables. It was a very pure way to eat. Everything was earthy, vegetal, herbaceous—you really tasted the land. There was nothing to disturb what it was.

I told my *songthiew* driver I wanted to find a place where they made rice noodles, *khao piak sen* (made with tapioca and rice flour, almost like Japanese udon) and *khao poon* (vermicelli made from fermented rice). He picked me up at dawn the next day and took me to a shophouse he knew, friends of his wife's.

The Somsack family has been making noodles here every morning for thirty years, a mom, two sons, and a daughter-in-law, in their covered backyard. The sons were shirtless and barefoot, the women in tank tops, flour everywhere, just like a daily routine. They ground their own rice flour, first time I'd ever seen rice flour being milled.

They soaked jasmine rice for twenty-four hours, then fed it into a mill that was almost like a juicer. The result was thick, starchy water (it looked like soy milk) collected in muslin bags. They put huge rocks on top of each bag and let them drain. That was the rice flour.

For the khao piak sen they didn't make their own tapioca starch, but had this ancient, belt-driven machine to mix it with fresh-milled rice flour in hot water. Everything was wood-fired. Nothing was measured out, nobody was checking temperatures. They banged out sheets of dough and cut them into noodles, every morning fifty kilos of khao piak sen and ten kilos of khao poon. They got bagged up and delivered to noodle stalls, or vendors stopped by to pick up a couple of bags. The whole process was over by eight in the morning, every morning. Things just didn't change here. It was astonishing.

It was a blessing to get to roll noodles with them, to touch the dough and feel how it was supposed to be. The whole operation was primitive, a noodle shop with an open fire and a partially open ceiling. It was beautiful. And the noodles were so good. I'd never seen khao poon made that way, so different from the fresh noodles we get in the Bay Area from our Vietnamese vendor. They had depth of flavor, a fermented bitterness, gently sour, and the color wasn't opaque white but a translucent off-yellow.

I met an aspiring culinary food guide named Sii. His family was ethnically Tai Lü, from a northern region where the cooking is more like the Lao food I'm accustomed to. Sii invited me to cook with his mother. It was a beautiful meal: dried fish soup; *gaeng nor mai*, the bamboo-shoot stew, but made with fresh yanang leaves; pork fried with MSG, oyster sauce, seasoning sauce, garlic, and black pepper—it started out cooking in water, but it evaporated as the fat rendered, so for the last stage of cooking the meat caramelized and fried. Everything was like a one-pot dish, one piece of equipment throughout the whole process.

We were cooking outdoors, in the wood-fired kitchen that ran beside their small house. It all made sense to me, my mom's efficiency and resourcefulness. It was really farm- or field-to-table cooking. There was an innocence about it, they didn't talk about proportions, it was just adding to taste. I was surprised when Sii's mother, who was doing most of the cooking, asked my opinion about the seasoning of the soup. I was thinking, *Are they testing me? Do you want more padaek in here or less?* It was an honor.

The meal at Sii's was a new benchmark for me—you tasted that innocence of a home-cooked meal, it wasn't penciled and papered and then made. I came to realize every meal cooked that way is a bespoke experience. I think if we were to go back tomorrow to Sii's family's house and said, "Hey, can we make those dishes again?" I'm pretty sure the taste would be different, but just as good. And that was my mom's cooking: Her *aws* were never the same twice, as far as seasoning. One might be spicier than the batch before; it was all just good. Sometimes being inconsistent is a good thing, if you know what you're doing. Same same but different.

It made me appreciate more than ever what you can produce having very few resources. At a noodle stall on the street— an outdoor kitchen put together with blocks and clay, scaffolding, whatever—they served pretty much the best noodles I'd ever had. Even with the lack of refrigeration, the fresh herbs are pristine, they bouquet up the mint, tie it with a bamboo splinter . . . all those little details. And a bowl of *khao soi* or *khao poon* was fifteen thousand kip, less than $2.00 U.S. It was like, wow—talk about overdelivering.

It made me realize how food is appreciated there, how everyone eats well there, that meals are wholesome. Laos is a poor country, but good food is almost a right, not a privilege. It's accessible to everyone on the street. If this auntie could make the best three bowls of noodles out of this open-air shophouse, in this alleyway, it shows how simple this food is. Spiritually it centered me. I felt very grounded. There's no need for excessive creativity or overthinking: just use what you have and make the best of it. There's genuine innocence to that. It's the difference between a home-cooked meal and a restaurant meal, the quality of freestyling.

It's the difference between a rapper spitting a written verse he's been working on for days, or just getting on the mic and letting go. Sometimes the freestyle turns out a lot better, more sincere, like he's shooting from the hip, you know? Cooking, using your senses, is not something you can distill to an absolute form, it has a life of its own. You just ride the wave.

I walked the high, steep steps to the temple on top of Mount Phousi in the center of Luang Prabang. Before starting, at the bottom, three women sold me offerings: a flower *stupa* (banana leaf and marigolds, in a tiered, tapering, conical shape), three sticks of red-tipped incense, and a little woven basket, a birdcage with a finger handle, holding two birds to set free at the top: a New Year's tradition.

Both of mine had a gray-blue patch on their throats, black beaks sticking out between the reeds, grazing my fingers, chirping loud. I walked up the steps, passed young monks who said hello and seemed to tell a little joke about me, laughing after I passed. At the top, I leaned on the railing, looking over the smoky city that seemed swallowed by the dirty amber air. This is the place, this region, that created the food I loved most, the laap and som tum, jaews and noodle soups.

Food I was given at birth, that I was now fully ready to accept and give myself over to, not try to overthink.

I entered the little temple at the peak, where there were candles for lighting. I looked for matches or a lighter to spark my candles as an offering. There were none. I went back outside to ask a man I saw smoking. I lit my candles and ran back outside to return the lighter. I lit the incense, stuck it in the ash, bowed three times. I went back outside to set my birds free.

It was hard to unweave the bottom of the cage. The birds popped their beaks out more aggressively. I felt a nip on my finger, not painful. Finally I got the cage open; one flew to the tree above me, high above the city. The second bird struggled a bit but finally flew free. I hoped the women down at the base of the steps wouldn't catch them and cage them all over again.

Walking down, halfway to the bottom, I noticed a series of planters on a terraced level. The plants they held had thick, thorny stalks, dull gray-brown, with occasional dusty leaves. On top, they sprouted simple geranium-like flowers of coral pink. Some plants had more flowers than others.

They were plants my mom always grew. The number of flowers is supposed to show the level of spirit in the home or temple they belong to. If you had a lot of flowers, Moms would always say, your spirit was strong. I smiled: I was ready to blossom out all over.

9

FAREWELL FUNK: AN EPILOGUE

Sometimes, just when things are getting good, something comes along to put an end to it all. A chef working up through the ranks of the kitchen once told me that a restaurant is only as good or bad as its last service. That stuck in my head; I often pass along that notion to my chefs and everyone else who works in my restaurants. Every night is an opportunity to finish strong.

In 2014 I started taking major notice of how the neighborhood around Hawker Fare in Oakland—my neighborhood—was changing. The transformation was both good and bad (maybe they always go hand in hand). The 'hood was no longer the 'hood. Families I grew up with were forced to move away because of rent increases. Larger businesses started setting up shop; construction cranes towered in the places where my personal history once stood. High-rent condo buildings began to rise.

Since November 2016, Hawker Fare Oakland had been on a month-to-month basis. Our landlord had no intention of renewing the lease. The building was for sale; a development group acquired it. With all the activity, the block was always hot! Suddenly, it was hot in a brand-new way, one that had everything to do with the temperature of Oakland's real estate frenzy.

On February 18, 2017, I made the decision to close Hawker Fare Oakland. It was bittersweet. Those last few

weeks of service I was there every day, soaking it all in, slowly saying my goodbyes. Also my thanks: Between Manyda and Hawker Fare, in the span of almost two decades, we'd had such a rewarding run. I wasn't done—like I said, I was determined to finish strong. Those last few weeks I was building momentum for the final days. Making a splash, sending the restaurant on its way and paying respect—it was now or never. Time to go hard in the paint.

We ran a few specials that last weekend, unapologetically unfiltered dishes that reminded me

of growing up and the reasons I started Hawker Fare in the first place. Raw shrimp, beef offal and bile with betel leaf and MSG—I called it the Farewell Funk Menu. These things never made it to the regular offerings because I knew they wouldn't sell on any normal evening—they were the dishes my mom was always scared to serve. But for the goodbye dinners I didn't worry about sales or guest reception. It was all about coming correct, paying my respects to the cuisine, my heritage, and a past that's always present: the story of this book.

10

HOW TO USE THE RECIPES IN THIS BOOK

Before you set out to cook one of the dishes in this book, here's one large piece of advice: Read the recipe all the way through first, then read it again.

A recipe should start to make sense in your head before you approach it. Build a game plan. As I realized myself while learning to cook this food, the more you cook a recipe the better you understand the food and the techniques that yield a better dish.

No recipe is perfect—I've learned that over years of cooking. Even at Commis, where ingredients are measured to the tenth of a gram, results can vary in another kitchen halfway across the country. Ingredients vary from season to season and place to place; so do stoves and pan sizes. Recipes are a guide.

Building a pantry is key. Shopping is the beginning of mise en place, and the most crucial part of the process of cooking food entirely foreign to you. Sourcing ingredients is going to take some effort, depending on where you live (the Internet can help). You'll be spending time in multiple Asian markets, walking down aisles amid a matrix of sauces. Substitutions are problematic. I'm not saying you should never substitute, but understand that the dish will not turn out as it's supposed to.

Brand recognition is key when buying prepared sauces like soy, fish, and oyster. The ingredients list in The Lao and Isan Pantry (page 328) will help. Please stick to the brands of bottled sauces I recommend, the ones I've calibrated these recipes to.

Get familiar with ingredients. Taste them on their own. Chew. Bite. Take a whiff. Fresh ingredients taste different from season to season, so taste before you add to a dish. Chiles are a perfect example—start with less (food should not be painful to eat); add more if you like that kick.

Several recipes in this book ask you to season to taste. Keep in mind that most dishes aren't meant to be eaten on their own, but with sticky rice or steamed vegetables and herbs, so the padaek or fish sauce and salt measurements are relatively high. General rule of thumb: If the recipe is bold in seasoning, it's meant to be eaten with rice for balance.

Staples like granulated sugar, eggs, and salt are standard. Use kosher salt unless the recipe calls specifically for, say, iodized salt. Squeeze citrus fruits fresh that day. Eggs should be large. Herbs and leafy vegetables should always be rinsed under cold water, then transferred to paper towels or a colander to drain.

Whenever a recipe calls for charred chiles, garlic, or shallots it means cooking them over a gas or charcoal grill (charcoal is better, since it adds a dimension of smokiness). If a recipe calls for fried cloves of garlic, deep-fry them in a sauté pan with just enough canola oil to allow them to float.

I specify a mix of standard and metric measurements, depending on the ingredient. There are volume measurements for liquids for ease. Weight measures note both grams and ounces. Meats and fish are in ounces/pounds. For making things like curry paste, where precision matters, I give gram measures. For example, 30 grams is a more accurate measure for whole garlic cloves than ½ cup. Grams are also best for measuring small amounts of minced garlic and sliced chiles. My 1 tablespoon of Thai chiles weighs in at 15 grams; someone else's might weigh 10 grams, because the dimensions of the cut are different. Buy a digital scale that can switch between grams and ounces—it saves time and makes cooking more enjoyable. A $20.00 scale is worth the investment. For common conversions, see pages 340–341.

BUILDING A LAO ISAN MEAL

Hearing the word *meal* taps something in my cook's reflexes. It's a trigger word for fulfillment and satisfaction, a complete experience. A meal is never just about food, it's about everything that surrounds it: the context, circumstance, atmosphere, guests, and service, even if it's casual. Any meal—from something à la carte to a lengthy tasting menu—should reinforce an idea. Context brings food to life, animates it.

Building the kind of Lao or Isan meal I grew up with is quite simple. My family had a template in the shape of a pyramid, a hierarchy of importance. At the top was sticky rice. Unlike Western meals, where a starch like potato, bread, or pasta is a side for meats, vegetables, or seafood, rice is paramount. Everything is subordinate to that. A Lao meal flips the typical American question, *What should I have with my steak?* to *What are we going to eat with sticky rice?* Rice is life. It's the center.

In a Lao meal, sticky rice (page 275) is the thing that everyone literally surrounds, whether sit-

ting on the floor, on a *saat*, or at a table in chairs. It's our version of breaking bread with family. So constructing a full-blown family meal is figuring out what dishes should circle the rice. It looks something like this:

> Sticky rice
> Jaew
> Steamed vegetables and herbs
> Salad (tum som or laap)
> Soup or stew
> Meat or fish, fried or grilled

The only major variation is when you have noodles or *khao mun gai*, full meals in their own right, when you don't need anything else. But actually, in reality, you can serve a fraction of the formulated meal and still engineer something that satisfies: sticky rice with papaya salad and beef jerky, or even just sticky rice plus jaew, no need for anything else. It all depends on the social situation and time of day, but remember: You can never cut out sticky rice.

TWO

RECIPES

11

SNACKS

FRIED RED PEANUTS WITH GARLIC, LIME LEAVES, CHILES, AND IODIZED SALT

KHUA MAK TUA DIN SAI KATIEM

Peanuts are one of those snacks that, once you start eating—full up in conversation, not noticing—the entire bowl is suddenly empty. Pops and Uncle would tear through a bowlful in no time, knocking back a cocktail of Rémy Martin Cognac and Thai original Red Bull on the rocks like it was a SmartWater, huddled on the saat playing blackjack on my birthday. Good times! These end up being almost twice cooked: once, dry, in the oven, then fried with garlic, chiles, and lime leaves. You'll notice the recipe calls for iodized salt, something I can't praise enough for seasoning fried foods. I think the flavor of iodized salt makes you crave whatever it touches, and the round granules coat things like peanuts better than kosher salt can. Whatever you might think about iodized salt, please use it in this recipe and see if you don't agree.

MAKES 2 CUPS

2 cups shelled peanuts (448 grams), with skins

5 fresh red Thai chiles (7 grams)

⅛ cup (25 grams) peeled garlic cloves

6 whole makrut lime leaves (2 grams; see page 332)

⅛ cup (18 grams) canola oil

1 tablespoon (15 grams) iodized salt

1. Preheat the oven to 350°F. Spread out the peanuts in a single layer on a rimmed baking sheet lined with parchment paper. Roast for 15 to 20 minutes, rotating the pan halfway through to ensure even toasting—the peanuts should be a light tan color, their red skins dry and papery. Cool the peanuts on the baking sheet.

2. Meanwhile, combine the chiles, garlic, and lime leaves in a mortar and pound to a coarse paste. Warm the oil in a wok over medium heat, add the chile paste and sweat until fragrant. Turn up the heat to medium-high, add the peanuts, and fry until you start to notice the toasted aromas of garlic and chiles (you might end up coughing—that's the sign to turn off the heat). At this point the pieces of garlic and lime leaves should be crisp. Add the iodized salt and toss to mix thoroughly. Transfer the peanuts to a bowl and allow to cool for a bit before serving with beer and booze. They'll keep in a sealed container for about 1 week, but they won't remain uneaten for that long. Trust me.

SOURED PORK SOM MOO

This is the Thai/Lao version of *salumi*, a great bar snack accompanied by peanuts, slices of ginger, and fresh Thai chiles. The pork sours with garlic and salt and the magic curing packets made by a Thai company called Lobo, available at Asian markets (I'm pretty sure they contain a curing culture, nitrates, and a bit of MSG). My mother would make this in twenty-pound batches in our apartment on Twenty-Fifth Street in Oakland. She'd form the farce into sausages and wrap them individually and very tightly in plastic wrap with a slice of raw garlic and a single Thai chile, securing the ends with rubber bands—a one-person assembly line. Moms used to roll them, collect them in a grocery bag, and tie the bag on the kitchen doorknob to let them cure and ferment. After a few days she'd give it to friends in the neighborhood, or slice them up and serve them with beer or whiskey sodas for entertaining or kicking back after work at the restaurant.

MAKES ABOUT 10 ROLLS

1 pound (454 grams) very lean ground pork	1 package Lobo brand nam powder	1 tablespoon (11 grams) kosher salt	4 peeled garlic cloves, thinly sliced (15 grams)
½ pound (226 grams) pork skin, blanched, fat shaved off, then thinly sliced	2 tablespoons (24 grams) finely minced garlic	1 tablespoon (12 grams) sugar	
		10 fresh red Thai chiles (15 grams)	

In a large mixing bowl, combine the ground pork, pork skin, nam powder, minced garlic, and salt. Massage the mixture with your hands, like kneading bread, for 5 minutes, until the pork gets tacky and sticky. Make sure to get rid of any lumps of pork (they can make the entire batch spoil). Divide and shape the mixture into 4-ounce balls. Place a ball in the center of a sheet of plastic wrap. By rolling the plastic wrap and applying pressure, shape the ball into a log about 1½ inches in diameter and about 5 inches long. Place 1 Thai chile and 2 garlic slices directly onto the log and push to embed them. Wrap up the log in the plastic and twist the ends to secure and tighten—the log should be very firm and in the shape of a sausage. Wrap the log with another layer of plastic wrap to keep the twisted ends from unraveling. Repeat with the remaining pork balls. To ferment, place the pork logs in a container. Place the sealed container in a dark, warm place in your kitchen, with a steady temperature of about 70°F (the top of the fridge is usually a good spot). Let the pork cure for 3 days. Check it on the fourth day: The pork should be pink and very firm to the touch. It's ready to be served. Store in the refrigerator, sealed in zipper-top bags to keep it dry, for up to 4 weeks.

LAO IMPERIAL ROLLS PUN GAI YAW

Very similar to Vietnamese imperial rolls. I like the use of taro in this recipe: It gives the rolls more weight, even for such small bites. I like to snack on them by themselves, without herbs or lettuce wraps (that's how I liked to eat them as a child). They were like Tater Tots for me. Serve these as a snack—just the rolls themselves, with the dipping sauce—or as a light meal with the lettuce, herbs, and rice vermicelli.

SERVES 6 TO 8 AS AN APPETIZER OR SNACK

FILLING

2 ounces (57 grams) bean thread noodles, soaked in cold water for 20 minutes, drained

10 ounces (283 grams) ground pork, finely ground

1 ounce (57 grams) carrot, peeled and coarsely grated on a box grater

2 ounces (56 grams) taro root, peeled and coarsely grated on a box grater

2 ounces (56 grams) fresh wood ear mushrooms, thinly sliced (see page 333)

½ tablespoon (6 grams) kosher salt

1 tablespoon (12 grams) fish sauce

Pinch of ground white pepper

1 tablespoon (11 grams) MSG (optional)

8 dried rice paper rounds, cut into quarters with scissors

2 quarts (1,640 grams) canola oil, for frying

GARNISHES

Red or green leaf lettuce leaves

Cucumbers, cut into bâtons

Cilantro sprigs

Mint sprigs

Rau ram sprigs

Vietnamese shiso

Rice vermicelli

CONDIMENTS

Hot, Sweet, and Sour Dipping Sauce for BBQ Chicken (page 301)

1. MAKE THE FILLING: Cut the bean thread noodles in 1-inch lengths and transfer to a mixing bowl. Add the ground pork, carrot, taro, wood ear mushrooms, and seasoning (salt, fish sauce, white pepper, and MSG, if using) and mix well by kneading, making sure everything is evenly distributed; the mixture should feel tacky. Cover and set aside at room temperature.

2. ASSEMBLE AND FRY THE ROLLS: Work on a plastic cutting board or tray. Fill a large bowl with cold water and place it next to your work surface. Working with 4 pieces of the quartered rice paper at a time, dip each piece individually into the water for 8 seconds and line them up side by side on the work surface with the widest part closest to you. Place about 1 tablespoon of the filling at the bottom of each piece of rice paper, at the widest part. Lift the round bottom edge of the rice paper up and over the filing. Roll away from you in a single turn to cover the filling. Now fold the left and right sides of the rice paper toward the center. Continue to roll as tightly as possible to the pointed tip, sealing the cylinder. Repeat with the remaining pieces of rice paper and filling.

3. Add canola oil to a deep, heavy pot for frying and heat it to 325°F. Set up a baking sheet or platter lined with paper towels and set aside.

4. Carefully fry 3 to 4 rolls at a time until they are light brown in color, 7 to 8 minutes; they don't have to be crispy at this point. Transfer the cooked rolls to the paper towel–lined baking sheet to drain and cool. Refrigerate for 24 hours, uncovered, so the skins dry out a little. Reserve the frying oil.

5. The next day, reheat the reserved frying oil to 375°F. Drop the cooked rolls back into the fryer, just as you did the first time. Fry for about 3 minutes; they should be crispier this time, with the skins ending up slightly caramelized. Drain well on paper towels and let cool for a bit. Serve them slightly warmer than room temperature with the garnishes and dipping sauce.

DA'S BLISTERED GREEN BEANS WITH BACON

PHAT PRIK KHING

Da (short for Davan) is my mother's name, and this recipe is hers. The family was on welfare support when I was growing up, so all of our groceries were limited to what she could get from supermarkets that accepted food stamps. This recipe is a personal reflection, Moms's alteration of a common Thai dish based on ingredients she could lay her hands on. In Ubon, she would have used pork shoulder or collar, but in Oakland that was out of range. Instead, she substituted ordinary presliced bacon from the supermarket. Remaking the dish made me realize how inspired my mother's adaptation was. Spice, sweetness, brininess, and smoke all support the taste of the green beans. Moms, you were an innovator in your own right!

SERVES 4

4 cups (454 grams) green beans, cut into 2-inch segments	2 ounces (56 grams) smoked bacon, cut into ¼-inch batons	1 teaspoon (1 gram) whole kaffir lime leaves, cut into julienne	3 tablespoons (45 grams) oyster sauce
2 quarts (1,640 grams) canola oil	1 tablespoon (35 grams) Prik Khing Curry Paste (recipe follows)		1 tablespoon (12 grams) sugar

Preheat the deep fryer to 350°F. Lower the green beans into the hot oil and fry until the skin blisters, about 30 seconds. Heat the wok to moderate heat. Add the bacon and let it render. Cook until the bacon is fragrant and slightly caramelized on the edges, then add the curry paste and lime leaves and fry until fragrant. Be careful not to burn the curry paste; lower the heat if it gets too hot. Add the green beans and seasonings to the wok. You may have to add a touch of water to allow the beans to steam and prevent the curry and sugar from burning. Toss all the ingredients in the wok until beans are coated in the sauce. Serve as a snack or with jasmine rice.

PRIK KHING CURRY PASTE NAAM PRIK KHING

The measurements for this recipe are in grams alone, so you'll need a kitchen scale. The balance of the ingredients is crucial, so weigh everything carefully.

MAKES 2 CUPS

100 grams dried red chiles

30 grams shrimp paste

4 grams coriander seeds, toasted

60 grams peeled garlic cloves

20 grams fresh galangal, thinly sliced

120 grams shallots, thinly sliced

40 grams lemongrass, thinly sliced

8 grams whole makrut lime leaves

30 grams krachai (Boesenbergia rotunda), also known as fingerroot or wild ginger (see page 335)

20 grams cilantro root or stems

20 grams kosher salt

115 grams water, more or less

Combine all the ingredients except the water in the blender. Turn the motor on, adding just enough water so that the blades catch the ingredients. (Add only as much water as you need—curry paste should be as dry as possible.) Puree until smooth. Transfer to an airtight container and keep in the refrigerator for up to 3 months.

FRIED CHICKEN WITH CHARRED CHILE JAM

GAI TOD NAAM PRIK PAO

We were resourceful in our household. We'd buy whole chickens because they were cheaper and use the legs and thighs for fried chicken. Moms would bone out the chicken thighs and use the bones for stock, even though she knew that fried chicken on the bone was much better—an economic compromise. The chicken was still delicious. It was something to come home after school to a plate of it—the aromas alone were addicting. Fried chicken was one of my favorite foods EVER. (If Moms didn't make it I'd have to make a Church's run, that's how much I loved fried chicken.) This simple recipe calls for a wet batter (we always had Perrier around for Pops's whiskey sodas, so that was the sparkling water of choice, by default). Unlike Southern fried chicken, no seasoning of the flour is required—it's all about marinating the meat. It's fantastic on its own, but I always find myself raiding the fridge for some sort of spicy condiment, and Crystal hot sauce wasn't an option. Charred chile jam (*naam prik pao*) is my go-to hot, along with Shark brand Sriracha straight out of the bottle.

SERVES 6 TO 8

MARINADE

½ teaspoon (1 gram) ground white pepper

2 tablespoons (10 grams) chopped cilantro roots or stems

1 tablespoon (12 grams) peeled garlic cloves

¼ cup (60 grams) oyster sauce

3 tablespoons (36 grams) fish sauce

2 pounds (907 grams) boneless chicken thighs, skin on, cut into quarters

BATTER

1 cup (100 grams) jasmine rice flour

1 cup (237 grams) soda water

1 gallon (3,280 grams) canola oil, for frying

SAUCE

¼ cup Charred Chile Jam (page 291)

1. In a stone mortar, pound the white pepper, cilantro roots or stems, and garlic to a paste. Transfer to a large mixing bowl, add the oyster sauce and fish sauce, and mix well. Add the chicken, cover with plastic wrap, and marinate in the refrigerator for a minimum of 2 hours (but no more than 12).

2. Preheat a deep fryer to 350°F. Line a baking sheet with paper towels. Make the batter by adding the rice flour to a medium mixing bowl. Add the soda water and whisk to form a smooth, loose batter. Drain the chicken from the marinade and place directly in the batter. Fry the chicken a few pieces at a time for 5 to 6 minutes, or until golden brown and fully cooked (check by cutting into a piece). Make sure not to crowd the fryer, or it might lower the temperature of the oil. Transfer to the paper towel–lined baking sheet to drain, then transfer to a clean mixing bowl. Add the charred chile jam and toss to coat. Heap on a platter and serve.

FRIED EGGPLANT AND MACKEREL WITH ACACIA-LEAF OMELET, GRILLED SHRIMP PASTE DIP

JAEW GAPI NUMM PLA TUU, MAK KUA TOD, KAI JIE PAK CHA OM

SERVES 6 TO 8

ACACIA-LEAF OMELET

4 large eggs
 (200 grams)

1 cup (60 grams)
 roughly chopped
 acacia leaves

1 tablespoon (12 grams)
 fish sauce

3 tablespoons
 (27 grams) canola oil

FRIED EGGPLANT AND MACKEREL

2 quarts (1,640 grams)
 canola oil, for frying

Eight ½-inch slices
 Chinese eggplant

1 large egg (50 grams),
 beaten

2 mackerel (see Note)

TO SERVE

Fresh Thai chiles

Pea eggplants

Shrimp Paste Dip
 (recipe follows)

Blanched or steamed
 yu choy greens

Blanched or steamed
 kabocha squash

1. **MAKE THE OMELET:** Crack the eggs into a small mixing bowl and beat with a fork as if for scrambled eggs. Fold in the acacia leaves, season with fish sauce, and mix thoroughly. Add the oil to an 8-inch nonstick sauté pan (cast iron is fine, too) and set over medium heat. When the oil is warm, add the eggs and tilt the pan to ensure the egg covers the bottom of the pan. Reduce the heat and cook the omelet for about 3 minutes, or until the top is cooked and has firmed up. If the omelet starts to color it means the pan is getting too hot—take the pan off the heat to cool it slightly. Once the top of omelet is firm flip it and cook over low heat for another minute. Slide the omelet out of the pan and onto a plate to cool. Serve at room temperature.

2. **FRY THE EGGPLANT AND MACKEREL:** Add the oil to a wok or deep, heavy pot and heat to 350°F. Line a baking sheet or platter with paper towels and set aside. First, fry the eggplant: Dip the slices into the

beaten egg and then gently lower them into the hot oil. Fry for about 3 minutes, flipping to ensure they brown evenly. Transfer to the paper towel–lined baking sheet to drain. Next, add the mackerel to the hot oil. Fry for about 5 minutes, depending on the size of the fish—the skin should end up crisp. Transfer to the baking sheet with the eggplant and cool to room temperature before serving.

3. ASSEMBLE THE DISH: Drop the chiles and eggplants onto the surface of the shrimp paste dip. On a platter, arrange the yu choy greens, kabocha squash, omelet, fried mackerel, and eggplant. Serve with a basket of warm sticky rice and dip away.

> **NOTE:** Find frozen Thai mackerel—presteamed and packaged in bamboo baskets—in the freezer aisle of Asian markets. You can substitute fresh sardines or American mackerel. Eviscerate the fish, rinse under cold running water, and pat dry before frying.

SHRIMP PASTE DIP JAEW GAPI

If you want funk then this is it, a sauce I call the tasty paste. In Thailand it's known as *naam prik gapi*. To me it smells *hom*—"fragrant"—but to some it's *min*, meaning "stinky." It's packed with umami, along with salt, spice, sweetness, and bitterness. Serve *jaew gapi* as a dip for sticky rice, or spoon it on some jasmine rice; it needs nothing else. You can also serve it with raw and steamed vegetables like kabocha squash and yu choy greens, also fried mackerel and fried eggplant. And *jaew gapi* is the classic accompaniment for an omelet of *cha om*, highly nutritious acacia leaves native to Laos and Thailand.

MAKES 2 CUPS

½ cup (45 grams) dried shrimp

1 banana leaf, trimmed into an 8-inch square

½ cup (140 grams) shrimp paste

⅛ cup (25 grams) peeled garlic cloves

5 fresh red Thai chiles (7 grams), stems removed

½ cup (100 grams) granulated sugar

¾ cup (180 grams) fresh lime juice

2 tablespoons (24 grams) fish sauce

Soak the dried shrimp in warm water for 30 minutes; drain and set aside. Preheat a gas or charcoal grill—try to maintain a medium-low temperature. Lay out the banana leaf square and place the shrimp paste in the center. Fold the leaf over the paste to form a neat parcel. Place the parcel on the grill and cook until the shrimp paste is fragrant, about 5 minutes. Remove from the grill and set aside. Add the garlic and chiles to a mortar and pound to a medium-fine paste. Add the soaked shrimp and the grilled shrimp paste and pound until smooth. Add the sugar, lime juice, and fish sauce and pound lightly to incorporate them; stir with the pestle to help dissolve the sugar. Transfer to a serving bowl.

CRISPY FRIED PORK RIBLETS KRA-TOOG MOO TOD

Growing up I ate a lot of fried meats. Most were the trim left from butchering for other dishes. Silverskin, tendon, bits with fat attached: It didn't matter, we liked texture. Moms seasoned them simply with salt and white pepper, and into the deep fryer they went. Like that, we had a meat dish to go with steamed and raw vegetables, some sort of jaew, and tum som—the everyday Lao dinner. To this day I don't care for braised meats. When it comes to things like these pork riblets, I like to pull, tug, and chew my way through. Just like chicken wings, these little spareribs have the perfect ratio of meat to bone, and the proper balance of tenderness and chew (the best part is the film of connective tissue that attaches meat to bone). Eat with the homies as a snack with beers, or add to a meal with sticky rice and Lao Green Papaya Salad (page 147).

SERVES 4 TO 6

2 tablespoons (30 grams) water	1½ tablespoons (12 grams) minced garlic	¼ teaspoon (1 gram) MSG (optional)	1 gallon (3,280 grams) canola oil, for frying
2 teaspoons (8 grams) kosher salt	1 tablespoon (15 grams) oyster sauce	1 pound (454 grams) pork spareribs, cut ½ inch wide	

1. MAKE THE MARINADE: In a medium mixing bowl, combine the water, salt, garlic, oyster sauce, and MSG, if using, and mix well to dissolve the salt; set aside. Next, separate the rack of ribs into individual ribs by cutting through the meat between the bones. Drop them into the marinade. Move the ribs around with your hands to ensure they're fully coated. Cover and refrigerate for 8 to 12 hours.

2. COOK THE RIBS: Line a baking sheet with paper towels. Add the oil to a deep, heavy pot or Dutch oven and heat to 350°F, adjusting as necessary to maintain an even temperature. Drain the ribs of any excess moisture and marinade. Carefully lower the ribs into the oil, making sure not to splash. Cook for about 5 minutes; the ribs should be coated with a crust but not be completely dried out. Transfer the ribs to the paper towel–lined baking sheet to drain. Cool for about 5 minutes and serve with Fried Red Peanuts with Garlic, Lime Leaves, Chiles, and Iodized Salt (page 113) and cold beer, or with a meal of various dishes.

FRIED LEMONGRASS-MARINATED BEEFSTEAK

This is both kid food and adult drinking food. Pops and his pals enjoyed this fried beef snack with beers and booze, dealing hands of single-deck blackjack; I had it for the first time at the age of three, over a ball of sticky rice. It was a tough cut of beef, but that's what made it delicious. I had tender, Tic Tac–size baby teeth, but I was able to experience it through my mom—she'd prechew the beef as a way to tenderize it before dropping it on a ball of sticky rice for me. One day I told this story to LyLy, a sous-chef at Commis and also Lao (she grew up in San Diego). She laughed; I thought she was making fun of me, but she'd had that same experience as a child, probably like many other Lao kids, too. Mother birds feeding their babies.

SERVES 6 TO 8 AS PART OF A MEAL; 8 TO 10 AS A SNACK

1½ pounds (680 grams) beef sirloin

½ cup (60 grams) thinly sliced lemongrass

⅛ cup (40 grams) finely chopped garlic

Pinch of freshly ground black pepper

2 tablespoons (24 grams) granulated sugar

1 teaspoon (4 grams) MSG (optional)

⅛ cup (30 grams) water

2 quarts (1,640 grams) canola oil, for frying

1. Trim the sirloin steak of any large pieces of silverskin and most (though not all) of the fat. Slice into ½-inch slices on a bias along the grain. Transfer to a mixing bowl. Add the lemongrass, garlic, black pepper, sugar, MSG, if using, and water and massage the meat with your hands until all the marinade is absorbed. Transfer to a sealed container or zipper-top bag and allow the beef to marinate, refrigerated, for 24 hours.

2. Heat the canola oil in a deep, heavy pot or Dutch oven to 350°F, adjusting the heat as necessary to maintain an even temperature. Line a baking sheet or platter with paper towels. Drain the marinade from the beef, then carefully drop the pieces of beef into the hot oil and fry for about 2 minutes; the meat should end up stringy and chewy, not dried and hard. Drain on the paper towel–lined baking sheet and serve warm or at room temperature. Enjoy with ice-cold beer (that is, beer with ice cubes in it) or some sticky rice with any jaew on the side.

SESAME BEEF JERKY, A.K.A. "HEAVENLY BEEF"

SEEN HANK (SEEN SAVAHN)

I recall going up to the rooftop of our apartment building with my mother to gather the shriveled slices of beef speckled with sesame seeds. The roof was a jerky zone for the whole community, a beef-preserving co-op space. Every family had a corner. Pops would serve this at his gatherings as a drinking snack, something to whet the appetite for more Heinekens and Cognac and sodas, but jerky wasn't really for snacking. Sometimes it was the protein highlight of the meal, especially if Moms was strapped for time. Sticky rice, dried meats, and some sort of jaew—that was it, a satisfying meal. My first taste came when I was two and newly arrived to the States.

MAKES 1 POUND

- 2 pounds (907 grams) beef top round
- 1 cup (200 grams) granulated sugar
- 2 tablespoons (24 grams) Gold Mountain brand seasoning sauce
- 2 tablespoons (20 grams) kosher salt
- 1 teaspoon (4 grams) MSG (optional)
- ¼ cup (60 grams) water
- ⅛ cup (20 grams) white sesame seeds
- 2 quarts (1,640 grams) canola oil, for frying

1. Trim the beef of any large pieces of silverskin and most (but not all) of the fat. Cut the beef into ⅛-inch slices on the bias and along the grain of the meat. Place the slices in a mixing bowl. Add the sugar, seasoning sauce, salt, MSG, if using, water, and sesame seeds and massage the meat with your hands until all the marinade is absorbed. Transfer to a sealed container or zipper-top bag and allow the beef to marinate, refrigerated, for 24 hours.

2. The next day, lightly coat roasting or drying racks with nonstick cooking spray and set them over baking sheets—you'll need enough racks to cover two full-size sheet pans. Spread the beef out on the racks and leave in a warm place with good air circulation until dried; the slices should no longer feel tacky. Avoid dehydrating the beef too fast in a warm place. For jerky with the best texture, the process should be slow and gentle. If it happens to be a warm, sunny day, you can dry the beef in the sun for one full day. Store the finished jerky in an airtight container for up to 4 weeks at room temperature; for longer storage, store in zipper-top bags in the refrigerator.

3. To serve, heat the canola oil in a deep, heavy pot or Dutch oven to 350°F, adjusting as necessary to maintain an even temperature. Carefully drop the jerky into the hot oil and fry for 5 to 10 seconds, depending on the dryness of the meat. The point is to cook out excess moisture from the beef, which escapes as bubbles. If you notice a lot of bubbles surfacing, it means there's a lot of moisture in the jerky—fry for the maximum time. You don't want to fry the jerky crisp; it should end up stringy and chewy.

"ONE SUNNY DAY DRIED FISH" PLA DAT DIEW

This is pretty much what the literal translation suggests: strips of fish dried for a full day in the sun, then fried. I had this for the first time in Ubon, on my first trip there at the age of twelve. It's best to use a lean, firm fish like bass, tilapia, snapper, or rock cod. Fatty fish like black cod or salmon won't yield the same results. After drying the fish, you fry it to crisp up the exterior (the interior stays moist). There's a bit of fermented funk from sitting in the sun all day. It travels well—it's food you send into the rice fields with a basket of sticky rice for lunch. Tackle this recipe when the sun cycle is longest where you live. For best results, you'll need a daytime temperature of at least 80°F (but less than 100°F), and very little to no humidity. Even if you don't plan to eat all the fish in one sitting, fry it all. The fried strips keep for 2 days, sealed airtight and refrigerated.

MAKES 1½ POUNDS

2 pounds (908 grams) boneless tilapia fillets, skin on

2 tablespoons (22 grams) kosher salt

1 teaspoon (4 grams) MSG (optional)

3 quarts (2,460 grams) canola oil, for frying

1. Cut the fish into strips the width of your index finger (the length doesn't matter). Toss the strips with the salt and MSG, if using, and let stand for 30 minutes at room temperature. Arrange the fish strips on a drying rack in a single layer. Check what time the sun rises the next day; set the fish out to dry (still on its rack) 30 minutes before sunrise. Let it dry, undisturbed, until the sun goes completely down that evening.

2. Add the oil to a deep, heavy pot or Dutch oven and heat to 375°F, adjusting as necessary to maintain an even temperature. Carefully drop the pieces of fish into the oil and fry for 2 minutes, or until the flesh is cooked and the exterior crisp. Drain on paper towels and let cool for a bit. Serve with sticky rice and Charred Tomato and Chile Relish with Fermented Fish (page 289).

TAPIOCA DUMPLINGS STUFFED WITH CARAMEL-COOKED PORK, SALTED TURNIP, AND PEANUTS SAKOO YUT SAI

I love dumplings. What I like about these is you don't need to make a dough or roll out wrappers: You enclose the filling in a network of small tapioca pearls (since tapioca contains no gluten, you can't roll it out like wheat-flour dough anyway). I find this the best way to make dumplings, since the ratio of filling to skin ends up being much higher. Moms would make these sweet-salty snacks only rarely, for Buddhist holidays and at Lao New Year. It's an easy recipe, but you need to pay extra attention when putting together the filling, which involves making a caramel; everything needs to be scaled and measured out before you start. Make sure to use ground pork that's not too fatty or your farce won't hold together, making it very difficult when it's time to wrap the dumplings. *Sakoo yut sai* taste best at room temperature. To eat, wrap each dumpling in a lettuce leaf with herbs and a bit of fresh chile, no dipping sauce needed. It's a great snack to socialize with, sure to spark conversation.

MAKES 32 DUMPLINGS; SERVES 6 TO 8 AS AN APPETIZER

TAPIOCA PEARL DUMPLING SKIN

10 ounces (28 grams) small white tapioca pearls

Cold water

FILLING AND STEAMING

3 tablespoons (27 grams) canola oil

7 ounces (200 grams) lean pork, finely ground

⅛ cup (22 grams) finely minced shallots

1 tablespoon (12 grams) finely minced garlic

5 tablespoons (63 grams) granulated sugar

2 ounces (56 grams) salted turnip, very finely chopped

½ cup (113 grams) finely ground roasted peanuts

¼ teaspoon (1 gram) finely ground black pepper

¼ cup (48 grams) fish sauce

½ tablespoon (5 grams) kosher salt

1 teaspoon (4 grams) MSG (optional)

Fried Garlic Oil (page 307)

GARNISHES

Red leaf lettuce leaves

Fresh red Thai chiles

Toasted dried arbol chiles

Cilantro sprigs

Mint sprigs

1. MAKE THE DUMPLING SKIN: Pour the tapioca pearls into a small mixing bowl and cover with cold water. Let them soak for 1 minute. Drain through a fine-mesh chinois or sieve and get rid of the water. Let the tapioca pearls drain in the chinois for 20 minutes, then transfer them to a medium mixing bowl; using your hands and fingers loosen and fluff the pearls as if fluffing rice. Cover the bowl with plastic wrap and set aside.

2. MAKE THE FILLING:

Place a medium-fine chinois or strainer over a bowl and set aside. Warm the oil in a large, preferably nonstick sauté pan over medium heat. Add the pork, shallots, and garlic and cook until the pork is cooked through, making sure no caramelization takes place. Stir frequently with a wooden spoon, scraping the bottom of the pan to prevent anything from sticking and burning. The pork needs to be fully cooked, with very little of the fat rendered. Scrape the cooked pork into the chinois or strainer to drain into the bowl; set aside the sauté pan for the next step. Give the chinois a firm shake or two to help it drain. Set aside.

3. MAKE THE CARAMEL:

Add the reserved fat from the pork to the same sauté pan and set over high heat. Add the sugar and begin to make a caramel, moving the sugar around the pan with the same wooden spoon you used for cooking the pork. You want the sugar to melt and cook to a rich, almost reddish-amber brown. When it reaches the right color, add the pork mixture and immediately stir, reducing the heat to medium-low. Add the salted turnip, peanuts, black pepper, fish sauce, salt, and MSG, if using, and stir to mix thoroughly. Cook for about 7 minutes on medium-low. You want the filling to absorb almost all of the liquid and end up very dry and sticky. Transfer the cooked filling to a platter or rimmed baking sheet to cool to room temperature. Spread the filling out in a thin layer to release steam and allow it to cool faster.

4. MAKE THE DUMPLINGS:

Oil the surface of a flat, perforated steaming pot or bamboo basket and set aside. Take a tablespoon of the filling (about 10 grams) and form it into a ball. If you're right-handed, hold the ball of filling in your left palm over the bowl of loose tapioca pearls. With your right hand pick up a good amount of the tapioca pearls and place it over the filling. With the ball of filling still in your left palm carefully transfer it—with the tapioca pearls—to your right palm. Now repeat the movement in the opposite direction. With every transfer from palm to palm give the tapioca ball a firm squeeze to make the pearls adhere. Go back and forth between your palms until the filling is covered in tapioca pearls. Make sure there isn't too much tapioca clinging to the filling—this will make your dumpling too large, throwing off the filling-to-wrapper ratio and making it taste bland. The finished dumpling should be of a single-bite size, weighing in at about 22 grams. Place the dumpling on the oiled steaming vessel. Repeat until all the filling is gone.

5. COOK THE DUMPLINGS: Bring the water in your steamer to a medium rolling boil. Set the perforated steaming vessel with the dumplings over the boiling water and cover. Let the dumplings steam for 11 minutes. Transfer the cooked dumplings to a flat plate, drizzle with fried garlic oil, and cool to room temperature. Serve with the garnishes of your choice.

6. TO ASSEMBLE A BITE: Place a dumpling in the center of a lettuce leaf, followed by your preferred chile and a few leaves of cilantro and mint.

FRIED AND SALT-CRUSTED GRILLED TILAPIA LETTUCE WRAPS WITH PADAEK AND PINEAPPLE JAEW WITH VERMICELLI NOODLES, HERBS, AND GARNISHES PUN MIENG PLA NIIN

When someone hosts a *pun mieng*, you know you're going to party big. It's a celebration all by itself, whose only reason for existing is to have a festive meal with friends and relatives, intense and at the same time chill. We always had two types of fish prepared different ways, and two sauces: one with a base of canned pineapple (please use chunks, not the kind packed in light syrup), the other with tamarind and padaek, more on the funk side of the rainbow.

Pun mieng takes some time to prepare, but once you're done shopping most of it is knife work. It's okay if you can't find all the garnishes listed here, but I urge you to try. And don't plan a pun mieng for less than 6 people—going big is what it's all about. It's a learning experience, everyone on the saat looking over the spread, strategizing where to begin, experimenting with creating perfect bites with the right combination of garnishes. The way to start is with a leaf of lettuce or cabbage. Add vermicelli (or not), followed by fish. Pick some herbs of your choice, putting them here and there with bits of garnishes. Spoon on one or both of the sauces and you're done—just remember to keep your creations to no more than two mouthfuls. There are really no rules; you choose your own adventure. The frustration is trying to remember the details of your favorite bite when you're on your tenth variation. Heinekens and Hennessy-and-sodas might not help with short-term memory, but they'll ensure you have a good time. Just writing about one makes me want to have a pun mieng jamboree.

A FEASTING PARTY FOR 6 TO 10 FRIENDS AND FOES

FRIED WHOLE TILAPIA

1 very fresh whole tilapia, about 3 pounds (1,360 grams), scaled
2 tablespoons (22 grams) iodized salt
1 gallon (3,280 grams) canola oil, plus more as needed

1. To gut the fish, use a sharp knife. Start just under the mouth, piercing the skin and continuing to cut just before the rear bottom fin. Remove the innards with your hands. The fish will bleed so you'll have to rinse the cavity under the tap until the water runs clear. Score

the fish on both sides in a crosshatch pattern by running a sharp knife into the flesh, slicing deep enough so that the tip of the knife hits the bones. Start at the top of the fish, cutting four evenly spaced diagonal slits. Repeat, going in the other direction. When you're finished, the fish should be scored in evenly sized squares. Flip the fish and repeat on the other side. Sprinkle the salt all over the fish, including in the belly cavity; set aside to marinate for 15 minutes.

2. Meanwhile, line a baking sheet or platter with paper towels. Heat the oil for deep-frying to 350°F in a rondeau or deep wok wide enough to hold the fish (add more oil if the pan is on the larger side). Holding it by the tail, carefully and gently slip the fish into the hot oil head first. Fry the fish for 4 to 5 minutes per side. Drain well on the paper towels and let rest and cool while you prepare the other fish.

GRILLED SALT-CRUSTED WHOLE TILAPIA

1 very fresh whole tilapia, about 3 pounds (1,360 grams)

4 lemongrass stalks (225 grams)

1 bunch (48 grams) cilantro

8 whole makrut lime leaves (3 grams)

2 cups (375 grams) coarse sea salt

2 tablespoons (30 grams) water

2 tablespoons (12 grams) all-purpose flour

1. When you buy your whole fish at the Asian market, do yourself a favor and ask the butcher to do two things that will save you time and agony. One is to remove the guts through the gills without slicing open the belly; and two, leave the scales on. Your fish is now ready for stuffing.

2. Beat and bruise the lemongrass stalks with something hard and heavy, like a mortar. This brings out the lovely flavor. Mix the cilantro and lime leaves together and begin stuffing the cavity of the fish (you may not end up using all of them). Stuff the fish halfway full. Fold the lemongrass stalks in half and begin stuffing them in the fish—the size of your fish will determine how many stalks of lemongrass you can fit. Start with 2 or 3 stalks and pack them in tightly, making sure you don't push them in so hard that you pierce the flesh. Set the fish aside.

(CONTINUED ON PAGE 142)

(CONTINUED FROM PAGE 139)

3. In a large mixing bowl or roasting pan, combine the salt, water, and flour and combine thoroughly, massaging with your hands until it's fully mixed. You want the salt to be a little moist so it sticks. Slip the fish into the bowl and start plastering it with the salt mixture. Pat and rub the fish with the salt, making sure to cover the entire surface and all over the head and tail. Set aside.

4. You want to grill the fish over steady, quite low heat. Make sure you build a good bed of coals. If they're too hot you can either tone them down with a scoop of ashes, or push the really hot coals to one side, away from where the fish is, using indirect heat. You can add more coals as you cook—the idea is to grill the fish, without burning the outside layer. Try to wait about 15 minutes before flipping the fish. If you flip too early, before the salt has dried out completely, the fish skin might stick to the griddle. Flip the fish as few times as possible. Keep roasting until the fish feels firm and the white salt-skin has turned crusty and golden, 30 to 40 minutes total.

THE SETUP

- 1 pound (454 grams) vermicelli noodles
- 2 heads green leaf lettuce
- 1 head green cabbage, quartered
- 2 cups (320 grams) cucumbers, sliced lengthwise into 1-inch strips
- 1 bunch (48 grams) cilantro, washed, left whole
- 1 bunch (48 grams) mint, washed, left whole
- 1 bunch (40 grams) rau ram, washed, left whole

- 1 bunch (36 grams) dill, washed, left whole
- 1 bunch (40 grams) Vietnamese shiso
- ½ cup (45 grams) dried shrimp, toasted in a dry wok
- ½ cup (100 grams) small-diced fresh ginger
- 4 ounces (112 grams) fried pork rinds or fried pig's ear
- 1 cup (224 grams) roasted skin-on peanuts
- 1 cup (100 grams) small-diced green mango

- 1 cup (150 grams) Fried Shallots (page 306)
- 1 cup (60 grams) thinly sliced scallions, green and white parts mixed
- 1 cup (120 grams) very thinly sliced lemongrass
- 1 cup (60 grams) fresh red and green Thai chiles
- ½ cup (23 grams) dried puya chiles, toasted whole
- 1 cup (160 grams) shallots, cut in small dice

- 1 cup (110 grams) green unripe plantains, unpeeled, split lengthwise and thinly sliced
- 1 cup (120 grams) small-diced Granny Smith apples
- Pineapple, Ginger, and Fish Sauce Dip (recipe follows)
- Padaek and Tamarind Jaew (recipe follows)

Prepare all the garnishes and set out on serving plates and in bowls.

PINEAPPLE, GINGER, AND FISH SAUCE DIP JAEW MAK NHUT

MAKES 2½ CUPS

1 cup (230 grams) canned pineapple chunks, drained

4 peeled garlic cloves (15 grams)

¼ cup (50 grams) ⅛-inch-thick slices fresh ginger, peeled

½ cup (100 grams) granulated sugar

¼ cup (48 grams) fish sauce

¼ cup (60 grams) fresh lime juice

1 teaspoon (4 grams) kosher salt

4 fresh red Thai chiles (6 grams)

Place everything in a blender and puree until smooth. Do not strain. Serve at once, or transfer to a sealed container and store up to 5 days in the refrigerator.

PADAEK AND TAMARIND JAEW JAEW MAKHAM

MAKES 2½ CUPS

¼ cup (60 grams) tamarind paste

½ cup (120 grams) water

½ cup (100 grams) granulated sugar

3 tablespoons (45 grams) padaek

2 fresh Thai chiles (3 grams)

2 peeled garlic cloves (6 grams)

1 tablespoon (12 grams) fish sauce

1. In small saucepan, bring the tamarind, water, sugar, and padaek to a boil. Remove immediately from the heat and set aside to stand for 20 minutes to let the tamarind hydrate.

2. Meanwhile, pound the chiles and garlic to a fine paste in a mortar; set aside. After 20 minutes strain the tamarind mixture through a medium chinois or sieve into a small mixing bowl. Use the back of a ladle to push as much juice through the pulp as possible; discard the pulp. Add the chile-garlic paste and season with the fish sauce. Stir with a spoon to mix, serve at once, or transfer to a sealed container and store up to 5 days in the refrigerator.

TUM SOM

12

LAO GREEN PAPAYA SALAD TUM SOM MAK HOONG

A Lao or Isan meal without some sort of tum som is almost unheard of. A pounded salad of fruit or vegetables ties a meal together, acting as a bridge between the sticky rice and grilled or fried meat or fish. *Tum som mak hoong* means "pounded papaya" in Lao. Though it's made its way to Thailand through human and cultural transport, tum som (*som tum* in Thai) originated in Laos. It was never on the menu at my mom's Thai restaurant, Wat Phou. "They won't understand," she'd say of our mostly non-Asian customers. "It has flavors and smells they're not accustomed to. It will scare them away." At food stalls on the streets of Laos and Thailand, there's always chatter between customer and tum som vendor. They're not talking about the weather, they're discussing the customer's tastes. Would you like it sweeter? Spicier? Exactly how many chiles? Crabs or no crabs? Heavy on the padaek or no padaek at all? It can be as bespoke an experience as you'd like. This recipe reflects how I like *my* tum som mak hoong. Start here, then play around. Use your taste buds as your guide, adjusting the seasonings. You can't go wrong.

SERVES 4 TO 6

- 6 whole dried Thai chiles (3 grams)
- 2 peeled garlic cloves (6 grams)
- ½ tablespoon (6 grams) shrimp paste
- 1 teaspoon (8 grams) Pantai Norasingh brand black crab paste
- ¾ lime, cut into thirds
- 1 ounce (28 grams) salted black crabs
- 6 ounces (168 grams) green papaya, shredded
- 3 ounces (84 grams) cherry tomatoes, halved
- 3 ounces (84 grams) Thai eggplant, thinly sliced
- 2 tablespoons (24 grams) fish sauce
- 2 tablespoons (30 grams) padaek
- 3 tablespoons (36 grams) granulated sugar

Drop the dried chiles into a clay mortar and pound into flakes. Add the garlic, shrimp paste, and black crab paste and pound some more. Add the lime wedges and salted black crabs and pound to extract the juices. Add the shredded papaya, cherry tomatoes, and eggplant and pound lightly to bruise the papaya, about 10 seconds. Add the fish sauce, padaek, and sugar and continue pounding firmly while moving the papaya around with a spoon held in your other hand. The correct motion is pound then stir, pound then stir—alternate between pounding and stirring. Do this repeatedly for 15 seconds. The goal is to gently bruise and macerate the papaya, without crushing the strands. You want to bruise the papaya just enough so it can absorb the dressing while extracting some of the juices of the tomato to add flavor to the dressing. Transfer to a serving plate; accompany with a wedge of crisp green cabbage and pork rinds.

MUDDLED CUCUMBER SALAD WITH RICE VERMICELLI AND DRIED SHRIMP

Cucumber is always delicious, always satisfying. For this salad I prefer larger slicing cucumbers with thick, dark green skins. They have the best flavor and the right texture for this dish. A tum som of cucumber is best with rice vermicelli noodles. It's a little trickier to make than other tum soms—since cucumber is composed mostly of water, it's quite easy to overdo the bruising in the mortar and end up with mush. The trick is finding the happy medium where the cucumber is bruised enough to give off juice that becomes part of the dressing but still keeps its integrity. Done right, it's one of the most flavorful and refreshing things you'll taste.

SERVES 4 TO 6

- 8 dried Thai chiles (4 grams)
- 2 peeled garlic cloves (5 grams)
- 2 tablespoons (20 grams) tamarind pulp
- 1 tablespoon (12 grams) granulated sugar
- 1 teaspoon (4 grams) MSG (optional)
- ¼ lime, cut lengthwise into two pieces
- 3 tablespoons (18 grams) dried shrimp
- 2 tablespoons (24 grams) fish sauce
- 2 tablespoons (30 grams) padaek
- 20 ounces (567 grams) cucumber, sliced lengthwise in strips
- 3 ounces (84 grams) cherry tomatoes, halved
- 2 cups (120 grams) cooked rice vermicelli noodles (see page 156)

Drop the dried chiles into a clay mortar and pound into flakes. Add the garlic and tamarind pulp and pound to a paste. Add the sugar, MSG, if using, lime wedges, and 2 tablespoons of the dried shrimp and pound to extract the lime's juice, then add the fish sauce and padaek to form a dressing. Add the cucumber and cherry tomato halves and pound firmly while moving the cucumber around with a spoon held in your other hand. The correct motion is pound then stir, pound then stir, done repeatedly. Be careful not to overpound the cucumber or it'll become too watery. You want to bruise the strands of cucumber and cherry tomato halves gently to release some of their juices and allow them to absorb the dressing, not crush them. Transfer to a serving plate and sprinkle with the remaining 1 tablespoon of dried shrimp. Offer the cooked rice vermicelli on the side for guests to mix their own salad to their liking.

MUDDLED LONG BEAN SALAD TUM MAK TUA

Thai long beans, Chinese long beans, snake beans, yard-long beans: The names are interchangeable. Unlike the normal "black-eyed" cowpea we're used to, the snake bean has delicious stringless pods you can eat like green beans, though in fact they beat the tar out of your run-of-the-mill Kentucky Wonders, since the pods are 18 inches or longer. There are different types. The fatter, paler beans contain more starch, and when you make tum som with these, the sauce becomes creamy. The skinnier and firmer and darker-skinned beans have less starch and a sweeter vegetable flavor, similar to green cabbage. Red long beans are harder to find; their flavor is similar to the paler green beans. I tend to favor the slender, darker beans because of their natural sweetness and firm texture—they hold up better in the mortar and pestle. Try both types and see.

SERVES 4 TO 6

- 3 dried Thai chiles (2 grams)
- 1 peeled garlic clove (4 grams)
- ½ tablespoon (17 grams) shrimp paste
- 3 tablespoons (36 grams) granulated sugar
- 1 teaspoon (4 grams) MSG (optional)
- ½ lime, cut into 4 wedges (50 grams)
- 1½ tablespoons (18 grams) fish sauce
- 1½ tablespoons (24 grams) padaek
- 8 ounces (226 grams) long beans, in 1½-inch bâtons
- 3 ounces (85 grams) cherry tomatoes, halved

Add the dried chiles to a clay mortar and pound into flakes. Add the garlic and shrimp paste and pound to a paste. Add the sugar, MSG, if using, and lime wedges and pound to extract the juice, then add the fish sauce and padaek to create a dressing in the mortar. Once you have the dressing add the long beans and tomato halves and pound firmly while moving the beans around with a spoon held in your other hand. The correct motion is pound then stir, pound then stir—do this repeatedly. The goal is to bruise the beans and slightly crush them, allowing them to macerate and absorb the dressing while extracting juices from the cherry tomatoes to combine with the dressing. Transfer to a serving plate and accompany with warm sticky rice and fried pig's ears, fried soured pork, or beef jerky.

DIP FOR TART, UNRIPE FRUIT JAEW JUM MAK SOM

Foraging? That was something my cousins and I were doing on our block long before New Nordic cuisine. Wild blackberries, plums, loquats, apricots—we trespassed in the yard of the apartment building behind us and pillaged whatever we could get our little paws on. Climbing trees and roof tops, hopping fences, breaking branches: We didn't care if the fruit was unripe—to be honest, we liked it better crisp and sour, dipped in this spicy-sweet and savory jaew. Moms contributed by picking up unripe guavas in East Oakland or buying supermarket Granny Smiths. *Jaew jum mak som* is still a sauce I make all the time, but I have to admit it's not quite as satisfying with fruit I haven't poached from a neighbor's yard. This dip goes with ripe fruit, too, but you'll want to reduce the sugar.

MAKES 1 CUP

- ½ cup (100 grams) granulated sugar
- ¼ cup (48 grams) fish sauce
- 2 tablespoons (30 grams) padaek
- 1 tablespoon (10 grams) Toasted Rice Powder (page 283)
- 1 tablespoon (5 grams) prik phong (ground toasted chile; see page 329)
- ½ tablespoon (3 grams) thinly sliced garlic
- 1 tablespoon (9 grams) thinly sliced shallots

FOR SERVING (ALONE OR IN COMBINATION)

- Green mangoes
- Green guavas
- Granny Smith apples
- Jujubes, aka Chinese red dates
- Unripe pears
- Unripe blackberries, red and firm
- Unripe wild plums

Combine the sugar, fish sauce, and padaek in a mixing bowl. Stir to dissolve the sugar. Add the toasted rice powder, prik phong, garlic, and shallots and stir to combine. Transfer to a serving bowl. Serve with fruit.

13

NOODLES AND SOUPS

FERMENTED RICE VERMICELLI

KHAO POON (KANOM JEEN)

When you talk about Lao noodles, you're talking *khao poon*.

These long, thin strands of fermented rice noodles have been around for centuries. Because of the labor involved, they were once made only for religious ceremonies, festivals, and special occasions like Lao New Year and birthdays. They always show up at Lao parties. Ever since machinery was introduced, the noodles have become more common. They're offered at markets for sale by the kilo, presented on banana leaves, piled up in coils. That's how you see them at Talat Sao, the morning market in the heart of Luang Prabang in Laos. The vendors set up by five every morning behind the retired Royal Palace, right outside Wat Mai Temple. A few feet down from the aunt selling khao poon, you can enjoy a bowl of khao poon nam prik or khao poon nam jaew. You'll find vendors eating at these shophouses in the market's alley—a closed-loop mini economy. I was there often in my visits to the city. It was the destination of my morning strolls.

I was humbled by the honor of being a commis one morning at a khao poon shophouse in the middle of a row of guesthouses in Luang Prabang, on the Nam Khan side of the peninsula. The Somsack family consisted of a mother, two sons, and a daugher-in-law. The family has been making noodles (including *khao piak sen*) daily for the last thirty-plus years in their covered backyard. Production starts at four a.m.; they're done by eight a.m., when noodle-stall shop owners come to pick them up. The Somsacks grind and make their own rice flour. The heat source is wood. The khao poon noodles are extruded through a machine that looks like a garden hose with a showerhead attached. They were the most flavorful sen khao poon I have ever had, whitish gray and very silky, with a nice tackiness to them. You can smell the fermentation and taste the tang. Mae Somsack served them to me with just fish sauce. It was all they needed. Simple, yet complex. So good.

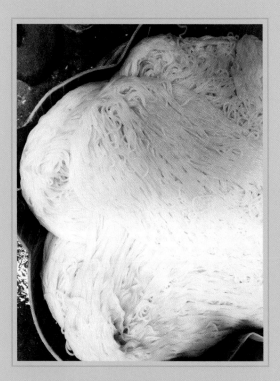

Unfortunately we don't have families here in the States producing such quality noodles. The closest thing we have are Vietnamese or Thai rice vermicelli, which come in various thicknesses. The noodles don't require soaking: You cook them like dried Italian pasta, but you want to cook them soft, not al dente. Every brand has its own directions for cooking (I suggest you follow them). While the noodles cook, grab a colander. When they're ready, drain and run warm water through them to wash off any excess starch and cool them. Once the water runs clear transfer the noodles to a large mixing bowl and fill it with lukewarm water to completely cover. Move the noodles around so they float freely and don't clump.

To begin coiling the noodles, find a plastic or metal mesh strainer, something you'd wash and drain vegetables in. Reach into the pool of water and grab about 2 ounces (56 grams) of noodles with the three middle fingers of your left or right hand. Keep the noodles in the cup of your fingers, not your palm. With the aid of your other hand wrap the loose ends and coil them around the three same fingers, holding the noodles. Now firmly squeeze out any excess water and slide them off your fingers to set them in the draining basket. Repeat with the rest of the noodles, stacking them partially overlapping, going clockwise around the basket. Fill the bottom before starting the next layer. Let them drain for about 30 minutes, then store the noodles by transferring the entire basket to a plastic bag and tying it. Store at room temperature. They'll stay flexible and soft this way. (Refrigeration hardens them.) They'll keep for 24 hours.

RICE VERMICELLI IN CHARRED CHILE AND SHALLOT BROTH WITH PORK OFFAL

KHAO POON NAAM JAEW

As a kid I didn't like offal, but the taste grew on me. Nowadays, this bowl of noodles and broth with pork innards makes me feel truly Lao. Don't limit yourself when shopping for pig's offal—use whatever parts you like. You can even substitute boneless skin-on pork belly or trotters for the neck. Go for it!

SERVES 10 TO 12

1 pound (454 grams) pig's intestine, whole

½ pound (227 grams) pig's liver, whole

½ pound (227 grams) pork neck collar, with skin if possible

1 gallon (3,785 grams) water

Four ¼-inch-thick fresh galangal slices (12 grams)

6 whole makrut lime leaves (4 grams)

½ cup (40 grams) sliced lemongrass, 1-inch bias cut

3 fresh Anaheim peppers (50 grams)

½ cup (90 grams) grilled serrano chiles (see page 329)

½ cup (64 grams) roasted garlic (see page 331)

1 cup (180 grams) roasted shallots (see page 334)

6 ounces (168 grams) cooked pork blood cake, in 1-inch cubes (see page 333)

1⅛ cups (215 grams) fish sauce

¼ cup (60 grams) padaek

2 tablespoons (22 grams) MSG (optional)

Kosher salt, to taste

GARNISHES

Rice vermicelli noodles, cooked according to package instructions, cooled

Shaved red and green cabbage, mixed

Shaved banana blossom

Thinly sliced long beans

Mung bean sprouts

Mint leaves

Rau ram leaves

Roughly chopped cilantro

CONDIMENTS

Lime wedges

Prik phong (ground toasted chile; see page 329)

Fresh Thai chiles

Shrimp paste

Long beans, in 6-inch pieces

1. Rinse the pork intestine, liver, and neck collar under cold running water; transfer to a colander to drain. Add the water to a large stockpot along with the galangal, lime leaves, and lemongrass and bring to a boil over high heat. Add the intestine, liver, and collar. Reduce the heat to maintain a gentle simmer and cover the pot. Simmer for about 1 hour, skimming impurities from the surface from time to time.

2. Meanwhile, char the Anaheims directly on the grill until they're softened and blistered. Transfer to a zipper-top bag, seal the top, and set aside to cool. Peel the Anaheims, seed them, coarsely chop the flesh, and add it to a mortar. Add the grilled serrano chiles, roasted garlic, and roasted shallots and pound to a medium-fine paste; set aside.

3. When the broth has simmered 1 hour, check the meats: Using a spider or a slotted spoon, remove the intestine, liver, and collar from the broth and transfer to a plate. Once they're

cool enough to handle, cut off a small slice of the intestine and give it a taste: It should be toothsome and tender while retaining some chew (if the intestine is ready, the other meats will be, too). If it needs more time, return the meats to the pot for an additional 20 minutes of simmering. When it's ready, cut the intestine into ½-inch pieces; cut the liver and collar into ¼-inch pieces. Return the cut-up meats to the simmering broth and stir in the pork blood cakes and the reserved chile mixture. Season with fish sauce, padaek, and MSG, if using. Taste, and add salt to your liking. Let the broth simmer for another 15 minutes.

4. To assemble a bowl of noodles, place two coils of vermicelli in a large individual soup bowl. Ladle over just enough broth to cover. Garnish to your liking with cabbage, banana blossom, sliced long beans, bean sprouts, mint, rau ram, and cilantro. Serve, adjusting at the table with the condiments to get the salt, spice, and acid just right. Dip a long bean into the shrimp paste, and take bites between slurps of noodles.

RICE VERMICELLI IN CHICKEN-COCONUT CURRY BROTH WITH PORK BLOOD KHAO POON NAAM GAI

If there was a favorite chicken noodle dish in our house, this was it. It showed up at weddings, birthdays, and Buddhist holidays. We never got sick of it. There'd be a large stockpot of broth keeping warm on the stove. Everyone would help themselves, building their own bowl as they liked.

SERVES 10 TO 12

2 pounds (907 grams) boneless chicken thighs with skin

10 ounces (284 grams) canned sliced bamboo shoots

2 quarts (1,893 grams) water

Three ⅛-inch slices fresh galangal (9 grams)

6 whole makrut lime leaves (2 grams)

3 quarts (3,120 grams) unsweetened coconut milk

1 cup (205 grams) canola oil

½ cup (140 grams) Red Curry Paste (page 301)

¼ cup (45 grams) finely minced shallots

2 cups (384 grams) fish sauce, plus more to taste

¼ cup (50 grams) granulated sugar

1 tablespoon (11 grams) MSG (optional)

8 ounces (226 grams) pork blood, poached (see page 333)

GARNISHES

Dried rice vermicelli, cooked, rinsed, and drained

Shaved red and green cabbage, mixed

Shaved banana blossom

Thinly sliced long beans

Mung bean sprouts

Mint leaves

Rau ram leaves

Roughly chopped cilantro

CONDIMENTS

Lime wedges

Prik phong (ground toasted chile; see page 329)

Fried Chile Oil (page 307)

Fish sauce

Fresh Thai chiles

Shrimp paste

Granulated sugar

1. Lay out the chicken thighs, with skin, on a cutting board. Using a cleaver, start chopping the chicken to the consistency of a medium grind. Stop when the texture is evenly rough, like coarsely ground hamburger. Set aside. Bring a medium saucepan of water to a boil. Add the canned bamboo slices and blanch 1 minute. Transfer to a colander to drain (no need to shock in ice water); set aside.

2. Combine the 2 quarts water, galangal, and lime leaves in a large stockpot, cover, and bring to a boil over high heat. When the water boils add the minced chicken and stir immediately to prevent clumping. Return to a boil and add the coconut milk; reduce the heat to maintain a gentle simmer. Meanwhile, warm the oil in sauté pan over medium heat. Add the red curry paste and shallots and cook until fragrant, stirring constantly to prevent burning, about 10 minutes. Carefully stir the fried curry mixture into the broth. Season with fish sauce, sugar, and MSG, if using. Add the reserved bamboo shoots and pork blood and lower the heat to

maintain a gentle simmer; cook for 45 minutes. Turn off the heat and taste, adjusting the seasoning with additional fish sauce, if necessary.

3. To assemble a bowl of noodles, place two coils of vermicelli in a large individual soup bowl. Give the broth a stir to mix. Ladle over just enough to cover the noodles. Serve with the garnishes and condiments, inviting your guests to build and season their bowls as they like.

LAO BEEF NOODLE SOUP, A.K.A. PHO LAO FER

Vietnamese cuisine influenced Lao food, and there's no better example than *pho* (pronounced *fer*). It's a great dish, varying from house to house and bowl to bowl, the base recipe always morphing. Anyone you serve a bowl of pho to should season according to taste, or how they feel that day. I like to dilute gapi shrimp paste in the broth, add fish sauce, a pinch of sugar maybe, a squeeze of lime, prik phong, even Sriracha. Then comes the green stuff: mint, cilantro, saw-tooth leaf, fermented cabbage, basils—the combinations are endless. I can't think of another dish modified so much *after* it hits the table. As with anything you build, you have to start with a solid foundation, in this case broth. A broth made solely with bones lacks depth; flavor comes from protein, especially the tougher cuts of meat. This recipe calls for beef brisket. Moms used trim that was fatty or otherwise unwanted from other beef dishes, banked up in bags thrown into the freezer. When she had enough to make a good amount of broth, she'd make pho and invite her friends over. You can find both beef meatballs (preferably the ones with tendon) and salted preserved cabbage (it comes in squat, bulbous plastic jars) at Asian markets.

MAKES 10 TO 12 BOWLS

BROTH

2 pounds (908 grams) beef brisket, in ½-inch cubes

1½ pounds (672 grams) beef neck bones

1½ gallons (5,677 grams) water

Three ¼-inch-thick slices fresh galangal (9 grams)

3 star anise pods (4 grams)

1 yellow onion (195 grams), peeled and halved

½ cup (24 grams) cilantro stems or roots

½ cup (130 grams) thin light soy sauce

½ cup (96 grams) fish sauce

1¼ cups (346 grams) black soy sauce

1½ tablespoons (15 grams) kosher salt

15 beef meatballs with tendon

GARNISHES

Thin dried rice noodles, preferably Three Ladies brand

Beef sirloin (about 2 pounds / 980 grams), thinly sliced, as if for stir-fry

Sliced scallions

Chopped Chinese celery

Chopped cilantro

Fried Garlic Oil (page 307)

Salted preserved cabbage

CONDIMENTS AND SIDES

Prik phong (ground toasted chile; see page 329)

Shrimp paste

Lime wedges

Granulated sugar

Mung bean sprouts

Thai basil sprigs

Saw-tooth herb

Fresh Thai chiles

Fish sauce

Long beans, cut in 6-inch pieces

1. Combine the brisket and beef bones in a large stockpot and cover with the water. Add the galangal, star anise, onion, and cilantro stems or roots, followed by the seasoning (thin soy, fish sauce, black soy, and salt). Bring the water to a boil over high heat, then lower the heat to maintain a very gentle simmer. Let the broth simmer for about 2½ hours; the brisket should be somewhat tender and you should be able to pick the meat from the neck bones fairly easily,

though it won't be meltingly tender. Don't skim impurities from the surface—they're protein from the blood, marrow, and juices, all of which contribute flavor. Once the brisket is somewhat tender, the broth is done. Remove the onion and discard; cut the meatballs in half and add them. Keep the broth just below a gentle simmer to keep it hot.

2. Soak and drain the dried rice noodles according to the package directions (if you can get your hands on fresh Chinese *ho fun* noodles, by all means use them in place of dried). Bring a small stockpot of unseasoned water to a boil over high heat. Place a fistful of noodles in a blanching basket and dunk in the boiling water for 5 seconds. Shake the excess water from the noodles and drop them into a soup bowl. Next, add some slices of beef sirloin to the basket and blanch 5 seconds; add them to the bowl with the noodles. Give the broth a stir, making sure you get a few meatball halves. Cover the noodles with the broth and garnish sparingly with scallions, chopped Chinese celery, and chopped cilantro, a spoonful of fried garlic oil, and preserved cabbage. Serve with the condiments and sides arrayed on the table. Tell your guests to have fun.

DRY-FRIED RICE NOODLES, A.K.A. PHAT LAO

Phat Thai is to Thailand as khua mee is to Laos (hence the name: *phat Lao*). To me, it will always be *khua mee* ("fried noodles"). The dish is as simple as the name. It's a drier style of noodle dish. It calls for making a caramel with oil (yes, oil): heating the sugar in oil until caramelized, adding aromatics, and seasoning with a mixture of sauces. You add soaked rice sticks and cook them in the sauce until they're tender and all the sauce is absorbed. This was a must-have at every Lao kid's birthday party when I was growing up, as important as the cake (if not more so). Adults loved it, too—it's just a good, simple noodle dish. A plate of khua mee dusted with prik phong still makes me smile.

SERVES 8 TO 10

OMELET (KHAI JIAO)

4 large eggs (200 grams)

1 tablespoon (12 grams) fish sauce

3 tablespoons (27 grams) canola oil

NOODLES

1½ pounds (672 grams) dried medium-wide rice noodles, preferably Three Ladies brand

½ cup (103 grams) canola oil

½ cup (100 grams) granulated sugar

¼ cup (40 grams) sliced shallots

2 tablespoons (24 grams) finely minced garlic

¼ cup (60 grams) water

2 tablespoons (30 grams) oyster sauce

2 tablespoons (24 grams) Gold Mountain brand seasoning sauce

¼ cup (48 grams) fish sauce

1 tablespoon (26 grams) sweet soy sauce

½ teaspoon (1 gram) freshly ground black pepper

1 teaspoon (4 grams) MSG (optional)

2 cups (133 grams) mung bean sprouts

1½ cups (75 grams) scallions, in 1-inch pieces

GARNISHES

Sliced omelet

2 tablespoons (20 grams) Fried Shallots (page 306)

½ cup (21 grams) chopped cilantro, stems included

1 cup (65 grams) mung bean sprouts

CONDIMENTS

Prik phong (ground toasted chile; see page 329) or Sriracha

1. MAKE THE OMELET: Crack the eggs into a small mixing bowl and add the fish sauce. Beat with a fork, as if making scrambled eggs. Add the oil to an 8-inch sauté pan over medium heat. When it's warm pour in the egg mixture and tilt the pan to ensure the egg covers the bottom. Continue to cook over gentle heat for about 3 minutes—you'll notice the top of the omelet firming up. (If it starts to color it means the pan is too hot; remove the pan from the heat.) Once the top is firm, flip and cook over low heat for another minute. Slide the omelet out of the pan and onto a plate to cool. Slice into ¼-inch slivers and reserve for garnishing.

2. MAKE THE NOODLES: Start by soaking the noodles in cold water according to the package directions—when done they should be opaque white and firm yet flexible. Transfer to a colander and drain well. Meanwhile, add the oil and sugar to a saucepan with a wide diameter and mix well; set over medium-high heat. As the oil gets hot the sugar will caramelize. Cook until the caramel turns a deep amber. Once it has reached the desired color turn off the heat, carefully add the shallots and garlic, and give it a stir with a spoon to sweat the aromatics—at this point your kitchen should smell very good. Sweat the aromatics for 1 minute, deglaze with the water, and stir well. Add the seasonings (oyster sauce, seasoning sauce, fish sauce, sweet soy sauce, black pepper, and MSG, if using) and mix well. Return the saucepan to medium heat and bring to a simmer. Add the drained noodles and cook, stirring constantly with a pair of tongs. Move the noodles as if tossing a salad—they'll wilt and slowly soak up the sauce. When the noodles have absorbed all the sauce and the pan is dry, with no residual sauce remaining, turn off the heat and fold in the bean sprouts and scallions, again like tossing a salad. Transfer to a large serving bowl or platter. Scatter the top with the omelet slices, fried shallots, and chopped cilantro, with a side of extra mung bean sprouts. Serve with prik phong or Sriracha.

RICE NOODLES IN BROTH WITH GROUND PORK COOKED IN LARD, WITH CHILES, TOMATOES, AND STINKY YELLOW BEANS KHAO SOI LAO

Don't confuse this with the well-known version from Chiang Mai. *Khao soi Lao* is totally different—not even a distant cousin. It has a thin broth with no trace of coconut milk, and is only ever made with pork. It's a staple in northern Laos, served everywhere in Luang Prabang, from breakfast through dinner. It's a simple noodle dish. You can make the ground pork sauce days in advance and keep it refrigerated until you have that craving. Crumble fried puffed sticky rice into your bowl for an effect similar to soup garnished with croutons. Some Asian markets sell freshly rendered pork lard; you'll find it in Mexican markets, too.

SERVES 10 TO 12

BROTH

- 2 pounds (908 grams) pork bones
- 1½ pounds (672 grams) pork spareribs, cut between the bones
- 1½ gallons (4,257 grams) cold water
- 1 head garlic (45 grams), unpeeled, split
- 6 whole scallions (112 grams)
- 1 medium yellow onion (195 grams), peeled and halved
- ½ cup (24 grams) cilantro stems or roots
- 1½ tablespoons (15 grams) kosher salt

PORK SAUCE

- 3 cups (420 grams) pork lard
- ¼ cup (20 grams) finely ground dried puya chiles
- ¼ cup (70 grams) Red Curry Paste (page 301)
- 3 cups (525 grams) halved red cherry tomatoes
- 1¼ pounds (560 grams) finely ground pork
- ¾ cup (175 grams) fermented yellow bean sauce (page 181)
- 2 tablespoons (24 grams) Gold Mountain brand seasoning sauce
- ½ tablespoon (5 grams) freshly ground black pepper
- 1 tablespoon (11 grams) kosher salt

TO ASSEMBLE

- Dried wide rice stick noodles, preferably Three Ladies brand, soaked and drained according to package instructions
- Shaved green leaf lettuce
- Sliced scallions
- Roughly chopped cilantro
- Fried Shallots (page 306)

CONDIMENTS AND SIDES

- Puffed sticky rice
- Lime wedges
- Prik phong (ground toasted chile; see page 329)
- Fried Chile Oil (page 307)
- Fish sauce
- Gold Mountain brand seasoning sauce
- Fresh Thai chiles
- Sliced banana blossoms
- Mint leaves
- Sliced scallions

1. MAKE THE BROTH: Combine the bones and spareribs in a large stockpot and cover with the water. Add the garlic, scallions, onion, cilantro stems or roots, and salt and bring to a boil over high heat. Reduce the heat to maintain a very gentle simmer. Let the broth simmer for about 3 hours; the ribs should be somewhat tender, and you should be able to pick the meat from the rib bones fairly easily. Don't skim impurities from the surface—they're protein from the blood, marrow, and juices, all of which contribute flavor. Strain the broth and reserve.

2. MAKE THE PORK SAUCE: Melt the lard in a large saucepan over medium heat. Add the ground puya chiles and red curry paste. Fry about 5 minutes until fragrant, stirring constantly so the paste doesn't burn. It should look broken and greasy. Add the cherry tomatoes and stew until they soften and break down to a paste. Add the ground pork and seasonings (yellow bean sauce, seasoning sauce, black pepper, and salt) and stir immediately to smooth out any clusters of ground pork, making sure everything is well incorporated. Reduce the heat to low and gently simmer the sauce for about 30 minutes, stirring occasionally. The end result should look somewhat dry, not moist like a stew. Don't worry about the amount of fat—the sauce should look greasy (the pork lard actually preserves it). Set aside to cool. You can make the sauce up to 3 days in advance and reheat when assembling.

3. TO ASSEMBLE A BOWL: Soak and drain the rice stick noodles according to the package directions (if you can get your hands on fresh Chinese ho fun noodles, by all means use them in place of dried). Heat the pork broth and bring a small stockpot of unseasoned water to a boil over high heat. Place a fistful of noodles in a blanching basket and dunk in the boiling water for 5 seconds. Shake the excess water from the noodles and drop them into a soup bowl. Give the broth a stir and make sure it is very hot. Ladle enough broth into the bowl to cover the noodles, followed by about ¼ cup of the pork sauce. Immediately top with a scant amount of shaved lettuce, scallions, chopped cilantro, and fried shallots and serve. Set out the condiments and sides on the table and invite your guests to season their bowls to taste.

PORK AND EGG DROP CURRY NOODLES

"Coconut milk noodles" is the literal translation of *mee katee*, but there's more to it than that. At Hawker Fare we don't have phat Thai on the menu, for several reasons. Don't get me wrong: I love phat Thai, but we wanted to introduce our guests to lesser-known mee katee. It has all the flavors and textures everybody likes in phat Thai (peanuts, tamarind, eggs, spice, shrimp, bean sprouts), only in soup form. The broth is fairly rich for pork, enriched with coconut milk, spiked with fermented soybean paste and fish sauce. It hits all the notes of deliciousness with one slurp of the spoon, flooding the palate with savory umami notes, tartness and sweetness, and fragrant curry-paste heat. What more could you ask for?

SERVES 10 TO 12

2 quarts (1,893 grams) water

Four ¼-inch-thick fresh galangal slices (12 grams)

6 whole makrut lime leaves (2 grams)

12 ounces (336 grams) boneless pork belly, with skin

12 ounces (336 grams) coarse-ground pork

5 cups (1,300 grams) unsweetened coconut milk

½ tablespoon (6 grams) MSG (optional)

¾ cup (195 grams) Tamarind Water (page 299)

¾ cup (154 grams) canola oil

¼ cup (70 grams) Red Curry Paste (page 301)

1 tablespoon (5 grams) sweet paprika

¼ cup (50 grams) minced shallots

1 cup (192 grams) fish sauce, plus more to taste

1 cup (200 grams) granulated sugar

1 cup (233 grams) fermented yellow bean sauce (see page 181)

¼ cup (45 grams) kosher salt

6 large eggs (300 grams), beaten

GARNISHES

Dried rice noodles, medium width, preferably Three Ladies brand

Mung bean sprouts

Sliced scallions

Chopped cilantro

Ground toasted peanuts

Fried Garlic Oil (page 307)

Lime wedges

Fried Chile Oil (page 307)

1. Add the water to a large stockpot along with the galangal and lime leaves, cover, and bring to a boil over high heat. Reduce the heat, add the pork belly, and simmer gently for 45 minutes. Remove the pork belly and set aside to cool.

2. Return the heat to high and bring the pork belly liquid back to a boil. Add the ground pork and stir immediately to prevent it from clumping. Bring the liquid back to a boil and add the coconut milk, MSG, if using, and tamarind water. Lower the heat to maintain a gentle simmer.

3. Meanwhile, warm the oil in a sauté pan over medium heat. Add the red curry paste, paprika, and shallots and cook until fragrant, about 10 minutes, stirring constantly to prevent burning. Carefully add the fried curry to the simmering broth and season with fish sauce, sugar, yellow bean sauce, and salt. Simmer gently for 30 minutes.

4. While the broth cooks, cut the reserved pork belly into ½-inch slices; add them to the broth. After 30 minutes, increase the heat to bring the broth back to a boil, making sure it doesn't boil over. Add the beaten eggs to the boiling broth in a stream, stirring clockwise with a long-handled spoon all the while to create egg droplets. When cooked, the egg droplets will float. Turn off the heat and let the broth rest for 30 minutes. Taste, and adjust the seasoning with additional fish sauce if necessary.

5. TO ASSEMBLE A BOWL: Soak the dried rice noodles according to the package directions. Drain and reserve. Bring a small stockpot of unseasoned water to a boil over high heat. Place a fistful of noodles in a blanching basket and dunk in the boiling water for 5 seconds. Shake the excess water from the noodles and drop them into a soup bowl. Give the broth a stir to make sure you get a good mixture of the fat, egg, and pork belly, and ladle some into the bowl to cover the noodles. Garnish with a scant amount of bean sprouts, scallions, ground peanuts, chopped cilantro, and a spoonful of fried garlic oil. Serve with a slice of lime and fried chile oil on the side.

FRESH RICE AND TAPIOCA NOODLES WITH SHREDDED CHICKEN, FRIED GARLIC OIL, AND DONUTS KHAO PIAK SEN

Chicken noodle soup: It's like a warm, fuzzy blanket. I could eat chicken noodle soup any time of day. Growing up, I did just that: early in the morning, half asleep, my eyelids glued shut; a quick lunch break, sometimes while walking; and for dinner, eating leftovers from lunch. It didn't matter. My best memories of khao piak are from a neighbor. It was the night of Sam's tenth birthday, and like every Lao after party the adults were gambling, Sam's living room turned into a card-game arena—it would go on for hours, into the early morning and well beyond sunrise. Moms and the aunties had stayed up all night to gossip. At six a.m. khao piak production began. The noodles were kneaded by hand and rolled out using a fish sauce bottle with the labels removed. The dough was cut by hand into noodles, as a large stockpot of chopped-up chicken carcasses and giblets simmered away, becoming broth. The air was filled with the welcoming smell of fresh-chopped cilantro and scallions, the sweet jasmine fragrance of rice flour, and the aromas of steam coming off the chicken broth. These were signs that breakfast was served, as surely as the smell of bacon cooking in a skillet, an official buzzer to signal that the gambling was heading into intermission.

SERVES 8 TO 10

NOODLES

1¾ cups (417 grams) water

1½ cups (160 grams) jasmine rice flour

1⅓ cups (160 grams) tapioca starch

BROTH

1 whole chicken, about 3 pounds (1,360 grams)

1 gallon (3,785 grams) water

8 whole scallions (80 grams), roots attached

4 celery stalks (170 grams), cut into large dice

1 large yellow onion (425 grams), peeled

1 bunch (48 grams) cilantro, stems included

Six ⅛-inch slices fresh ginger (22 grams)

2 tablespoons (22 grams) kosher salt

⅓ cup (65 grams) fish sauce

1 tablespoon (11 grams) MSG (optional)

TO ASSEMBLE

Roughly chopped cilantro, stems included

Sliced scallions, green and white parts mixed

Fried Garlic Oil (page 307)

CONDIMENTS

Lime wedges

Pickled Serrano Chiles (page 306)

Gold Mountain brand seasoning sauce

Granulated sugar

Fish sauce

Fried Chile Oil (page 307)

Pa Tong Go, a.k.a. Chinese Donuts (recipe follows)

1. MAKE THE NOODLES: Bring the water to a boil in a medium saucepan. Sift the rice flour and tapioca starch together into a large mixing bowl. You'll be adding the water to the flour mixture in three additions—make sure the water is boiling during every addition. Carefully add the first third of the water to the flour mixture, using a wooden spoon. Once lumps are formed and the water is fully absorbed, add the second third; at this point it will start to resemble dough. Add the last third of boiling water and mix carefully, taking care not to scald yourself. While the dough is still hot, turn it out onto a wooden board and start kneading by hand as if for bread; it should come together in a smooth mass. Knead for about 10 minutes.

2. Let the dough rest on the bench or cutting board for 15 minutes, covered with a towel to keep warm. (Do not use plastic to cover or it will condensate and add unwanted moisture to the dough.) Dust your work surface with a fair amount of tapioca starch. Cut off a piece of the dough the size of a tangerine and start rolling the noodles either in a pasta rolling machine or with a rolling pin. Roll the dough about ¼ inch thick and 2 inches wide. Stack the rolled dough pieces with a dusting of tapioca between each so they will not stick to one another. Do not stack more than 3 sheets of dough. With a sharp knife cut the noodles into ¼-inch strands and dust with more tapioca starch. Store the noodles flat on a tray and refrigerate until needed.

3. MAKE THE BROTH: Rinse the chicken—including the neck and innards—inside and out under cold running water. Place the chicken, neck, and innards in a medium stockpot and cover with the water. Bring to a boil over high heat, skimming the impurities and fat that rise to the surface as you go, to achieve a clear broth. When the water boils, add the scallions, celery, onion, cilantro with stems, and ginger slices. Adjust the heat to maintain a gentle simmer. Cook for 3 hours.

4. After 3 hours, remove the chicken, drain it well, and transfer to a large bowl. When the chicken is cool enough to handle but still warm, pick off the meat into coarse threads, reserving the skin. Transfer the picked chicken to another bowl and cover with plastic wrap to keep the meat warm and prevent it from drying out. Season the broth with the salt, fish sauce, and MSG, if using.

5. TO ASSEMBLE A BOWL: Bring the broth to a gentle simmer. Shake off excess starch and flour from the noodles. Add 2 cups loosely packed noodles to a blanching basket and cook in the broth for approximately 1 minute, using chopsticks to move them around and prevent clumping. Transfer the noodles from the basket to a large soup bowl. Add about ⅛ cup of the picked chicken to the bowl and ladle over just enough broth to cover. Garnish with chopped cilantro, scallions, and fried garlic oil. Serve with the condiments, encouraging your guests to season and garnish their bowls as they like, including pa tong go, a.k.a. Chinese donuts, cut into pieces with scissors.

PA TONG GO, A.K.A. CHINESE DONUTS

MAKES 6 DONUTS

3 cups (405 grams) all-purpose flour, plus more for rolling

2 tablespoons (24 grams) granulated sugar

2 tablespoons (22 grams) baking powder

½ teaspoon (1 gram) baking soda

1 teaspoon (4 grams) kosher salt

1 egg yolk (20 grams)

2 tablespoons (18 grams) canola oil

1 cup (237 grams) boiling water

1 gallon (3,460 grams) canola oil, for frying

1. In a large mixing bowl, sift together the flour, sugar, baking powder, baking soda, and salt. Make a well in the center of the dry ingredients and add the egg yolk and oil. Using a wooden spoon, mix the dough lightly to combine the ingredients. Next, add ½ cup of the boiling water and continue to mix with the wooden spoon. When the water is absorbed, add the remaining ½ cup boiling water and continue to mix. When it's cool enough to handle, turn the dough out onto a floured surface and knead for 2 minutes to form a smooth ball. Wrap it in plastic and let rest in the refrigerator for 12 to 16 hours.

2. The next day, flour a work surface and roll out the dough to a 6-inch x 10-inch rectangle, ½ inch thick. Cut the dough into twelve 1½-inch strips. Gently score the center of each strip with a knife or dough cutter, being careful not to cut through the dough. Wet a pastry brush with water and brush the tops of 6 strips. Stack the remaining 6 strips on top and press down firmly. Let the strips of dough rest for 15 minutes while you heat the oil for frying.

3. Line a plate with paper towels and set aside. Add enough oil to come halfway up the sides of a large, wide, and deep pan or wok. Set the pan over medium-high heat and bring the oil to 350°F, using a thermometer to gauge, raising or lowering the heat as needed to maintain a steady temperature. When the oil is ready, carefully drop in 2 donuts and fry, turning them often and using a spider to make sure they are submerged beneath the oil. Fry for about 5 minutes. Transfer to the paper towel–lined plate. When the oil comes back to temperature, repeat, until all the donuts are fried. Serve warm or at room temperature. They're best on the day they're made.

RICE CONGEE WITH PORK MEATBALLS AND FRIED GARLIC OIL KHAO DTOM MOO SUUP

Weirdly, my mother once tried to Americanize our diets, starting with the first (and most important) meal of the day. She bought Eggo waffles, breakfast sausages, and maple-flavored pancake syrup. She served it to us one morning, but my brother and I weren't having it. Except for dipping our fingers in the syrup and dabbing it on our tongues, we didn't touch it—we'd been spoiled by bowls of rice congee every morning. As breakfast food, it's hard to top. What was Moms thinking?

SERVE 6 TO 8

- 5 ounces (141 grams) coarsely ground pork
- 1 tablespoon (12 grams) Gold Mountain brand seasoning sauce
- ½ teaspoon (2 grams) MSG (optional)
- Pinch of ground white pepper
- 1 teaspoon (4 grams) kosher salt

- 3 tablespoons (6 grams) finely sliced scallions
- 1 quart (946 grams) water
- Three ⅛-inch slices fresh ginger (12 grams)
- ½ cup (115 grams) raw jasmine rice
- 1 tablespoon (12 grams) fish sauce

GARNISHES
- Roughly chopped cilantro
- Sliced scallions
- Fried Garlic Oil (page 307)

CONDIMENTS
- Fish sauce
- Gold Mountain brand seasoning sauce
- Lime wedges
- Prik phong (ground toasted chile; see page 329)
- Fried Chile Oil (page 313)

Place the ground pork in a mixing bowl. Add the seasoning sauce, MSG, if using, white pepper, salt, and scallions and knead to incorporate; set aside. Combine the water and ginger slices in a medium soup pot and bring to a boil over high heat. When the water is at a rolling boil, add the jasmine rice and lower the heat to maintain a gentle simmer. After 20 minutes of simmering, add the pork mixture in teaspoon-size pieces. Let the porridge simmer for another 15 minutes, then add the fish sauce. Dish the porridge into small serving bowls and garnish with chopped cilantro, scallions, and fried garlic oil. Serve with condiments on the table.

NOTE: You can make congee from leftover cooked jasmine rice, though the final consistency will be a bit thinner. Reduce the amount of water and cooking time.

POACHED CHICKEN AND RICE KHAO MUN GAI

This simple, one-pot sibling of the Hainanese chicken and rice served at hawker stalls in Singapore is good at any hour, in any situation. My childhood memories alone make me crave it daily. When I opened Hawker Fare Oakland in 2010, I knew *khao mun gai* had to be on the menu, but I knew I had to make it marketable. I was mindful of what guests liked. And let's face it:

1. Most people these days prefer white-meat chicken over dark and do not like to eat around bones.
2. People freak the fuck out and go batshit crazy when they see chicken cooked pink.
3. A lot of people avoid chicken skin that isn't as crispy as a Lay's potato chip.

But white meat is boring and tasteless and often overcooked, turning stringy and dry. And chicken is pink near the bone *because* it is properly cooked—the marrow leaches out, staining the flesh. (The texture of foods is a cultural thing.) So I really wanted to make khao mun gai the O.G. way: When it's time to serve it you chop the chicken through the bone; the red marrow runs, but so what? The focus of perfectly cooked chicken is the flesh, not the marrow in the bones.

Still, we had a major challenge: How to cook chicken breasts juicy and moist without ending up pink? The answer was sous vide (duh!): poaching chicken on the bone in a vacuum-sealed bag filled with chicken stock, in a precise, temperature-controlled water bath. Cheating, but not really. It came out great and people loved it. On Yelp, customers said it was the moistest chicken breast they'd ever had. We sold a lot . . . built up a following for it. It was delicious, but it didn't hit the mark for me. I thought it was just okay.

So I switched it up, ditching sous vide and poaching bone-in chicken thighs the old-school way. Once cooked, I removed the bone, chopped the meat, and placed it over the rice. It was the best way I knew to check all the boxes, and make both diners and myself happy.

But here's the O.G. recipe I always wanted to do, the way I make khao mun gai for myself at home: moist, pink, bony, and delicious.

SERVES 4

POACHED CHICKEN

1 whole chicken, about 3 pounds (1,360 grams)

1 gallon (3,785 grams) water

8 whole scallions, roots attached (80 grams)

2 lemongrass stalks (85 grams), cut in 3-inch lengths, crushed

1 large yellow onion (425 grams), peeled

Six ⅛-inch slices fresh ginger (22 grams)

1 bunch cilantro, stems included (48 grams)

1 tablespoon (11 grams) MSG (optional)

2 tablespoons (22 grams) kosher salt

⅓ cup (65 grams) fish sauce

1½ cups (300 grams) raw jasmine rice

½ cup (144 grams) raw sticky rice

1 quart (910 grams) broth from poaching the chicken

1 teaspoon (3 grams) Knorr brand chicken bouillon powder

1 teaspoon (4 grams) Fried Garlic Oil (page 307; use the oil only, no garlic bits)

Fermented Yellow Bean Sauce (recipe follows)

Cucumber slices

Roughly chopped cilantro

Sliced scallions

1. POACH THE CHICKEN: Remove the innards from the cavity of the chicken and reserve. Rinse the chicken under cold running water inside and out; transfer to a colander to drain for 5 minutes. Rinse the innards (they're optional). Combine the water, the chicken, and the innards, if using, in a medium stockpot (make sure the chicken is completely submerged or it won't poach properly). Add the rest of the poaching ingredients and bring the water to a simmer over medium heat. As the water heats, constantly skim off the impurities that rise to the surface; this will ensure a crystal-clear broth. As much as you can, try not to remove the rendered fat that rises. Once the water is at poaching temperature—a very, very gentle simmer (around 175°F)—set a timer for 35 minutes. After 35 minutes turn off the heat and let the chicken rest in the broth for another 20 minutes. Remove the chicken and innards to a large plate or cutting board to cool. Strain the broth through a fine chinois or sieve into a bowl; set the bowl in a larger container of ice water to rapidly cool it to room temperature. Set aside while you prepare the rice.

2. MAKE THE RICE: Combine the jasmine and sticky rices in the insert of an electric rice cooker; mix and cover with cold water. Polish the rice by rubbing handfuls between your two palms in the water for about 15 seconds. Pour out the water, add fresh cold water back to the rice, and repeat the polishing. Repeat the process two more times, until the water runs pretty clear (this rinses away any unwanted excess starch, making the final cooked rice fluffy). Strain the rice and return to the rice cooker insert. Add the chicken broth, bouillon powder, and fried garlic oil, cover, and turn the rice cooker to the "cook" setting. Depending on your rice cooker, it should take 20 to 30 minutes. While waiting, make the fermented yellow bean sauce.

3. TO SERVE: When the rice is cooked, butcher the poached chicken by cutting the legs from the carcass. Separate the thighs from the drumsticks. Chop the chicken into approximately 1-inch pieces, straight through the bones. Fluff the rice with a plastic or bamboo rice paddle, releasing excess steam trapped in the network of kernels. Scoop about 1 cup of rice onto a serving platter and place the pieces of chopped poached chicken on top. Garnish the sides of the dish with cucumber slices and cilantro. Serve with a side of the sauce and a bowl of the warm chicken broth sprinkled with scallions.

FERMENTED YELLOW BEAN SAUCE

MAKES ABOUT 3 CUPS

¼ cup (50 grams) granulated sugar

¼ cup (56 grams) distilled white vinegar

1 cup (233 grams) fermented yellow beans

¾ cup (141 grams) Gold Mountain brand seasoning sauce

⅔ cup (150 grams) sweet soy sauce

2 tablespoons (55 grams) finely minced fresh ginger

1 tablespoon (12 grams) finely minced garlic

8 thinly sliced fresh red and green Thai chiles (12 grams)

Combine the sugar and vinegar in a small mixing bowl and stir to dissolve the sugar. Add the remaining ingredients and mix well. The sauce will keep for up to 1 week, sealed airtight and refrigerated.

MAMA NOODLES WITH POACHED EGG

The jump-off dish of my career—and my first crush in cooking—was a package of Mee Mama instant ramen noodles. I recall I was eight years old when I first made this for myself: Had to use a homemade step stool fashioned from 2-by-4s to see into the small pot on top of our Kenmore range. There are a few different Mama flavors available, but for me it's always the ground pork, in the yellow-orange package. We were never short of it at home. Once the box was down to six packages Moms replenished our stock on our next Khanh Phong Supermarket run in Chinatown. On school nights when Moms and Pops were working in the restaurant, my brother and I were pretty self-sufficient. Grandma (my father's mother) sometimes cooked for us, but there were nights we told her we'd take care of ourselves. The recipe is so basic, the older I got the fancier it became. I'd add pork cake, ground pork, scallions, napa cabbage, frozen corn, peas—the possibilities were endless, depending on what was in the fridge or freezer. At Commis I'd make it for staff meals now and then, adding vegetables and finishing with herbs. At times it became my compost bin for emptying out the fridge. I found there was no bad combination, no matter what. Almost thirty years later I still cook this for myself after a long day bouncing around between restaurants. I make it for my kids and they help (Emma always wants to drop the noodles in the boiling water). Even uncooked, Mee Mama is excellent, munched like a snack bag of potato chips. Open the bag, add the seasoning (minus the packet of garlic oil), give the bag a firm squeeze and a shake, and snack away. An instant classic, my Chef Boyardee.

SERVES 1

1½ cups (356 grams) water
1 package Mee Mama instant noodles
1 large egg (50 grams)

Add the water to a small saucepan and place on the stove over high heat. Open the package of Mama noodles and remove the seasoning packets. Open the packet of garlic oil and the soup base (the larger, dry packet) and add to the water. Remove the noodles from the bag and snack on the crumbs. Carefully drop the noodles in the boiling water. Cook at a rapid boil for about 30 seconds. Remove the noodles with a slotted spoon or fish spatula and place in a serving bowl. Return the soup to a boil. Crack in the egg and cook 1 minute. Turn off the heat and pour the soup, along with the egg, over the noodles. Open the last packet of seasoning— the prik phong (toasted ground chile)—and sprinkle on top. Eat immediately. Don't make more than two packets at a time.

BEEF SOUP WITH OFFAL, BETEL LEAVES, AND BILE DTOM KEUNG NAI KWUAY

The weekly beef slaughter was a ritual for many Lao families in the 'hood. It was pretty much a combination Groupon purchase and CSA subscription: You'd place your order for a share of the cow on Friday, then pick it up at the Lao market on Saturday by noon (if there were enough orders, the rancher would stop by the block to make a direct delivery). Everyone received a mystery bag of bones and various cuts of muscle, but you could always count on getting a nickel bag of beef bile from the first and secondary stomachs and a dime bag of fresh blood, still warm to the touch. (All butchery was done under the table, dodging the man—a.k.a. the USDA—just like back home.) The prime, tender cuts of beef were marinated and grilled, or mixed with tougher muscles and chopped to make *laap diep*, raw beef salad. The offal required different cuts. The tripe, liver, kidneys, and spleen were sliced into ¼-inch slices. Everything else got turned into soup: nose-to-tail cookery and then some, nothing wasted, everything ending up delicious.

SERVES 4 TO 6

- 1 quart (946 grams) water
- Two ⅛-inch fresh galangal slices (18 grams)
- ½ cup lemongrass (40 grams), 1-inch bias cut
- 15 whole makrut lime leaves (5 grams)
- 6 fresh green and red Thai chiles (10 grams)

- ¾ cup (60 grams) shallots, peeled and split in half
- 3 ounces (113 grams) beef shank or brisket, cut into ½-inch dice
- ½ tablespoon (5 grams) kosher salt
- 3 ounces (85 grams) beef offal (tripe, kidney, spleen, tendon, sweetbreads, intestine, lung, alone or mixed), sliced or diced

- 2 tablespoons (30 grams) padaek
- ½ teaspoon beef bile from the second intestine (optional)
- ½ teaspoon prik phong (ground toasted chile; see page 329)
- ¼ cup (10 grams) scallions, green and white parts mixed, in 1-inch pieces

- ¼ cup (12 grams) roughly chopped saw-tooth herb
- ¼ cup (7 grams) torn betel leaf

1. Fill a medium soup pot with the water and add the aromatics (galangal, lemongrass, lime leaves, chiles, and shallots) along with the meat and salt. Bring the water to a boil, then reduce the heat to achieve a simmer. Skim off excess foam and impurities and discard. Let the soup simmer gently, partially covered, over very low heat for about 60 minutes. Check the beef shank or brisket: It should be tender but still have some chew (don't let it cook to a braise-like softness).

2. When the beef is tender, add the offal and padaek and simmer 20 minutes more. For the optional bile, start with a few drops and taste before adding the full amount; simmer 5 minutes. Add the prik phong, scallions, and herbs, and transfer the soup to a large serving bowl. If you're not adding bile, stir the scallions and herbs into the soup without additional simmering, transfer to the bowl, and serve right away.

HOT AND SOUR SOUP OF PORK-RIB CARTILAGE

DTOM ZAAP KRA-TOOG MOO

The Lao, like Thais and other Asians, appreciate texture in food. We're so crazy about it we create dishes around the act of chewing bones, sidelining the meat itself. This soup is the perfect example. The cartilage comes from pork rib tips, the soft bones that run along the bottom set of ribs on the opposite side of the spine (you can easily cut through them with a sharp knife). Finding the right pork ribs for this soup is key—cartilage renders its gelatin faster than bones, lending richness to the broth without long simmering. Herbs and lime juice make the flavor bright and light.

SERVES 6 TO 8

4 whole shallots (45 grams)

1 pound (454 grams) pork sparerib tips with cartilage, cut into 1-inch pieces

2 quarts (1,893 grams) water

½ cup (56 grams) sliced lemongrass, 1-inch bias cut

Eight ⅛-inch slices fresh galangal (18 grams)

8 whole makrut lime leaves (3 grams)

3 tablespoons (36 grams) fish sauce

1 teaspoon (4 grams) MSG (optional)

¼ cup (60 grams) fresh lime juice

Kosher salt, as needed

1 tablespoon (5 grams) prik phong (ground toasted chile; see page 329)

½ tablespoon (5 grams) Toasted Rice Powder (page 283)

¼ cup (15 grams) scallions, green and white parts mixed, cut in 1-inch pieces

¼ cup (12 grams) roughly chopped cilantro

¼ cup (10 grams) torn saw-tooth herb

1. Start by charring the shallots: Grill the whole, unpeeled shallots over medium heat, turning occasionally so they don't completely burn and dry out, 10 to 12 minutes. You want them to cook slowly in their skins and end up with soft interiors and smoky aromas from the burnt skins. Cool and peel the shallots; discard the skins. Don't worry about any bits of ash that remain on the shallots after peeling.

2. Place the ribs in a colander, rinse under cold water, and drain. Transfer to a large soup pot, add the water and all the aromatics (the charred shallots, lemongrass, galangal, and lime leaves). Bring to a boil over high heat, then reduce the heat to maintain a gentle simmer. Add the fish sauce and MSG, if using. Cook at a gentle simmer, skimming occasionally, for 45 minutes to 1 hour; the ribs should be tender but retain some chew. When the ribs are cooked, remove the pot from the heat and stir in the lime juice. Taste; adjust the seasoning with salt if necessary. Transfer to a large, deep serving bowl. Sprinkle with the prik phong, toasted rice powder, scallions, and herbs. Serve immediately.

SIMPLE COUNTRY-STYLE GUINEA HEN SOUP

DTOM GAI BAAN

Roughly translated, this dish sounds boring: "chicken soup." But *gai baan* means "home chicken," the resident birds frolicking in your yard. That could mean a guinea hen or rooster: both yield soups far more deeply flavored than your typical egg-laying young hen. This soup exemplifies country life surrounded by rice fields, where the mantra of life is radically simple—there isn't even any spice or acid to distract from the purity. *Dtom gai baan* always reminded my mom of the Isan village she left for California. It was her remedy for homesickness, and it has become my own personal elixir whenever I crave honest comfort. If you can get hold of a rooster, by all means use it for this soup. You'll need to simmer it longer to tenderize its flavorful muscles.

SERVES 6 TO 8

1 guinea hen, about 1½ pounds (680 grams)

1 quart (946 grams) water

1½ cups (100 grams) lemongrass, crushed and cut in 1½-inch pieces

Eight ¼-inch slices fresh galangal (24 grams)

9 whole makrut lime leaves (3 grams)

5 tablespoons (50 grams) fish sauce

Kosher salt, to taste

¼ cup (10 grams) sliced scallions, white and green parts mixed

¼ cup (12 grams) roughly chopped cilantro

Remove the innards (if any) from the cavity of the guinea hen and reserve. Rinse the bird and innards under cold running water and transfer to a colander to drain for about 3 minutes. Remove the head and discard it. Cut off the feet and set aside. Using a cleaver, chop the bird, including the skin and bones, into 1-inch-wide pieces; set aside. Add the water, lemongrass, galangal, and lime leaves to a large soup pot. Cover and bring the water to a boil over high heat. Add the guinea hen pieces, innards (if you have them), the feet, and fish sauce to the simmering water; lower the heat to achieve a gentle simmer. Cook at this constant temperature for 45 minutes, skimming occasionally to keep the broth as clear as possible. After 45 minutes check a piece of guinea hen for tenderness—it should be softly chewy rather than meltingly tender. If it seems too firm, cook up to 15 minutes longer. If you've been careful to skim the surface, the soup should look clear. When the guinea hen is done, give the broth a taste; add salt if necessary. Transfer the soup to a large serving bowl and sprinkle with the scallions and cilantro.

HOT AND SOUR DRIED AND GRILLED FISH BONE SOUP DTOM KLONG PLA HANK

One of the many reasons my mother purchased whole fish (especially live, to be as fresh as possible) was this soup. She knew it would provide another meal after she turned the flesh into other dishes, one way to keep within our tight welfare budget. After breaking down the fish she'd collect the bones between the collar and tail (she cooked the head separately, for a soup served that day) and dry them in the sun on the rooftop of our apartment or in a south-facing window. Later she'd toast them in the open flame of our miniature hibachi grill, set up at the bottom of the stairs, outside the fire exit. Grilled dried fish bones add a smoky nuance—drying the bones first preserves them, and ensures they'll toast rather than cook on the grill. The flavor also changes, ending up richer and more complex, with a certain weight. You can use pretty much any fish (but avoid smaller, very oily ones like mackerel, sardines, and anchovies or herring).

4 large shallots, unpeeled (100 grams)

7 peeled garlic cloves (25 grams)

6 cups (1,422 grams) water

6 ounces (170 grams) fish bones, dried and grilled (see Note)

½ cup (40 grams) lemongrass, thinly sliced on the bias

Three ⅛-inch-thick slices fresh galangal (9 grams)

6 fresh green Thai chiles (10 grams)

6 whole makrut lime leaves (2 grams)

3 tablespoons (36 grams) fish sauce

1 tablespoon (15 grams) padaek

2 teaspoons (8 grams) MSG (optional)

Kosher salt, as needed

2 tablespoons (30 grams) fresh lime juice

2 scallions, green and white parts, in 1-inch pieces (25 grams)

1 cup saw-tooth herb, in 2-inch pieces (18 grams)

2 tablespoons (6 grams) roughly chopped fresh dill, stems included

½ cup (24 grams) roughly chopped cilantro, stems included

1. Roast the unpeeled shallots by threading them onto a skewer and grilling over an open flame until the interior is soft; give them a firm squeeze to tell when they're done. You can also roast them in a dry cast-iron pan over low heat, making sure to move them around often so the skins brown evenly. Peel the cooled shallots and set aside. Repeat with the peeled garlic cloves, roasted either on skewers over the grill or in a dry skillet.

2. In a medium soup pot, combine the water, grilled fish bones, roasted shallots, garlic, lemongrass, galangal, chiles, and lime leaves. Bring to a boil over medium heat, then lower the heat to maintain a gentle simmer. Simmer for 30 minutes, skimming occasionally to remove impurities from the surface to ensure a clear soup.

3. After 30 minutes add the fish sauce, padaek, and MSG, if using, and simmer for 15 minutes more. Remove from the heat. Taste and add salt as needed. When the soup is seasoned to your liking stir in the lime juice, scallions, and herbs. Transfer to a large serving bowl.

NOTE: To dry and grill fish bones, remove the head of the fish carcass and discard or save for another use. The bones don't have to be completely clean of flesh. Put them in an area with direct sunlight, dry them on a roasting rack in a 150°F oven, or place them in a dehydrator. I prefer drying bones in sunlight on a warm day, either by hanging the fish carcass or laying it out on a roasting rack left on a sunny counter. Once the bones are dried, grill the carcass: You're not cooking it, but giving it a light toast and a bit of char to pick up some concentrated fish aromas. It's best to grill over open fire (you can do this over the flame on a gas range, or even in the fireplace). Once the bones are completely dried they'll keep for about a year, stored in an airtight container in a dry place.

14

LAAP AND GOI

CRISPY RICE BALL SALAD NAM KHAO TOD

In a culture where nothing goes to waste, it's a sin to throw away food, especially rice. Leftover jasmine rice always transforms into another dish. My mother never served *nam khao tod* at her restaurant, but it was always present in large quantities in aluminum trays at parties and other functions—it was popular in the Lao 'hood. The rice balls themselves can stand alone as a snack, like Italian arancini. I love this dish because it's a different way to enjoy rice, herbs, and toasted dried chile, wrapping them up together in lettuce leaves to form a very delicious package. If you aren't planning to make your own soured pork, go to a Lao or Thai market and ask for *som moo* or *nam*. Often the owner will have some for sale by a local home cook. You can find something similar at Vietnamese markets, but it tends to be sweeter, less tart. Serve this salad the day you make it.

SERVES 4 TO 6 AS AN APPETIZER

RICE BALLS

- 2 cups (300 grams) cooked jasmine rice, at room temperature
- ¼ teaspoon (2 grams) Red Curry Paste (page 301)
- 2 tablespoons (34 grams) fresh coconut meat, grated
- ½ teaspoon (2 grams) kosher salt
- 3 quarts (2,460 grams) canola oil, for frying

SALAD

- 2 tablespoons (28 grams) crushed toasted peanuts
- 2 tablespoons (4 grams) thinly sliced scallions
- ½ tablespoon (3 grams) prik phong (ground toasted chile; see page 329); plus more to taste

- 2 ounces (56 grams) Soured Pork (page 114), crumbled
- 1 tablespoon (15 grams) fresh lime juice
- 1 tablespoon (12 grams) fish sauce
- 1 tablespoon (12 grams) granulated sugar

GARNISHES

- Fried dried chiles
- Lime wedges

SIDES

- Bibb lettuce leaves
- Mint sprigs
- Cilantro sprigs
- Cucumber slices

1. MAKE THE RICE BALLS: Place the rice in a large mixing bowl and add the red curry paste, coconut, and salt. With your hands, gently mix everything together—work the rice by doing a rotating folding motion, at the same time getting rid of any lumps that may form between your fingers. Try not to overmix—if you do, the rice will become firm, with broken grains. The individual rice grains should remain intact; the whole mixture should end up fluffy. Form the mixture into two equal round balls.

2. FRY THE RICE BALLS: Line a baking sheet with paper towels and set aside. Add the oil to a large, heavy saucepan or Dutch oven. Set the pan over medium-high heat and bring the oil to 350°F, raising or lowering the heat as needed to maintain a steady temperature. Carefully lower the rice balls into the hot oil. Fry for about 5 minutes, or until they're a rich golden color with a firm crust. Transfer to the paper towel–lined baking sheet to drain and cool slightly.

3. ASSEMBLE THE SALAD: With your hands, crush the warm fried rice balls into a large mixing bowl—they should look like fried rice when you're finished. Toss in the crushed peanuts, scallions, prik phong, and crumbled soured pork. Add the lime juice, fish sauce, and sugar and taste; adjust the heat to your liking with additional prik phong. Toss well. Garnish with fried chiles and lime wedges. Serve with a basket of Bibb lettuce leaves, mint, cilantro, and cucumber. Eat by rolling up the rice ball salad with garnishes in lettuce leaves.

LAO DUNGENESS CRAB SALAD PHON PUU

The best way to describe *phon* is a *jaew*—a spicy chile dip—mixed with protein and herbs. It's always made with seafood, usually a whole fresh fish (tilapia, snapper, bass, or catfish), poached with aromatics to create a stock. You remove the cooked fish and pick the flesh, muddle grilled Thai eggplants, green chiles, shallots, and garlic into a paste to combine with the fish. Season with padaek and fish sauce, loosen the texture with some of the stock, fold in the herbs, and you've got phon. This recipe, made with Dungeness crab, is a bit of a curveball. Sometimes Pops wouldn't come home until six in the morning—he'd meet up after work with some pals to go crabbing in the bay. He'd walk in with as many as ten Dungeness, a luxury for us in the early days (we'd see live crabs in the tanks in Chinatown but could never afford them). We'd have crab boils with *jaew som* for dipping, but Moms would change things up with this phon. Since it's soupy, I love having a bowl of warm jasmine rice to absorb all the flavors. This is best the day it's made.

SERVES 6 TO 8

1 live Dungeness crab, about 2½ pounds (1,134 grams)

¼ cup (23 grams) whole unpeeled shallots

2 peeled garlic cloves (25 grams)

½ tablespoon (3 grams) prik phong (ground toasted chile; see page 329)

1 tablespoon (12 grams) fish sauce

¼ cup (8 grams) thinly sliced scallions, green and white parts mixed

¼ cup (12 grams) roughly chopped cilantro

GARNISHES

Lime wedges

Mint sprigs

Cucumber slices

Long beans

Lettuce leaves

Whole fresh Thai chiles

1. Bring a large pot of unsalted water to a boil. While the water is heating, make an ice bath, a mix of ice cubes and cold water, in a large bowl. Once the water in the pot begins boiling rapidly, carefully lower in the crab, turn off the heat, cover the pot, and cook for 12 minutes. Remove the crab with a pair of tongs and immediately plunge it into the ice bath; let cool for 10 minutes.

2. To clean the crab, remove the top shell from the body by peeling it off, like removing a hat. Have a small bowl nearby to catch all the liquid from the cavity. Depending on the crab, the cavity under the shell will contain the roe (sometimes referred to as the "butter" or "miso"). With a spoon, scrape away the roe and add it to the bowl with the liquid. Clean the rest of the crab and remove the meat, using a cracker and a pair of scissors to penetrate the shell. Set the meat aside separately from the roe and liquid. When done, you should have about 6 ounces (170 grams) of crabmeat and 6 ounces (170 grams) of crab liquid and roe.

3. Place the unpeeled shallots on a medium-hot grill. Cook slowly until the flesh is soft; check by giving each shallot a firm squeeze. When the shallots are done set them aside to steam in their skins and cool. Peel when you're able to handle them comfortably; coarsely chop and set aside. Add the garlic cloves to a dry cast-iron skillet over medium heat. Cook, stirring often, until the garlic is soft and toasted. Set aside to cool.

4. Combine the shallots and garlic in a mortar and pound to a paste. Add the crab and roe mixture and lightly muddle and stir with the pestle for 30 seconds. Add the prik phong and fish sauce; stop pounding and simply stir with either the pestle or a spoon to combine. Fold in the scallions and cilantro. Transfer to a bowl and serve with the garnishes and hot jasmine rice.

BRAISED SHREDDED BAMBOO SALAD WITH SESAME SEEDS SOOP NAW MAI

The first time I ate bamboo shoots was in this dish. Whenever my dad bought a dress shirt from Sears on Telegraph Avenue, my mother would ask him to save the pins that kept it folded—she wanted them for shredding bamboo shoots. Sometimes she used bamboo skewers (toothpicks were too short), but they'd break and get dull. Back home in the village, a thorn from a citrus tree or other plant would do, but in Oakland, a shirt pin was her favorite tool. This dish is a salad with the texture of a ragout, moist and thick, the bamboo like a network of noodles bundled together. The bamboo shoots come in a tall can—look for the very young, slender ones about the diameter of your pinky, between 3 and 6 inches long. Knorr chicken bouillon powder adds protein richness (liquid stock would dilute the flavor and make the dish watery). The combination of sticky rice steaming hot out of the *thip khao* and *soop naw mai* yields something I can only describe as *yum*.

SERVES 4 TO 6

8 ounces (227 grams) thin young bamboo shoots

1 cup (250 grams) Yanang Leaf Water (page 300)

3 tablespoons (23 grams) thinly sliced lemongrass

1 tablespoon (15 grams) padaek

1 tablespoon (12 grams) Knorr chicken bouillon powder

½ tablespoon (3 grams) prik phong (ground toasted chile; see page 329)

2 tablespoons (20 grams) white sesame seeds, toasted

3 tablespoons (8 grams) sliced scallions, green and white parts mixed

¼ cup (8 grams) torn mint leaves

¼ cup (12 grams) roughly chopped cilantro, stems included

1 tablespoon (8 grams) thinly sliced shallots

1. Hold a bamboo shoot firmly by the thick end. Hold a bamboo skewer in your other hand, like a pencil. Start running the pointed end of the skewer along the flesh of the bamboo shoot, making deep scratches in the direction of the grain to shred the flesh. Transfer the shreds to a medium saucepan. Repeat with the remaining shoots. Cover the shredded bamboo with cold water and bring to a rapid boil over high heat. Drain in a colander and rinse under cold running water. With your hands, squeeze out as much water from the shoots as you can. Return the shoots to the saucepan and add the yanang leaf water; set aside.

2. Add the lemongrass to a mortar and pound to a paste; add to the saucepan. Bring the bamboo mixture to a boil and simmer gently for 5 minutes. Season with the padaek and chicken bouillon powder and simmer for another 3 minutes. Turn off the heat, then mix in the prik phong. Transfer to a platter and cool about 15 minutes. Just before serving, sprinkle with the sesame seeds, scallions, mint, cilantro, and shallots. You can also serve this at room temperature. It keeps for 3 days, refrigerated.

LAAP

In Lao Isan, *laap* refers to the action of mincing meat. Some Thai menus spell it *laab*. Also *larb*. Laap probably originated in southwest China before migrating to Laos, the Isan region, on to Bangkok, and all over Thailand.

It's categorized as a salad because you prepare it like one, tossing together minced meat, internal organs, and other cuts with spice blends, seasonings, and herbs. You serve it with a rich assortment of vegetables, herbs, and tender leaves. But laap is not salad as we think of one in the West: You don't eat it by itself at the beginning of a meal, or alone, in a big bowl, for lunch. Laap is a cluster of flavor bombs, and always needs something neutral—sticky rice and ice-cold beer!—to buffer the explosion.

The foundation of laap is minced animal protein, raw or cooked. Depending on the type of laap and the region, you add the skin of the animal, offal, blood, bile, and gastric juices. You season with fish sauce alone or just padaek, sometimes both. Spices and herbs can be simple or complex.

Like so much food in Asia, laap is more than just a dish. It's an integral part of the culture, a way of life. It represents the relationship between people, nature, and the social fabric, a symbol of well-being. Laap is a more complicated dish to prepare than it looks to the naked eye—it's both time- and labor-intensive—and calls for expensive ingredients, like whole ducks. Making laap in a traditional Lao community is a big deal, and a social exercise. You invite friends and relatives to take part, literally to lend their hands.

The process of making laap—from securing, say, freshly slaughtered beef, to the tedious job of chopping by hand, and the social drinking that follows—points to the ceremonial aspects of laap, its place at the center of a Lao or Isan village's social activity, and its status as an offering to important guests. The whole thing is supposed to bring good health and better fortune (in Isan, a word with the same pronunciation as laap—though with a slightly different spelling—means *unexpected gains*, *windfall profits*, or *good luck*). Even here in America, far from village life, laap should be the heart of happiness, good times with relatives, friends, and neighbors.

There was always something macho about laap, especially the raw versions. Consider the huge effort to process large amounts of meat for a ceremony: the men sitting in a circle, each holding two knives, pounding out beats like it's some bloody drum circle. The sound was an invitation for neighbors to join the fest.

Laap was probably the only dish a Lao man would ever make—it wasn't popular with women, at least raw. Raw laap is a dish full of testosterone, a bonding event for the manly brotherhood: butchering an animal, sharing the bravery by eating it uncooked with your buddies, and drinking a lot of alcohol. In my household in Oakland, far from village chopping circles, laap was always accompanied by Heineken or Cognac and Red Bull on the rocks.

Alcohol and laap have a close relationship—they're strong enough to stand up to each other, a natural complement. Booze is believed to kill parasites in raw meat (science does not bear this out). And the bitterness of laap seasoned with bile and the accompanying vegetables facilitates smooth drinking. Together, laap and booze are strong folk medicine, nutritionally rich and a boost for male vitality, potency, and strength. Anyway, that's the myth of laap.

When my brother and I were kids, the grown-ups wouldn't let us eat raw laap for fear of parasites. My mom or an auntie would toss a lump into a wok, without oil or liquids, and cook it for us, resulting in *laap khuaa* or *laap sook*, which translates to "laap for the kids' table."

The key to good laap is mincing the meat to the right consistency. The old-school method calls for a knife, a wooden chopping block, and the plain force of muscle. Mincing happens gradually, through repeated pounding with the knife blade. At times, with raw laap, I've seen my mother or an uncle add small amounts of fresh blood to adjust the consistency and add richness as they chop.

Skin and offal are thoroughly cleaned and boiled in water with aromatics—crushed stalks of lemongrass, makrut lime leaves, and galangal—until they're soft and tender, then sliced into bite-size pieces. (Don't throw away the poaching liquid. You can season it into a soup called *dtom kueng nai*—the intention of making one dish turns into two plates of food.) In the case of chicken or duck laap the skin can be seasoned with salt and then fried to a crisp for crackling that is later crushed on top of the laap.

Serve laap with a wide range of herbs and vegetables: cucumber slices, a wedge of cabbage, tomatoes, leaves of lettuce or mustard greens, sprigs of rau ram and mint, raw long

beans and eggplant (pea, Thai, or apple), and the list goes on. Aromatic, sour, and bitter leaves are all welcome on the plate, depending on what type of laap you're serving. There are no rules.

Types of laap vary a lot from region to region, from one city to another, and even from house to house. The biggest difference is the type of animal protein at its heart, but spicing tells you a lot about laap styles. In the Lanna region of northern Thailand, in the cities of Chiang Mai and Chiang Rai, laaps have a rich blend of dried spices called *nahm prik laap*, originally imported to the region by trade caravans from India and China back in the day.

Laap from Isan is fresh, spicy, salty, and a bit sour sometimes, with nutty hints from roasted rice powder. It's simple, seasoned with just a few ingredients: pulverized dried chile, fish sauce, padaek, ground toasted rice (which also serves as a binder), and sometimes lime juice. Since the ancient trade routes never made it through Isan, aromatic spices are almost never present. But laaps of raw beef or water buffalo in Isan include fresh blood and bile, added for their rich bitterness, which magically enhances the intrinsic sweetness of the meat.

All laaps, regardless of meat or region of origin, get a lift from herbs and alliums: coriander, spring onions or scallions, shallots, mint leaves, and rau ram, among others. They add freshness and fragrance to the dish.

To complement the soft texture of the minced meat, just before serving, sometimes laap gets a sprinkling of crunchy elements: brittle fried dried chiles, deep-fried shallots and garlic, bits of fried internal organs and crispy skins, even deep-fried fish scales.

Some types of laap:

LAAP ISAN/ลาบอีสาน

Isan cooks make this from almost any animal protein they can get, including beef, water buffalo, pork, chicken, duck, birds, fish, shrimp, lizard, the eggs of fire ants, and more. The seasoning is simple: pounded dried chiles, ground toasted rice, lime juice (sometimes), and fish sauce or padaek. Once seasoned, the mixture gets spring onions, mint, and coriander leaves.

KOY/ก้อย

Mainly with fish and beef. The meat is thinly sliced rather than minced.

LAAP LEUUAT/ลาบเลือด

Similar to *luu* from the Lanna region of northern Thailand (including both Chiang Mai and Chiang Rai) and the *sohk lek* of Northern Isan, made with minced beef or water buffalo meat with blood added to fill the plate.

NAM DTOHK/น้ำตก

This is made from barbecued pork (usually the neck) sliced into bite-size pieces. You bring the meat to a boil in stock to create a sauce, then turn off the heat and add sliced shallots, ground toasted rice, powdered chile, lime juice, and fish sauce, along with shredded coriander leaves, spring onions, and mint.

DTAP WAAN/ตับหวาน

Similar to nam dtohk, but instead of barbecued pork neck, you use a semicooked liver.

NORTHERN ISAN LAAP (NAKORN PANOM PROVINCE)

SOHK LEK/ซกเล็ก

The Isan version of luu, a lot spicier than the Lanna version.

LEUUAT BPLAAENG/เลือดแปลง

Popular in northern Isan with people of Vietnamese descent, this is a laap made with the cooked internal organs of a pig or duck, served with fresh pork blood. You season fresh blood with fish sauce and stock, then pour it over the minced meat; as the blood coagulates, it sets like panna cotta.

FRIED PORK LAAP MEATBALL LETTUCE WRAPS

Here's a different take on laap, with a different way of eating it: in Bibb lettuce cups. It's more of a snack, drinking food, if you will. This is one laap you won't need to accompany with sticky rice unless, like me, you want sticky rice with everything. The pork meatballs are fairly easy to make and highly rewarding. You can make them a day ahead, even freeze some of the mixture and defrost, shape, and fry when you're ready. To eat, build a cup with a leaf of Bibb lettuce. Place a laap fritter in the center, followed by cucumber and picked leaves of mint, cilantro, and rau ram. Spoon on a bit of *naam jim gai yang* sauce and eat. Repeat, trying to down them faster than the person sitting next to you.

SERVES 6 TO 8

- 1 ounce (28 grams) pork skin
- 1 quart (946 grams) water
- Pinch of salt
- 2 quarts (1,640 grams) canola oil, for frying
- 1 pound (454 grams) finely ground pork
- 2 tablespoons (30 grams) thinly sliced lemongrass

- ¼ cup (40 grams) thinly sliced shallots
- 1 tablespoon (8 grams) minced fresh galangal
- 6 makrut lime leaves (2 grams), in fine julienne
- 2 tablespoons (20 grams) Toasted Rice Powder (page 283)
- ¼ teaspoon (1 gram) MSG (optional)

- ½ tablespoon (3 grams) prik phong (ground toasted chile; see page 329)
- 3 tablespoons (8 grams) sliced scallions, green and white parts mixed
- 2 tablespoons (24 grams) fish sauce
- 1 tablespoon (15 grams) padaek

GARNISHES

- 2 heads Bibb lettuce, leaves separated, washed, and dried
- 1 bunch cilantro
- 1 bunch mint
- 1 bunch rau ram
- 1 cucumber, thinly sliced

1. Rinse the pork skin under running water, place in a small saucepan, and cover with cold water. Lightly salt the water. Bring to a gentle simmer over medium heat and cook for 30 minutes. Drain and cool under cold running water. With a sharp knife shave excess fat from the skin, then dice into ⅛-inch cubes. Transfer to a large mixing bowl and set aside.

2. Add the oil to a large, heavy saucepan or Dutch oven; it should come no more than halfway up the sides. Set the pan over medium-high heat and bring the oil to 350°F, adjusting the heat as needed to maintain a steady temperature. To the mixing bowl with the pork skin, add the ground pork, lemongrass, shallots, galangal, lime leaf julienne, toasted rice powder, MSG, if using, prik phong, scallions, fish sauce, and padaek. Knead the mixture with your hands, smoothing out any lumps of ground pork, to make an evenly seasoned sausage farce. Clean off your hands, moisten them with water, and form some of the laap mixture into a golf ball–size lump. Smooth between both palms and transfer to a baking sheet. Repeat until all the farce is used.

3. Line a plate with paper towels and set aside. Using a spider, gently lower 6 laap balls at a time into the hot oil. Fry for 3 to 4 minutes, until they turn a dark amber color with crispy exteriors. Transfer the cooked laap balls to the paper towel–lined plate to drain. Serve immediately with the garnishes and Hot, Sweet, and Sour Dipping Sauce for BBQ Chicken (page 295).

LAO MINCED PORK SALAD LAAP MOO

Pork on pork on pork—what more can you ask for in a salad? Don't be tempted to remove any of the fat from the pork shoulder: It renders as it cooks, to become an essential part of the dressing. Since you need only a small amount of pork skin for this recipe, cook a piece that's 2 ounces or so, set aside ½ ounce, and freeze the rest in a zipper-top bag. Serve this laap with freshly steamed sticky rice so hot it's hard to handle. The combination of warm salad with hot rice is perfect.

SERVES 4 TO 6

2 ounces (56 grams) thinly sliced pork skin

Pinch of salt

10 ounces (283 grams) pork shoulder with fat

1 ounce (28 grams) pork liver, thinly sliced

¼ cup (40 grams) thinly sliced shallots

1 tablespoon (10 grams) Toasted Rice Powder (page 289)

2 fresh Thai chiles, thinly sliced (3 grams)

1 tablespoon (5 grams) prik phong (ground toasted chile; see page 329)

1½ tablespoons (18 grams) fish sauce

2 tablespoons (30 grams) padaek

¼ teaspoon (1 gram) MSG (optional)

3 tablespoons (6 grams) thinly sliced scallions, green and white parts mixed

¼ cup (8 grams) torn mint leaves

¼ cup (12 grams) chopped cilantro, stems included

⅛ cup (6 grams) saw-tooth herb, in ½-inch segments

GARNISHES

Green cabbage heart wedges

Cucumber slices

Long beans, in 1½-inch pieces

Fried pork rinds

1. To prepare the pork skin, rinse it under cold running water. Place it in a small pot and cover with cold water. Lightly salt the water and bring to a boil; reduce the heat to achieve a gentle simmer. Cook for 8 to 10 minutes. Drain, and rinse under cold running water to cool. With a sharp knife shave excess fat from the skin and discard. Slice the blanched skin into very thin strips.

2. With a cleaver, chop the pork shoulder to a medium-coarse texture, like loose pork sausage. Warm a large sauté pan over medium heat. Add the chopped pork shoulder and sliced liver to the dry pan and cook, stirring constantly, breaking up the meat to keep it from clumping. After about 3 minutes, the pork should be cooked; transfer it, along with the juices, to a large mixing bowl. Cool the meat until it's lukewarm to the touch, about 2 minutes. Add the blanched pork skin, the shallots, toasted rice powder, fresh chiles, prik phong, fish sauce, padaek, and MSG, if using. Using your hands, mix thoroughly. Add the scallions and herbs and mix again. Transfer to a serving platter and garnish with raw cabbage wedges, cucumber slices, long bean pieces, and fried pork rinds and serve right away with hot sticky rice.

DUCK LAAP: SPICY, HERBACEOUS MINCED DUCK SALAD LAAP PED

Duck laap was a rare treat when I was growing up, a ceremonial event in the Laotian ghetto, like Thanksgiving. You'd hear through the grapevine that someone was planning to slaughter a duck for laap. Soon everyone on the block invited themselves to the party, and that original single duck had become several. The party would start with killing the ducks in the communal empty lot. I was seven the first time I witnessed one drained through a slit in its neck, the blood collecting in a plastic pan for the finished laap. I helped pluck feathers after my dad plunged a carcass into scalding water. It stoked my curiosity about cooking. I was amazed—it was the beginning of my education about where food comes from and how it's processed. Duck laap was an event! It was fun! I've left the blood out of this recipe but none of the richness or herbal aromas. Next time you're wondering what to make for a Thanksgiving potluck, consider *laap ped*, a dish with a history of bringing people together. Serve right after it's made.

SERVES 4 TO 6

11 ounces (310 grams) boneless duck meat with skin

½ cup (103 grams) canola oil

Kosher salt

2 ounces (56 grams) duck offal (liver and gizzards), or extra duck meat

3 tablespoons (8 grams) thinly sliced lemongrass

¼ cup (40 grams) thinly sliced shallots

2 tablespoons (20 grams) Toasted Rice Powder (page 283)

1 tablespoon (5 grams) prik phong (ground toasted chile; see page 329)

1½ tablespoons (18 grams) fish sauce

1 tablespoon (15 grams) padaek

½ teaspoon (2 grams) MSG (optional)

3 tablespoons (8 grams) thinly sliced scallions, green and white parts mixed

¼ cup (8 grams) torn mint leaves

¼ cup (12 grams) roughly chopped cilantro, stems included

GARNISHES

Green cabbage wedges

Cucumber slices

Long bean bâtons

Green Thai eggplant slices

1. Remove the skin from the duck. To make cracklings, place the oil in a small saucepan and get it hot over medium heat. Salt one half of the duck skin lightly, then fry it in the canola oil until it's browned and crisp. Set aside to cool on paper towels. You should have 3 tablespoons (10 grams) of crackling. With a cleaver, chop the duck meat to a medium-coarse, hamburger-like texture. Using a sharp knife, thinly slice the offal and the remaining skin and mix it with the duck meat.

2. Set a large sauté pan over medium heat. Add the duck mixture to the dry pan and cook, stirring constantly, breaking up the meat to keep it from clumping. After about 3 minutes, the duck should be cooked. Scrape the cooked meat and all of the juices into a large mixing bowl.

Cool until the mixture is lukewarm to the touch, about 2 minutes. Add the lemongrass, shallots, toasted rice powder, prik phong, fish sauce, padaek, and MSG, if using, and mix thoroughly with your hands. Add the scallions, mint, and cilantro and mix again. Arrange on a serving platter, sprinkle with the duck cracklings, and garnish with raw cabbage wedges, cucumber slices, long bean bâtons, and slices of Thai eggplant. Serve with hot sticky rice.

RAW BEEF LAAP LAAP SEEN DIP

As a kid I wasn't supposed to eat raw beef laap because of the risk of food-borne infection, but I always managed to sneak a morsel anyway, propped on my ball of sticky rice like a piece of nigiri sushi. The bitterness of the bile didn't bother me at all—in fact, it made me salivate, wanting more. I loved it. This dish would have been impossible to make without the weekly subscription goodie bag from the Lao rancher who raised and butchered cows for the community under the table, as it were. It's the only way my mom and aunties could get the fresh blood and organ meats unavailable in American markets. The assortment of offal in the weekly delivery was always a little different, so *laap seen dip* varied. For this recipe, I kept the selection to leaf tripe and calf's liver, but if you find a reliable underground source for beef off-cuts, by all means get adventurous. Just make sure you rinse the offal and blanch it first in boiling water (offal should always be cooked, even for raw beef laap). Include the raw beef blood (2 tablespoons) only if you can get it very fresh. Serve this laap with hot sticky rice, cold beer, and for a double-down celebration of the cow, the beef and offal soup called Dtom Keung Nai Kwuay (page 186). For a kids'-table version, omit the bile, and cook the finished laap in a sauté pan over medium heat until thoroughly done.

SERVES 4 TO 8

- 2 ounces (56 grams) beef leaf tripe, thinly sliced
- Pinch of salt
- 2 ounces (56 grams) calf's liver, thinly sliced

- 10 ounces (280 grams) beef sirloin
- ¼ cup (40 grams) thinly sliced shallots
- 2 fresh Thai chiles, thinly sliced (3 grams)

- 1 tablespoon (10 grams) Toasted Rice Powder (page 283)
- 1 tablespoon (5 grams) prik phong (ground toasted chile; see page 329)

- 2 tablespoons (24 grams) fish sauce
- 2 tablespoons (30 grams) padaek
- ½ teaspoon pasteurized beef bile (optional; see page 328)

1 tablespoon (12 grams) raw fresh beef blood (optional)

¼ teaspoon (1 gram) MSG (optional)

3 tablespoons (8 grams) thinly sliced scallions, green and white parts mixed

¼ cup (8 grams) torn mint leaves

¼ cup (12 grams) chopped cilantro, stems included

¼ cup (12 grams) roughly chopped rau ram leaves

GARNISHES

Green cabbage heart wedges

Cucumber slices

Long beans, in 1½-inch pieces

Whole fresh Thai chiles, green and red

Green Thai eggplant wedges

Rinse the tripe under cold running water. Bring a pot of water to a boil and lightly season with salt. Blanch the tripe for 1 minute, remove with a slotted spoon, and transfer to a large plate to cool. Blanch the liver in the same water for 30 seconds; it should end up slightly pink. Drain and transfer to the plate with the tripe to cool. Using a sharp vegetable cleaver or large chef's knife, chop the sirloin to a medium-coarse, hamburger-like texture; transfer to a large mixing bowl. Once the offal is cool to the touch, add it to the chopped beef along with the shallots, fresh chiles, toasted rice powder, prik phong, fish sauce, padaek, beef bile, blood, and MSG, if using, and mix thoroughly with your hands. Add the scallions and herbs and mix again. Transfer to a serving platter and garnish with cabbage wedges, cucumber slices, long bean pieces, chiles, and Thai eggplant wedges. Serve immediately with hot sticky rice and ice-cold beer.

MINCED CHICKEN SALAD WITH HERBS AND TOASTED RICE POWDER LAAP GAI

Let's be real: With meats of all kind, the tougher the muscle, the better the flavor. That means dark-meat chicken is always moister and more succulent than white. The roots of this Lao salad feature a scrappier bird than American farmed chicken. In my mom's Isan village, they make *laap gai* with wild chicken, guinea hen, even rooster, including the breast meat—the flavor rivals duck for richness. At Hawker Fare, we use what's accessible: boneless chicken thighs with the skin, plus gizzards and hearts, a delicious approximation of a farm dish. Eat laap gai with balls of sticky rice chased by lettuce and cucumber slices, or wrap up pinches of laap in lettuce leaves. Either way, you should serve it right after making the laap.

SERVES 4 TO 6

- 10 ounces (283 grams) boneless, skin-on chicken thigh meat
- 2 ounces (56 grams) mixed chicken hearts and gizzards
- ¼ cup (40 grams) thinly sliced shallots
- 2 tablespoons (16 grams) thinly sliced lemongrass
- 3 fresh Thai chiles, thinly sliced (6 grams)

- 2 tablespoons (20 grams) Toasted Rice Powder (page 283)
- 1 tablespoon (5 grams) prik phong (ground toasted chile; see page 329)
- 1½ tablespoons (18 grams) fish sauce
- 2 tablespoons (30 grams) padaek

- ¼ teaspoon (1 gram) MSG (optional)
- 3 tablespoons (8 grams) thinly sliced scallions, green and white parts mixed
- ¼ cup (8 grams) torn mint leaves
- ¼ cup (12 grams) roughly chopped fresh cilantro

GARNISHES

- Leaves of green leaf lettuce
- Rau ram
- Cucumber slices
- Long beans, cut into 1½-inch pieces
- Fresh Thai chiles

Using a cleaver, chop the chicken thighs into a medium-coarse texture; set aside. With a sharp knife, cut the chicken hearts and gizzards into thin slices. Set a large sauté pan over medium heat. Add the chopped chicken and sliced innards to the dry pan and cook, stirring constantly, breaking up the meat to keep it from clumping. Sauté for about 3 minutes; the chicken should be thoroughly cooked. Transfer the cooked chicken and all of the juices to a large mixing bowl. Cool the chicken until it's lukewarm to the touch. Add the shallots, lemongrass, fresh chiles, toasted rice powder, prik phong, fish sauce, padaek, and MSG, if using, to the cooled chicken and mix thoroughly with your hands. Add the scallions and herbs and mix again. Transfer to a serving platter and garnish with lettuce leaves, rau ram, cucumber slices, and long bean pieces, and Thai chiles. Serve with hot sticky rice.

POUNDED RAW SHRIMP LAAP LAAP GOONG LAIL

I admit this is not the prettiest laap in my mom's repertoire: The combination of raw shrimp, grilled eggplant, chiles, toasted rice powder, seasonings, and herbs ends up a brownish-gray puree. But homely food can taste really delicious. My first encounter with *laap goong lail* was at a very young age, swiping a ball of sticky rice through the pile (my curiosity had won out over the fact that, as kids, we were forbidden raw proteins). That initial bite raised my eyebrows and made me chew faster so I could get the next bite. The smooth texture, the saltiness framing the umami taste—I thought it was out-of-this-world delicious. I didn't care what it looked like. Lesson learned: Never judge a dish by its color. This recipe makes more broth than you need; freeze the remainder for next time.

SERVES 4 TO 6

½ cup (40 grams) sliced lemongrass

Two ¼-inch slices fresh galangal (6 grams)

3 whole makrut lime leaves (1 gram)

1½ cups (357 grams) water

¼ cup (60 grams) padaek

2 ounces (56 grams) whole, unpeeled shallots

2 ounces (56 grams) Thai eggplant, grilled whole

4 ounces (112 grams) raw shrimp, 26/30 size, fresh or previously frozen, peeled and deveined

1½ tablespoons (18 grams) fish sauce

1 tablespoon (5 grams) prik phong (ground toasted chile; see page 329)

1 tablespoon (10 grams) Toasted Rice Powder (page 283)

¼ cup (12 grams) thinly sliced scallions, green and white parts mixed

¼ cup (12 grams) finely chopped cilantro, stems included

GARNISHES

Cucumber slices

Long beans, cut into 1½-inch pieces

Green Thai eggplants, cut into thin wedges

Mint sprigs

Rau ram leaves

1. Begin by making the broth: In a small saucepan combine the lemongrass, galangal, lime leaves, water, and padaek. Bring to a boil and immediately remove from the heat. Set aside and allow the aromatics to steep and the broth to cool to room temperature.

2. Meanwhile, grill the unpeeled shallots over medium heat, turning occasionally so they don't completely burn and dry out, 10 to 12 minutes. You want them to cook slowly in their skins and end up with soft interiors and smoky aromas from the burnt skins. Cool and peel the shallots; discard the skins. Don't worry about any bits of ash that remain on the shallots after peeling.

3. With a mortar and pestle, pound the grilled eggplant, shallots, and raw shrimp to a fine sticky paste, the stickier the better. Add ¼ cup of the cooled broth and pound lightly to incorporate the liquid completely; work carefully so you don't splash too much. Make sure the

paste is very smooth. Stir in a circular motion with the pestle, making sure the paste is thick and sticky. If it seems too dry, add a bit more broth—it should have a consistency like smooth guacamole. Add the fish sauce, prik phong, toasted rice powder, scallions, and cilantro and stir with the pestle to incorporate. Transfer to a shallow serving bowl and garnish with cucumber slices, long bean pieces, Thai eggplant edges, mint sprigs, and rau ram leaves. Serve with sticky rice.

TART AND AROMATIC FISH SALAD GOI PLA

Goi is a variation of laap, but instead of being minced, the central protein—in this case, fish—is sliced paper thin. As with ceviche, the striped bass or snapper is "cooked" by marinating in citrus juice. The aromatics are plentiful, yielding a very light and refreshing dish. I like to eat *goi pla* with hot jasmine rice, but it's just as good wrapped in lettuce leaves.

SERVES 4 TO 6

1 pound (454 grams) striped bass or snapper fillets, skin and pin bones removed

¼ cup (60 grams) fresh lime juice

⅓ cup (50 grams) very thinly sliced lemongrass

1 teaspoon (3 grams) finely minced fresh galangal

¼ cup (40 grams) thinly sliced shallots

1 tablespoon (2 grams) thinly sliced makrut lime leaves

1 tablespoon (10 grams) Toasted Rice Powder (page 283)

3 to 4 fresh Thai chiles, thinly sliced (5 grams)

3 tablespoons (36 grams) fish sauce, plus more to taste

½ teaspoon (2 grams) MSG (optional)

½ teaspoon (2 grams) granulated sugar

⅓ cup (100 grams) very thinly sliced long beans

¼ cup (5 grams) lemon basil leaves

¼ cup (8 grams) torn mint leaves

¼ cup (10 grams) roughly chopped cilantro leaves

¼ cup (5 grams) roughly chopped saw-tooth herb

GARNISHES

Cucumber slices

Whole fresh Thai chiles

Green leaf lettuce leaves

1. With a sharp knife slice the fish paper thin; transfer the slices to a mixing bowl. Add the lime juice and mix well. As the fish cures, it will go from translucent to opaque. After 5 minutes, add the aromatics and seasonings (lemongrass, galangal, shallots, lime leaves, toasted rice powder, chiles, fish sauce, MSG, if using, and sugar). Using your hands, lightly mix all the ingredients together without breaking up the fish. Taste, and add more fish sauce or sliced chile as needed.

2. Just before serving, lightly mix in the sliced long beans and herbs. Garnish with slices of cucumber, whole chiles, and lettuce and serve immediately.

SHREDDED CHICKEN SALAD WITH HERBS, FISH SAUCE, AND LIME YUM GAI

What do you do when you have leftover chicken from *khao mun gai* or *gai yang*? You turn it into a dish befitting the situation. My mother did that best, letting very little go to waste. You could poach chicken just for this salad and it would be delicious, especially if you serve it slightly warm. What's even better, the next time you make khao mun gai, poach extra chicken to make *yum gai* the next day. If you're not starting with leftovers, poach raw chicken according to the instructions for Poached Chicken and Rice (page 181). Pick the meat off the bones and tear it into strands. I like adding the skin—it provides richness and moisture, the way oil does in Western salads. Slice it into thin strands.

SERVES 4 TO 6

8 ounces (227 grams) shredded poached chicken, with sliced skin

¼ cup (32 grams) paper-thin red onion slices

4 fresh red Thai chiles, thinly sliced (7 grams)

3 tablespoons (36 grams) fish sauce

2 tablespoons (24 grams) granulated sugar

¼ cup (60 grams) fresh lime juice

¼ cup (15 grams) sliced scallions

¼ cup (8 grams) torn mint leaves

¼ cup (12 grams) roughly chopped cilantro

¼ cup (10 grams) rau ram leaves

GARNISHES

Fried Shallots (page 306)

Cucumber slices

Green leaf lettuce leaves

In a small mixing bowl, combine the chicken, red onion, chiles, and seasonings (fish sauce, sugar, and lime juice). Mix gently with a spoon or, even better, your hands. Fold in the scallions, mint, cilantro, and rau ram. Transfer to a serving platter and sprinkle with fried shallots. Garnish with cucumber slices and lettuce leaves.

FRIED EGG SALAD YUM KHAI DAO

There are many ways to cook eggs; I think frying them the Thai and Lao way is best. It's the opposite of how you fry eggs sunny-side up in Western cooking, which is all about gentle heat. The Thai/Lao way is to grip it and rip it (well, almost). You start by heating a fair amount of oil in a wok (a rounded-bottom wok works better than a flat pan) to near smoking point. Slip in the egg and watch the white bubble and start to engulf the yolk—it'll brown and seal in the yolk, creating a crispy skin: my favorite way to cook an egg. You get the textural layers of a crunchy exterior over a softer, gelatinous white and an oozing yolk. This dish comes together once the yolk breaks and mixes with the rest of the ingredients. It was very popular at Manyda, my mother's Thai restaurant in Oakland, and continues to be so at Hawker Fare. Note that you'll end up with extra dressing, but it keeps for about 2 weeks. Once you have some on hand, it's very easy to make this salad.

SERVES 2 TO 4 AS AN APPETIZER

DRESSING

1½ cups (300 grams) granulated sugar

1¼ cups (300 grams) fresh lime juice

1 cup (192 grams) fish sauce

15 fresh red Thai chiles, thinly sliced (25 grams)

¼ cup (50 grams) peeled garlic cloves

3 tablespoons (2 grams) thinly sliced makrut lime leaves

FOR THE SALAD

2 large eggs (100 grams)

¼ cup (51 grams) canola oil

3 ounces (84 grams) cherry tomatoes, halved

⅛ cup (8 grams) thinly sliced red onion

⅛ cup (10 grams) thinly sliced Chinese celery, leaves included

2 tablespoons (15 grams) Fried Shallots (page 306)

¼ cup (12 grams) chopped cilantro

1. MAKE THE DRESSING: In a small bowl, combine the sugar, lime juice, and fish sauce; stir to dissolve the sugar. Pound the chiles and garlic to a paste in a mortar. Stir the paste into the lime juice mixture along with the lime leaves. Set the dressing aside.

2. MAKE THE SALAD: Crack each egg into its own small bowl. Warm the oil in a wok over high heat to just below the smoking point; it should be hot enough so that when the egg hits the oil the white immediately bubbles. Cautiously slip an egg into the wok and cook until the white is brown and crispy and the yolk is still runny, as with an egg cooked sunny-side up. Transfer the cooked egg to a large plate. Repeat with the remaining egg.

3. ASSEMBLE THE SALAD: Scatter the halved cherry tomatoes, sliced onions, and Chinese celery around the fried eggs and spoon over 1 ounce of the dressing. Garnish with a scattering of fried shallots and chopped cilantro and serve immediately, while the eggs are still warm. At the table, break up the yolks and mix into the salad.

BEAN THREAD NOODLE SALAD WITH CHILE JAM

YUM SEN LOWN (YUM WOON SEN)

This was #26 on the menu at Wat Phou, my mother's first restaurant. All the kitchen tickets would be expedited on the written numeric ordering system, a way of communicating between servers and cooks that worked very well. My mother knew the numbers by heart; she expedited to the rest of the kitchen crew. The order that came up most (after #5, pad Thai) was #26. Once I started to get my handles and earn my cooking chops, this simple noodle salad with prik pao chile jam came off my station—I never got tired of making (and tasting) it. Bean thread noodles are fun to slurp, even in a salad.

SERVES 4 TO 6

- 5 ounces (141 grams) bean thread noodles
- 1½ ounces (42 grams) fresh wood ear mushrooms, sliced (see page 333)
- 4 ounces (114 grams) medium shrimp, peeled, deveined, and minced
- 4 ounces (114 grams) coarsely ground pork
- 4 tablespoons (116 grams) Charred Chile Jam (page 285)
- 2 tablespoons (30 grams) fresh lime juice
- 2 tablespoons (24 grams) fish sauce
- ¼ cup (8 grams) torn mint leaves
- 2 tablespoons (6 grams) sliced scallions
- ¼ cup (12 grams) roughly chopped cilantro
- 3 tablespoons (6 grams) Fried Shallots (page 306)
- Prik phong (ground toasted chile; see page 329)

1. Soak the bean thread noodles in cold water for 1 hour; transfer to a colander to drain (you can do this the day before and store the drained noodles in the refrigerator).

2. Bring a pot of unsalted water to a boil. Combine the soaked noodles and the wood ear mushrooms in a blanching basket, chinois, or cone-shaped colander. Blanch in the boiling water for about 5 seconds—the noodles will become limp immediately. Shake off excess water and empty the noodles and wood ear mushrooms into a medium mixing bowl. Add the minced shrimp to the basket and blanch in the same water for 10 seconds, moving the shrimp around with a spoon to break up the lumps and ensure even cooking. Add the cooked shrimp to the bowl with the noodles. Wait for the water to return to a boil, add the ground pork to the blanching basket, and cook the same way as the shrimp. The pork might take a bit longer; about 30 seconds. Make sure to stir as it cooks to break up the lumps. Drain well, shaking the basket to rid the pork of excess water that would dilute the dish, and add to the rest of the ingredients in the bowl. Stir while everything is still warm, then set aside to cool to lukewarm. Season the salad by adding the charred chile jam, lime juice, and fish sauce. Toss it around to mix well. Fold in the mint, scallions, and cilantro and transfer to a large serving platter. Finish by sprinkling with fried shallots and prik phong.

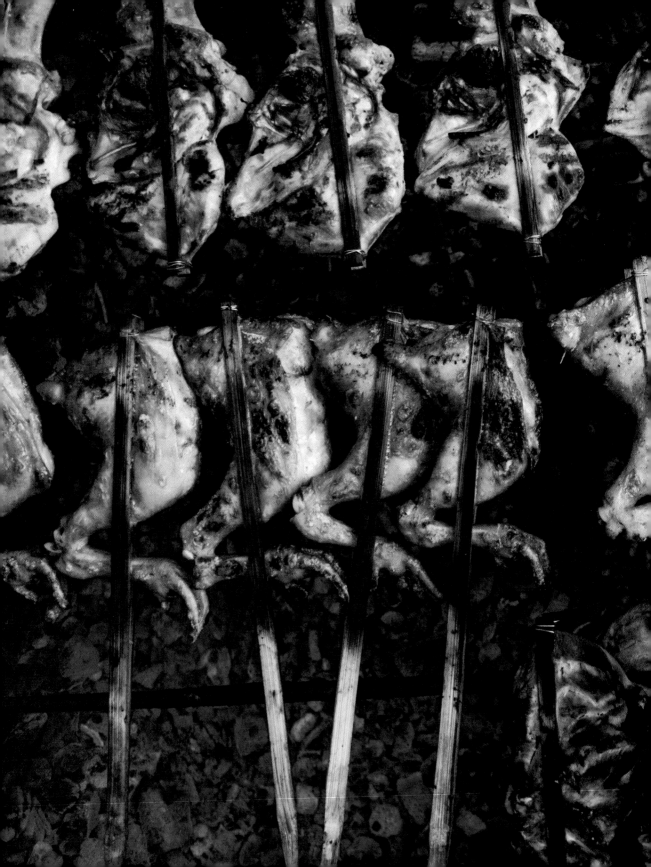

15

MEATS

CHEWY FLAVORFUL GRILLED BEEF BRISKET

SEEN PING

Brisket: We automatically think of corned beef, pastrami, and barbecue, the tenderer the better. I'm a fan of all three. In the West, we think of brisket as a tough cut that needs some major intervention to become tender and chewable, easy to consume. We apply low-temperature cooking for long periods to achieve melting results. But the divide over texture is one of the main differences between the cuisines of East and West. In Southeast Asia we prize chewiness, flavorful cuts in their natural state, tough muscles that pack a lot of flavor. This "un-tender" grilled brisket was a staple of outdoor barbecues when I was growing up. We'd cook it over glowing charcoal briquettes, not hardwood or mesquite charcoal but straight-up Kingsford black hockey pucks ignited with lighter fluid. It's still the smell of summer for me, backyard parties with Heineken beers and Molam music. At Hawker Fare we include a menu disclaimer that our *seen ping* is cooked medium-rare for a flavorful chew; we still get complaints that it's tough. Oh well. A bit of 7UP in the marinade adds sweetness.

SERVES 6 TO 8

¼ cup (30 grams) peeled garlic cloves

2 tablespoons (30 grams) water

2 tablespoons (30 grams) oyster sauce

2 tablespoons (30 grams) 7UP

½ teaspoon (2 grams) MSG (optional)

1 tablespoon (9 grams) canola oil

2 pounds (908 grams) beef brisket steaks, ½ inch thick, fat cap on

Kosher salt

1. Pound the garlic to a sticky paste in a mortar. Transfer to a large mixing bowl with the water, oyster sauce, 7UP, MSG, if using, and oil. Mix to combine. Add the brisket and massage it with your hands for 2 minutes to break up the muscle tissue. Transfer the meat and its marinade to a large zipper-top bag or nonreactive container. Let it rest in the refrigerator for 24 hours.

2. The next day, heat an outdoor grill to very hot, preferably using charcoal briquettes. Cook the brisket for about 2 minutes on each side (it should be medium rare—beyond medium, it's way too tough), sprinkling with salt as it cooks. Transfer to a cutting board and let stand for 1 minute. Chop into large bite-size pieces and serve with cucumber slices and Charred Chile Dip with Beef Bile (page 284), or any dip you prefer.

GRILLED PORK CHOPS MOO PING (MOO YANG)

Moo ping (*moo yang* in Thai—Isan use both names) are the grilled pork chops we serve at Hawker Fare, the same ones on the menu at Wat Phou, my mom's original restaurant, where it was one of the most popular orders. I understand why—I love pork chops when they're done well. These are thin—they absorb the marinade quicker and cook fast over high heat so the sugars caramelize before the meat overcooks. On the street in Laos and Thailand you see pieces of pork grilling on bamboo skewers; it's called moo ping, and is offered with sticky rice. More than likely the next vendor over is making green papaya salad (suggestive marketing, maybe). The street becomes a one-stop shop to put together a complete, delicious meal. I highly recommend using the shoulder end of the pork loin for this dish (it's what we use at Hawker Fare). It has a majority of dark meat—avoid the lighter, leaner end of the loin or the chops will end up dry. Another option is pork shoulder, or pork butt, sliced into thin steaks. Freeze the shoulder briefly to firm it up enough to get clean, straight cuts.

SERVES 6 TO 8

1 tablespoon (4 grams) coriander seeds	½ cup (120 grams) oyster sauce	6 tablespoons (72 grams) granulated sugar	2 pounds (908 grams) ¼-inch-thick pork shoulder chops
⅛ cup (40 grams) minced garlic	2 tablespoons (24 grams) fish sauce	3 tablespoons (27 grams) canola oil	2 tablespoons (33 grams) honey
½ teaspoon (1 gram) ground white pepper			

1. Toast the coriander seeds in a dry sauté pan over medium heat until they're fragrant; set aside to cool. Pound the toasted coriander seeds to a fine texture in a mortar. Add the garlic and pound to a paste; transfer to a large mixing bowl. Add the white pepper, oyster sauce, fish sauce, sugar, and oil to the bowl and mix well to incorporate. Set aside ⅛ cup of this marinade. Add the pork chops to the bowl. Using your hands, rub the marinade into the meat in a gentle massaging motion. Transfer the meat and its marinade to a large zipper-top bag, or simply cover the mixing bowl with plastic wrap. Marinate in the refrigerator for a minimum of 6 hours, and no more than 24.

2. Preheat a gas, charcoal, or wood grill to medium-high. Place the pork chops on the grill, reserving the marinade. Cook 2 minutes per side. After the chops are about 80 percent cooked through, baste lightly on both sides with the reserved marinade mixed with the honey. Continue to cook the meat all the way through, allowing the marinade to caramelize. Serve with Lao BBQ Dipping Sauce (page 288) and sticky rice.

BEEF SHORT RIBS SATAY SATAY KRA-TOOG NGUA

When the Korean supermarket opened in our Oakland neighborhood it was a godsend. Like the chef she is, Moms scoured the butcher counter for product to play with, and ended up bringing home Korean-style short ribs, something foreign to Thai and Lao cooking. At the restaurant, she made satay short ribs as a special. They had a built-in skewer: the bones. Grilled medium or medium rare, the delicious meat pulls from the bones, and you salivate even more as your teeth work to chew the gristle, a plus with most Asian meats. I put these on the menu at Hawker Fare, and just like back in Moms's day, people love them.

SERVES 4 TO 6

MARINADE

¼ cup (40 grams) thinly sliced lemongrass

⅛ cup (25 grams) peeled and sliced fresh ginger

¼ cup (40 grams) sliced shallots

5 peeled medium garlic cloves (15 grams)

2 tablespoons (18 grams) canola oil

2 tablespoons (30 grams) oyster sauce

1 tablespoon (12 grams fish sauce

¼ teaspoon (1 gram) turmeric powder

⅓ cup (87 grams) unsweetened coconut milk

1 pound (454 grams) beef short ribs, cut Korean *kalbi* style, ¼ inch thick

FOR THE BASTE

⅓ cup (87 grams) unsweetened coconut milk

Kosher salt, to taste

FOR SERVING

1 cup Satay Peanut Sauce (page 297)

1 cup Cucumber Ajat (page 298)

1. In a mortar, combine the lemongrass, ginger, shallots, and garlic; pound to a semismooth paste. Stir in the oil, oyster sauce, fish sauce, turmeric, and the ⅓ cup coconut milk and mix well. Reserve ¼ cup of this mixture and set aside. Transfer the rest to a large mixing bowl and add the short ribs. Toss the ribs to coat, cover the bowl, and let them marinate in the refrigerator for 24 hours (you can get away with marinating for 6 hours at a minimum, though the satay will have less depth of flavor).

2. When it is time to cook the ribs, preheat your grill until very hot. I highly recommend cooking satay on an outdoor grill over charcoal briquettes, but gas will suffice (cook them indoors in a grill pan only if you have a very good exhaust system, since they generate a lot of smoke). Make the baste by mixing the reserved ¼ cup marinade with the ⅓ cup coconut milk. Grill the ribs for about 2 minutes on each side (a little more or less, depending on how you like your meat). As they cook, brush the ribs with the basting liquid and a sprinkling of salt. Let the cooked ribs rest for 2 minutes before serving with the satay peanut sauce and cucumber ajat. Accompany with jasmine or sticky rice or slices of toasted white bread.

FRIED FERMENTED PORK JOWL SOM MOO TAWN

Fried fermented pork steaks might sound unappetizing, but think of Italian salumi, where time and fermentation build complexity and flavor. At her restaurant, Moms would sometimes be left with more pork than she could sell fresh. With all the freezer space already taken, she had to figure something out. *Som moo tawn* was a no-brainer (I'm pretty sure she learned the technique back home in her village, when a pig was slaughtered and parts had to be preserved). After fermenting the sliced jowl at room temperature you pop it in the fridge, where it can last six weeks. This is totally clutch when you have to put a delicious meal together with very little time, an ace in your pocket when people drop in. Everyone wins! As part of a meal, serve with sticky rice and any of the chile relishes or dips in this book. For snacking, serve with roasted peanuts, slices of ginger, and whole Thai chiles.

SERVES 6 TO 8

3 pounds (1,360 grams) pork jowl, skinless

¼ cup (45 grams) kosher salt

½ tablespoon (6 grams) granulated sugar

Pinch of freshly ground coarse black pepper

½ teaspoon (2 grams) MSG (optional)

⅛ cup (24 grams) finely minced garlic

3 tablespoons (20 grams) cooked sticky rice, rinsed and drained

Canola oil, for shallow frying

Cilantro sprigs

Dried shallots

1. Slice the pork jowl into ½-inch-thick steaks and place in a mixing bowl. Add the salt, sugar, black pepper, MSG, if using, garlic, and sticky rice and massage the steaks for 3 minutes. This helps tenderize the meat and allows the marinade to penetrate. In a small glass or stainless steel bowl (even a casserole dish will work), arrange the steaks flat in an even layer; repeat, stacking the steaks on top of each other. Lay a piece of plastic wrap directly on the surface of the meat (this prevents it from drying during the fermentation process). Find a place in your kitchen away from direct sunlight where the temperature is consistently 65° to 70°F (the top of the refrigerator is usually a good spot). Place the vessel of meat there and let it ferment for 24 to 36 hours. Check it after 24 hours: What you're looking for is a pleasantly sour aroma, similar to Italian salumi. The meat itself should have a slightly pinkish appearance. If you notice those things, transfer the meat to the fridge. If not, let it keep fermenting in the warm spot for up to 12 hours more.

2. To shallow-fry the pork, add a good amount of canola oil to a cast-iron skillet or wok and heat to about 350°F. Carefully add the pork to the oil—make sure not to add too much meat at one time or it will make the oil temperature dip. Cook the steaks on the first side for 3 minutes, then, using a pair of tongs, flip and cook on the other side for another 3 minutes. Transfer the steaks to paper towels to drain. Continue until all the pork is cooked. Chop into bite-size pieces and serve garnished with cilantro and shallots.

ISAN BBQ CHICKEN GAI PING (GAI YANG)

BBQ chicken is everywhere on the streets and in the markets of Isan. You can smell it from afar, like a smoke signal commanding you to come and eat. Chicken, roasted or barbecued, just spells comfort. It's easy and delicious. And with *gai yang*, sticky rice, and tum som, you've got a complete meal.

SERVES 8 TO 10

BRINE

1 gallon (3,785 grams) water

½ cups (90 grams) kosher salt

½ cup (100 grams) granulated sugar

2 whole chickens, about 2½ pounds (1,200 grams) each, split in half, backs removed

MARINADE

¼ cup (30 grams) thinly sliced lemongrass

2 tablespoons (16 grams) peeled garlic cloves

¼ cup (12 grams) cilantro root or stems

1 teaspoon (2 grams) coriander seeds

1 tablespoon (4 grams) yellow curry powder

⅛ teaspoon (1 gram) MSG (optional)

2 tablespoons (30 grams) oyster sauce

1 tablespoon (12 grams) fish sauce

2 tablespoons (18 grams) canola oil

½ tablespoon (5 grams) kosher salt

1. BRINE THE CHICKEN: In a large pot, combine the water, salt, and sugar. Bring to a boil to dissolve the sugar and salt, then turn off the heat and let the brine cool completely. Transfer to a container large enough to hold both chickens and fit in the fridge. Add the chickens to the brine and refrigerate for 24 hours.

2. MARINATE THE CHICKEN: In a mortar, pound the lemongrass, garlic, cilantro root or stems, and coriander seeds to a paste. Stir in the curry powder, MSG, if using, oyster sauce, fish sauce, oil, and salt and mix well. Remove the chicken halves from the brine and drain well; transfer to a large mixing bowl. Add the marinade and toss to coat. Marinate, refrigerated, for at least 8 hours, but no more than 16.

3. COOK THE MEAT: Preheat a grill to low, using gas, charcoal, or wood. Grill the chicken halves over low heat, flipping and watching carefully—it will take about 1 hour. To help with even heating and creating a sort of hot smoker, you can cover the chicken with a lid as it cooks. To tell if the chicken is done, check the color of the flesh between the thigh and the breast: The juices should run clear and the meat look opaque. Once done, the chickens can be hacked through the bones with a Chinese cleaver. Serve with Hot, Sweet, and Sour Dipping Sauce for BBQ Chicken (page 295) or Charred Tomato and Chile Relish with Fermented Fish (page 289), sticky rice, and Lao Green Papaya Salad (page 147).

AROMATIC LAO HERB SAUSAGE
WITH PORK SKIN SAI OUA

Sai oua is an addictive sausage that makes my mouth water just thinking about it. This was the high-value trading token in the Lao 'hood. It was always a staple at barbecues, as it is today at my house (I got my kids hooked). Before she opened her first restaurant my mom made this sausage once a week for our own consumption, and also to barter for other Lao foods in our apartment complex. Everybody wanted to trade for my mother's sausage—you could say she was holding the hot hand. Making sausage as she did was truly a labor of love, you could taste it. She didn't need any fancy F. Dick hand-crank stainless steel sausage stuffer: Her stuffing apparatus was a funnel, home-made from a two-liter plastic 7UP bottle with the top cut off and the pour spout to hold the casing. It got the job done, in 10-pound batches at a time. What made Moms's sausage unique were the braised pork skins: gelatinous pops of juiciness. The best!

SERVES 10 TO 12

- 1 pound (454 grams) pork skin
- 1 gallon (3,785 grams) water
- 1 tablespoon (11 grams) kosher salt
- ⅓ cup (40 grams) lemongrass, tender parts, thinly sliced
- Nine ¼-inch slices fresh galangal (27 grams)

- ¼ cup (40 grams) thinly sliced shallots
- ¼ cup (50 grams) whole peeled garlic
- 15 whole makrut lime leaves, center stems removed (5 grams)
- 8 whole fresh red Thai chiles, stemmed (12 grams)

- 2 pounds (908 grams) pork, 70:30 fat ratio, medium grind
- ½ cup finely chopped cilantro, stems included (24 grams)
- ¼ cup (48 grams) fish sauce
- 2 tablespoons (24 grams) Golden Mountain seasoning sauce

- 1 tablespoon (11 grams) MSG (optional)
- 6-foot (1.8-meter) length natural hog casing

1. Add the pork skin to a medium pot. Cover with the water and salt; bring to a boil over medium heat and simmer for about 45 minutes, uncovered. To test the skin's doneness, give it a pinch: It should break between your fingers. Once cooked, transfer the skin to a plate or baking sheet and allow it to cool. Once it's cool, cut the skin into a small dice—you'll need 6 ounces (170 grams) for this recipe. Set it aside, and reserve the remaining pork skin for another recipe.

2. With a mortar and pestle, make an herb paste: Start with the lemongrass and galangal, pounding them to a semifine paste. Add the shallots and garlic and pound to a semifine paste; add the lime leaves and Thai chiles and return the mixture to a semifine consistency.

3. In a large mixing bowl, combine the ground pork, pork skins, the herb paste, cilantro, fish sauce, seasoning sauce, and MSG, if using. Mix with your hands, making sure to get rid of any lumps that may go underseasoned and cause the sausage to spoil during fermentation.

4. Using a sausage stuffer, fill the hog casing with the pork mixture and twist off each link at 6-inch (15-centimeter) intervals. Tie the sausage at the last link. You can also leave the sausage as a single long coil—it all depends on how you want to serve it. For a backyard barbecue with lots of guests, leave it as a large coil. It makes for a cooler, more dramatic presentation, plus it'll be easier to cook. Cook immediately, or freeze the sausages in zipper-top freezer bags.

5. To cook, preheat an outdoor grill with charcoal briquettes. Prick the sausages with a needle before placing them on the grill; this ensures the casings will not break. Cook over a medium flame. I really enjoy sai oua with Charred Tomato and Chile Relish with Fermented Fish (page 289) or Roasted Green Chile Relish (page 290) and, of course, sticky rice.

SOUR FERMENTED PORK SAUSAGE SAI GOK

Fermenting pork: From our point of view in the States, it seems daring, if not plain off, especially when you don't use curing salt. But it works—garlic, salt, and rice do the job. This is a sausage you'll find mostly in Isan and Laos, and it was ubiquitous in our household. Links would dangle from clothes hangers by the water heater, our apartment's optimal place for fermentation, with a temperature and humidity perfect for allowing bacteria to do their thing to create rich, savory, tart, and addictive sausages. (In Ubon, sausages would hang outdoors in the shophouse.) *Sai gok* is a great drinking snack, paired with peanuts, sliced shallots, and peeled fresh ginger.

SERVES 10 TO 12 AS PART OF A MEAL

6-foot (1.8-meter) length natural hog casing

1 cup (300 grams) cooked sticky rice

½ cup (160 grams) minced garlic

1 tablespoon (11 grams) kosher salt

2 pounds (908 grams) pork, 70:30 fat ratio, medium grind

1 tablespoon (10 grams) ground white pepper

1 tablespoon (11 grams) MSG (optional)

1 tablespoon (12 grams) Golden Mountain seasoning sauce

1 teaspoon (5 grams) coriander seeds, ground

1. Rinse the hog casings under cold water and let them soak. In a small mixing bowl, soak the sticky rice in warm water for 30 minutes. Drain well.

2. With a mortar and pestle, pound the garlic and salt to a fine paste; set aside. In a large mixing bowl, combine the ground pork with the drained sticky rice, garlic paste, white pepper, MSG, if using, seasoning sauce, and coriander. Mix well with your hands, making sure to get rid of any lumps that might go underseasoned and cause the sausage to spoil during fermentation.

3. Using a sausage stuffer, fill the hog casing with the pork mixture and twist off each link at 2-inch intervals. Tie the sausage at the last link. Hang the linked sausages in a warm area (about 68°F) for 2 to 3 days to ferment. The sausages should become firm and have a pleasant sour aroma. Once fermented, store in the refrigerator in a sealed container or bag.

4. To serve, heat the sausages on a charcoal grill over a medium flame, or deep-fry them at 350°F. Serve warm with peeled fresh ginger slices, sliced shallots, and cilantro, alone (with beer) as a snack, or with sticky rice and any type of jaew as a meal.

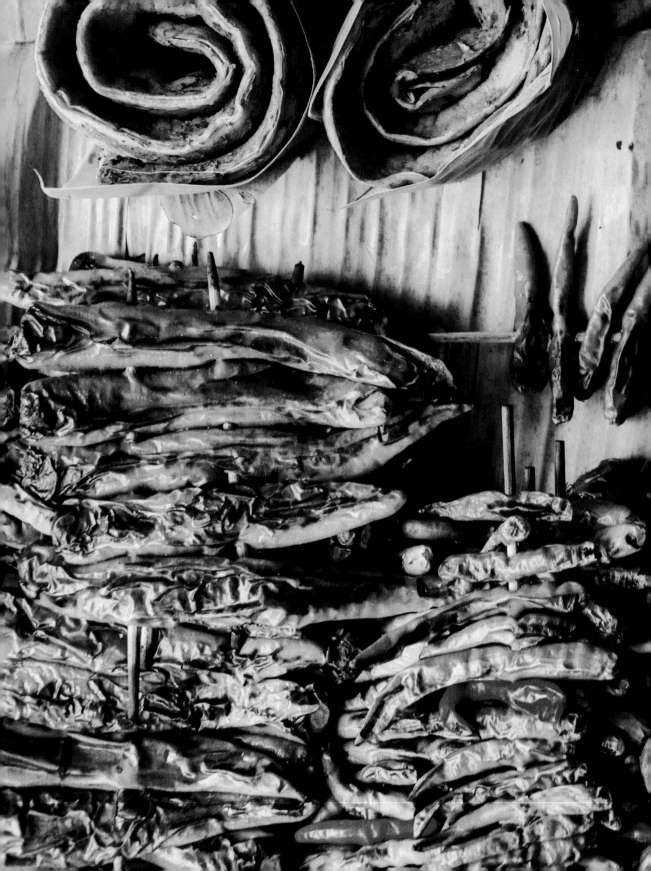

16

AWS AND MOKS

GELATINOUS CHICKEN WINGS STEWED WITH PEPPER WOOD, MORNING GLORY, AND LEMON BASIL AW PIK GAI

Chicken wings have an ideal ratio of skin to meat to bone in a small package; the best part are the tips. Skin is a crucial element for succulence in this stew—long cooked in broth, it lends a gelatinous quality. And when you hack up chicken wings you expose a small amount of the marrow. Lemongrass and lemon basil give this dish beautiful citrus aromas.

SERVES 6 TO 8

- 1 pound (454 grams) whole chicken wings, chopped in 1-inch pieces
- 3 peeled garlic cloves (10 grams)
- ¼ cup (40 grams) shallots, thinly sliced
- 3 fresh Thai chiles (5 grams)
- 3 tablespoons (27 grams) canola oil
- 1 quart (946 grams) water
- ½ cup (40 grams) lemongrass, thinly sliced
- 1 cup (85 grams) ¼-inch wedges Thai eggplant
- Two 2-inch pieces pepper wood (sakahn; 8 grams; see page 333)
- 6 whole makrut lime leaves (2 grams)
- 3 tablespoons (54 grams) raw sticky rice, soaked for 24 hours in cold water
- 1 cup (80 grams) 1-inch slices green cabbage
- 1 cup (80 grams) morning glory leaves, cut into 1-inch pieces, stems included
- 1 teaspoon (4 grams) MSG (optional)
- 2 tablespoons (24 grams) fish sauce
- 2 tablespoons (30 grams) padaek
- 6 scallions, cut into 2-inch pieces (45 grams)
- 1 cup (33 grams) lemon basil leaves

1. Rinse the chicken wings well under cold running water. Transfer to a colander and leave to drain thoroughly.

2. With a mortar and pestle, pound the garlic, shallots, and chiles to a paste. Warm the oil in a saucepan over medium heat; add the chile-garlic paste and cook until fragrant. Add the chicken and sauté for 3 minutes. Add the water, lemongrass, eggplant, pepper wood, and lime leaves and bring to a boil. Adjust the heat to achieve a gentle simmer and cook for 30 minutes.

3. Meanwhile, pound the soaked and drained rice to a starchy paste resembling a thick slurry. When the chicken is done, add the rice paste and raise the heat just a touch to achieve a gentle boil; if the stew boils too rapidly the starch will cook out instead of thickening. Once you notice the broth start to thicken, let it simmer for 3 minutes. Add the cabbage, morning glory, MSG, if using, fish sauce, and padaek. Give the pot a stir and simmer 5 more minutes; remove from the heat. Stir in the scallions and lemon basil just before serving.

UBON KASSOD-LEAF CURRY WITH WATER BUFFALO SHANK GAENG KEE LEK

This is difficult to make outside Ubon Ratchathani because of the ingredients, but I feel a family obligation to share it. In my family's village, walking toward the lake in Baan Nong Jam Nak, you pass rice fields on the left and, lining the dirt path to your right, evergreen trees called *kassod*, or *kee lek*. They're everywhere, almost invasive in the local landscape. Kassod leaves are edible but extremely bitter—before cooking they have to be boiled and washed multiple times. The leaves are also believed to have medicinal properties (lowering cholesterol, aiding digestion, and relieving sore throats). My family ate them often, in different versions of curry: sometimes with fish, or pork—even with the fresh, milky ant eggs extracted from the mango tree on our property. It's a dish with a sense of place, Ubon terroir. My mother's travels from Ubon with bags and bags of the dried leaves and buds have been a means of transport for kassod. She always brings a piece of home back with her.

This version of curry does not involve coconut milk, and the meat will not be meltingly tender like a braise, but it has texture and some chew. The taste of kassod is vegetal, like braised collard greens or kale, in addition to smelling meaty and aromatic. I've tried substituting dino kale for the kassod leaves, and it comes out delicious, though not as bitter or complex.

SERVES 4 TO 6

- 8 ounces (226 grams) kassod tree leaves from Ubon, dried
- 2 cups (454 grams) Yanang Leaf Water (page 300)
- 10 ounces (283 grams) water buffalo or beef shank meat
- Kosher salt
- 1 stalk lemongrass, smashed and cut into 2-inch lengths (50 grams)
- 6 whole makrut lime leaves, torn (2 grams)
- Four ⅛-inch slices fresh galangal (12 grams)
- 2 ounces (57 grams) cow or buffalo skin, sliced ¼ inch thick
- 1 teaspoon (4 grams) MSG (optional)
- 2 tablespoons (24 grams) fish sauce
- 2 red Thai dried chiles (3 grams)
- 2 tablespoons (36 grams) raw sticky rice, soaked for 24 hours in cold water

1. Soak the dried kassod leaves in cold water for 24 hours. Drain well in a colander and squeeze to remove excess water. Preheat a grill to a very hot temperature (wood or charcoal yields better flavor than gas). Put the kassod leaves in a medium pot and cover with cold water. Place the pot over high heat and bring to a rapid, rolling boil for 10 minutes. Drain the leaves in a colander and rinse under cold running water; return to the pot and cover with cold water again. Repeat the same process two more times to leach out the harsh bitterness of the leaves. After the third time, let the leaves sit in the colander for 20 minutes to drain well,

then squeeze the residual blanching water out with your hands, discarding the water. Place the leaves in a blender with the yanang leaf water. Pulse to puree the leaves to a coarse chopped texture. Do not strain the puree; transfer to another pot and set aside.

2. Lightly season the buffalo shank with salt. Sear the meat on the grill over high heat for about 5 minutes to achieve a wonderful smoky flavor. Don't worry about cooking the meat; it will be simmered afterward. Let the meat rest for 10 minutes. Cut into ¼-inch-thick slices and transfer to the pot with the kassod puree. Add the lemongrass, lime leaves, galangal, cow or buffalo skin, MSG, if using, and fish sauce and bring it to a gentle simmer over medium heat. Let the curry simmer for 1 hour, partially covered. While the curry is simmering, in a mortar and pestle pound the chiles and the soaked and drained sticky rice to form a paste. Add the paste to the pot after the hour of simmering and let it simmer an additional 15 minutes, uncovered. Taste and adjust the seasoning with salt as needed. Let the curry cool for about 15 minutes, uncovered, and serve with steamed jasmine rice.

EARTHY BEEF SHANK STEW WITH BITTER PEA EGGPLANTS, WOOD EAR MUSHROOMS, AND DILL AW LAM SEEN

My favorites in the aw family of stews contain rich proteins or game, like this one made with beef or water buffalo shank. *Aw lam seen* is the earthiest, heartiest, bitterest, and most fragrant of the type—full of in-your-face flavors and textures. For me, the spicier the better, but I've kept this recipe on the low-burn level for maximum accessibility. Feel free to go hotter. Other stewing cuts (like brisket) work, but the tendon and connective tissues in beef shank add to the richness. Boneless beef shank is common in Asian supermarkets. You can also use meat from the calf muscle. If you're not shopping at an Asian market, ask your butcher for osso buco (save the bones to add to the stew). I've had versions of this stew finished with cow's blood; I remember them with affection. This dish keeps for three days, and tastes better on day two. If you plan on making it ahead, wait until just before serving to add the scallions and dill.

SERVES 6 TO 8

1 peeled garlic clove (5 grams)

¼ cup (40 grams) sliced shallots

2 tablespoons (16 grams) sliced lemongrass

3 fresh Thai chiles (5 grams)

3 tablespoons (27 grams) canola oil

8 ounces (226 grams) boneless beef shank, in 1-inch cubes

2 cups (474 grams) water

3 ounces (85 grams) Thai eggplant, sliced ¼ inch thick

Two 2-inch pieces pepper wood (sakahn; 8 grams; see page 333)

6 whole makrut lime leaves (2 grams)

1 tablespoon (18 grams) raw sticky rice, soaked for 24 hours in cold water

2 ounces (56 grams) fresh wood ear mushrooms, in bite-size pieces (see page 333)

¼ cup (60 grams) pea eggplants

1 tablespoon (11 grams) MSG (optional)

3 tablespoons (45 grams) padaek

4 scallions, in 1-inch pieces (20 grams)

½ cup (12 grams) roughly chopped fresh dill, stems included

1. With a mortar and pestle, pound the garlic, shallots, lemongrass, and chiles to a paste. Warm the oil in a large saucepan over medium heat. Add the chile-garlic paste and cook until fragrant. Add the beef cubes and sauté for 3 minutes. Add the water and deglaze, scraping up the bits from the bottom of the pan, using a wooden spoon. Add the sliced Thai eggplant, pepper wood, and lime leaves. Bring to a boil, then reduce the heat to achieve a gentle simmer. Cover and cook for about 90 minutes, or until the beef is tender.

2. Meanwhile, add the soaked and drained sticky rice to a mortar and pound it to a paste resembling a thick slurry. When the beef is done, add the sticky-rice paste and raise the heat just a touch to achieve a gentle boil. Once you notice the broth starting to thicken slightly, let it simmer for 3 minutes. Add the mushrooms, pea eggplants, MSG, if using, and padaek. Give the pot a stir and simmer for 5 minutes.

3. Just before serving, stir in the scallions and dill. Transfer to a serving bowl.

BRAISED PORK TROTTERS AND BELLY IN CARAMEL WITH TOFU AND EGG DTOM KHEM

One of the homiest dishes I know—comfort food for sure. A lot of Lao and Thai kids can definitely relate to this craveable distant cousin of Chinese red-braised pork belly. Pork, hard-boiled eggs, and tofu braise in seasoned caramel. Time is a key factor for flavor development: After cooking, the ingredients sit to allow the flavors to mellow and harmonize. My mother always made a huge batch to make sure there'd be leftovers for days, kept on the stovetop for self-service, an all-hours buffet. (You'll want to have leftovers, too; store them in the fridge.) Serve with jasmine rice and Sriracha or pickled chiles.

SERVES 6 TO 8

Twelve 2-inch cubes medium-firm tofu

8½ cups (1,743 grams) canola oil

2 cups (400 grams) granulated sugar

1 pound (454 grams) pork trotters, in 1-inch pieces

1 pound (454 grams) skin-on boneless pork belly, in 2 pieces

1 quart (946 grams) water

6 hard-boiled eggs (see Note)

⅛ cup (30 grams) peeled garlic cloves

¼ cup (40 grams) ¼-inch slices peeled fresh ginger

1 teaspoon (3 grams) whole black peppercorns

3 whole star anise pods (5 grams)

½ cup (96 grams) fish sauce

¼ cup (47 grams) Gold Mountain Brand seasoning sauce

1. Drain the tofu well, then transfer to a layer of paper towels for 15 minutes to remove as much water as possible.

2. Line a plate with paper towels. Add 8 cups of the oil to a large heavy saucepan or Dutch oven. Set the pan over medium-high heat and bring the oil to 350°F, regulating the heat as necessary to maintain a steady temperature. Carefully drop 3 or 4 pieces of tofu into the hot oil; fry 4 to 5 minutes, until it develops a crisp, tan crust. Remove the tofu from the hot oil with a slotted spoon or spider and transfer to the paper towel–lined plate to drain and cool. Repeat until all tofu cubes are fried.

3. Add the remaining ½ cup oil and sugar to a medium saucepan, mix well, and set over medium-high heat. As the oil gets hot the sugar will caramelize. Once the caramel reaches a deep amber color, turn off the heat and carefully add the trotters and belly. Stir to coat the meat with the caramel, then add the water to deglaze. Add the eggs, tofu, garlic, ginger, peppercorns, star anise, fish sauce, and seasoning sauce and bring the mixture to a gentle

simmer. (At this stage, there's no need to skim the surface). Let the pork braise, partially covered, for 2½ hours—the pork should be tender but not falling apart. Skim off excess fat and impurities.

NOTE: To hard-boil eggs, place room-temperature eggs in a deep saucepan and cover with cold water—make sure there's at least 2 inches of water to cover. Don't cover the pan. Bring the water to a boil as quickly as possible over high heat. Once it achieves a rolling boil, turn off the heat, cover the pot, and set a timer for 8 minutes. After 8 minutes, pour off the hot water and run the eggs under cold water to cool to room temperature. Lightly crack the shells against a hard surface, then submerge the eggs in water. They should be very easy to peel.

STEAMED BAMBOO-SHOOT CASSEROLE WITH PORK BELLY AND COCONUT MILK COOKED IN BANANA LEAF MOK NAW MAI

Pork, shredded bamboo, and coconut milk steam together in a banana leaf for a rich, flavorful dish. The pork fat renders as it steams, melding with a small amount of coconut milk to create a cooking medium. The bamboo shoots are sold in bulk in the produce section of Asian markets. Look for shoots with solid stalks and a diameter of about 1½ inches at the base. Avoid mature bamboo for this dish—as the shoots get older they develop segmented hollow pockets. Jasmine rice is best to serve with *mok naw mai*—you need something to spoon the delicious cooking juices onto.

SERVES 6 TO 8

- 12 ounces (340 grams) slender young bamboo shoots
- 2 tablespoons (20 grams) thinly sliced lemongrass
- 2 tablespoons (2 grams) thinly sliced shallots
- 2 fresh Thai chiles (3 grams)
- 2 peeled garlic cloves (6 grams)
- 2 tablespoons (36 grams) raw sticky rice, soaked for 24 hours in cold water
- 4 ounces (112 grams) skinless pork belly, cut in ¼-inch dice
- ¼ cup (56 grams) Yanang Leaf Water (page 300)
- 1 tablespoon (12 grams) fish sauce
- 2 tablespoons (30 grams) padaek
- ¼ teaspoon (1 gram) MSG (optional)
- ⅛ cup (33 grams) unsweetened coconut milk
- ⅓ cup (12 grams) roughly chopped fresh dill, stems included
- 1 banana leaf (see page 328), trimmed to a 10-inch square
- 1 tablespoon (5 grams) prik phong (ground toasted chile; see page 329)

1. Using a wooden skewer, shred the bamboo shoots: Take the sharp end of the skewer and scratch a shoot lengthwise, in the same direction as the fibers. Continue until all the shoots are shredded. Bring a large pot of water to a boil. Add the shredded bamboo and blanch for 15 seconds; drain in a colander and rinse under cold running water until cool. Remove excess water by squeezing small handfuls of the shreds firmly between your palms; transfer to a mixing bowl.

2. With a mortar and pestle, pound the aromatics (lemongrass, shallots, chiles, and garlic) and soaked and drained sticky rice to a coarse paste. Add the paste to the bowl with the bamboo, along with the pork belly, yanang leaf water, fish sauce, padaek, MSG, if using, coconut milk, and dill. Mix thoroughly.

3. Place a 12-inch-square sheet of aluminum foil on a work surface. Spread out the banana leaf square in the center, glossy side up. Place the bamboo mixture in the center of the leaf. Fold the bottom of the leaf toward the center to cover the mixture; do the same with the top. Fold in the sides to create an envelope. Wrap with the foil just as you did with the banana leaf, folding in the bottom, top, and sides to form an envelope. Secure by crimping the top and bottom edges of the foil.

4. Add about 2 inches of water to a wok or other pan large enough to hold a metal or bamboo steamer. Set the steamer insert in place and bring the water to a boil over medium-high heat. Place the packet in the steamer and cook for 40 minutes. Transfer the packet to a serving platter; cool for 10 minutes, still wrapped. Open the packet and sprinkle with prik phong.

BAMBOO SHOOTS STEWED IN YANANG LEAF WATER WITH FERMENTED FISH SAUCE

GAENG NAW MAI

I was very excited about this dish when we put it on the menu of the new San Francisco location of Hawker Fare in 2015, but some customers just couldn't get into it. I admit that a bowl of bamboo shoots cooked with yanang leaf water isn't for everyone—it has vegetal, straw-like flavors, and the color is a challenge. For me it's a connection to childhood. Moms would make a large cauldron and leave it out on the turned-off stove overnight, sometimes for as long as two days. We'd help ourselves at all hours. I'd come home to jasmine rice on the keep-warm setting, drop a few spoonfuls of stew on top, and dig into an instant meal, nothing else needed. I keep telling myself customers will come around someday, figuring out what I've always known: that *gaeng naw mai* is delicious. I'm still keeping the faith. The bamboo shoots come in a tall can. The ones you're looking for are very young, slender ones, about the diameter of your pinky, 3 to 6 inches long. Common in Vietnamese cuisine as *ngo om*, paddy leaf herb has small, serrated, arrow-shaped leaves with succulent stems; the aroma has hints of cumin, citrus, and cucumber.

SERVES 6 TO 8

- 12 ounces (340 grams) thin young bamboo shoots
- ¼ cup (30 grams) thinly sliced lemongrass
- ¼ cup (40 grams) sliced shallots
- 3 fresh Thai chiles, roasted over the fire (5 grams)
- 3 cups (680 grams) Yanang Leaf Water (page 300)
- 2 tablespoons (30 grams) padaek
- 3 ounces (85 grams) kabocha squash, peeled, cut into large dice
- 1 tablespoon (18 grams) raw sticky rice, soaked for 24 hours in cold water
- 1 ounce (28 grams) fresh wood ear mushrooms (see page 333)
- 1 ounce (28 grams) enoki mushrooms
- 1 ounce (28 grams) canned straw mushrooms, rinsed in cold water
- ¼ cup (8 grams) roughly chopped paddy leaf herb
- Fish sauce, to taste

1. Begin by blanching the bamboo to remove some of its bitterness: Put the bamboo shoots in a medium saucepan with just enough cold water to cover. Bring to a boil over high heat. Immediately remove from the heat, drain, and give them a quick rinse under cold running water. Return to the pot and set aside.

2. With a mortar and pestle, pound the lemongrass, shallots, and roasted chiles to a coarse paste. Add to the bamboo shoots along with the yanang leaf water, padaek, and squash. Bring to a boil over medium heat, then reduce the heat to achieve a gentle simmer. Let the stew cook for 15 minutes.

3. Meanwhile, pound the drained sticky rice in a mortar until it resembles a thick slurry. After the stew has cooked, add the mushrooms and rice paste, stir well, and simmer for 5 more minutes; remove from the heat. Just before serving, gently stir in the paddy leaf herb and season with fish sauce.

CHICKEN WINGS IN RED CURRY GAENG PHET PIK GAI

A simple recipe that satisfies. Typical of red curries from Isan, this curry with sharp flavors does not contain coconut milk. The richness comes from the gelatinous quality of the wings. If, like Moms, you can make this recipe with wing tips only, it'll end up being that much more succulent. I say make a triple batch and have leftovers for the next two days. I promise you'll enjoy it even more on day three.

SERVES 6 TO 8

1 pound (454 grams) whole chicken wings, including the tips

½ cup (65 grams) canola oil

¼ cup (50 grams) minced shallots

¼ cup (70 grams) Red Curry Paste (page 301)

2 tablespoons (10 grams) ground dried Thai chiles

½ cup (40 grams) ¼-inch slices lemongrass, cut on the bias

Five ¼-inch slices fresh galangal (15 grams)

12 whole makrut lime leaves (4 grams)

½ tablespoon (6 grams) kosher salt, plus more as needed

2 cups (474 grams) water

3 tablespoons (36 grams) fish sauce

2 teaspoons (8 grams) MSG (optional)

1 cup (200 grams) Thai eggplants, cut in eighths

1. Rinse the wings under cold water and drain well. Using a meat cleaver or heavy kitchen knife, chop into 1-inch pieces. Set aside.

2. Warm the oil over medium heat in a heavy-bottomed soup pot. Add the shallots and sweat until fragrant. Add the red curry paste and ground chiles and cook until fragrant, about 5 minutes. Add the wing pieces, lemongrass, galangal, limes leaves, and salt and cook for 5 minutes, stirring. Add the water, fish sauce, and MSG, if using, and bring to a gentle simmer. Add the sliced eggplants and stir to incorporate. Partially cover the pot and continue to simmer gently over low heat for 45 minutes—the chicken and eggplant should be pleasantly tender but not melting. Taste and adjust the seasoning with more salt if needed. Let the wings rest for 30 minutes at room temperature to let the flavors marry, then serve with steamed jasmine rice.

LAO PORK-RIB STEW WITH PEPPER WOOD, DILL, AND SQUASH VINES AW KRA-TOOG MOO

Fresh dill makes most people automatically think of salmon, bagels, and Scandinavia. It seems jarring in the context of Southeast Asian cuisine, or really with any traditional food from the Southern Hemisphere. But the first time I tasted dill was in this stew. It combines here with padaek and fish sauce to reinforce the savory qualities of pork. The licorice flavor gives a numbing freshness that allies with chiles, a combination that always makes me salivate. *Opo,* or "fuzzy melon," is long (typically 10 to 15 inches) and cylindrical. Its smooth skin varies from light green to chartreuse and encases a creamy white flesh and petite seeds. When cooked it becomes soft and silken and turns a bit transparent. The flavor is like cooked cucumber, though the texture is firmer, less watery. You can find both opo squash and vines at Asian groceries and some farmers' markets.

SERVES 6 TO 8

- 1 pound (454 grams) pork ribs
- 1 tablespoon (10 grams) peeled garlic cloves
- ¼ cup (40 grams) thinly sliced shallots
- 3 tablespoons (21 grams) thinly sliced lemongrass
- 1 tablespoon (8 grams) whole dried Thai chiles

- 3 tablespoons (27 grams) canola oil
- 1 quart (946 grams) water
- 6 whole makrut lime leaves (2 grams)
- Two 2-inch pieces pepper wood (sakahn; 8 grams; see page 333)

- 2 tablespoons (36 grams) raw sticky rice, soaked for 24 hours in cold water
- 1 cup (255 grams) opo squash, in 1-inch dice
- 2 cups (105 grams) tender opo vines, in 2-inch pieces
- 3 tablespoons (36 grams) fish sauce

- 2 tablespoons (30 grams) padaek
- ½ teaspoon (2 grams) MSG (optional)
- 1 cup (60 grams) scallions, green and white parts, in 1-inch pieces
- ½ cup (12 grams) roughly chopped fresh dill, stems included

1. Cut the pork ribs into ½-inch pieces, cutting between the bones; set aside.

2. With a mortar and pestle pound the garlic, shallots, lemongrass, and chiles to a paste. Warm the oil in a medium saucepan over medium heat. Add the chile-garlic paste and cook until fragrant. Add the pork and sauté for 3 minutes. Add the water, scraping with a wooden spoon to deglaze the pan. Add the lime leaves and pepper wood and bring to a boil. Reduce the heat to achieve a gentle simmer; cover and cook for 90 minutes.

3. Meanwhile, pound the soaked and drained rice to a starchy paste resembling a thick slurry. After the soup has cooked, add the slurry, adjusting the heat to achieve a gentle boil. You'll notice the soup starting to thicken: simmer for 3 more minutes, then add the opo squash, squash vines, fish sauce, padaek, and MSG, if using. Give the soup a stir and simmer 5 minutes more. Stir in the scallions and dill just before serving.

STEAMED CHICKEN CASSEROLE WITH AROMATICS AND SHAVED BANANA BLOSSOM MOK GAI

Moms always made dishes whose only purpose was to be leftovers—cook it in bulk and you're set for the week. Steaming boneless chicken thighs in a banana leaf not only retains moisture but lends flavor and aroma. *Mok gai* is best the next day—time allows the flavors to meld, and enhances the scent of the banana leaf. Steam it the day before you want to serve it, let it cool, and reheat in the steamer just before serving. This recipe calls for cooking the chicken thighs in one big banana leaf package, but you could also make smaller, single-serving bundles. Steam them together and keep in the fridge until you have that craving.

SERVES 4 TO 6

- 1 pound (454 grams) boneless, skin-on chicken thighs
- ¼ cup (40 grams) thinly sliced lemongrass
- 3 fresh red Thai chiles (4 grams)
- 2 tablespoons (16 grams) peeled garlic cloves
- 6 whole makrut lime leaves (2 grams)
- ¼ cup (40 grams) thinly sliced shallots
- 2 tablespoons (6 grams) roughly chopped cilantro stems
- 2 tablespoons (36 grams) raw sticky rice, soaked for 24 hours in cold water
- 2 tablespoons (24 grams) fish sauce
- 1 teaspoon (4 grams) MSG (optional)
- 4 ounces (112 grams) banana blossom, thinly sliced and rinsed
- 1 banana leaf, trimmed to a 10-inch square (see page 328)

1. Rinse the chicken with cold water and drain well. Transfer to a mixing bowl; set aside.

2. With a mortar and pestle, pound the aromatics (lemongrass, chiles, garlic, lime leaves, shallots, and cilantro stems) to a coarse paste. Add the soaked and drained sticky rice and pound everything to a semifine paste; stir in the fish sauce and MSG, if using. Add to the bowl with the chicken thighs. Add the sliced banana blossom and mix, making sure the chicken is evenly coated.

3. Clean the banana leaf by wiping with a damp towel. Place a 12-inch-square sheet of aluminum foil on your work surface. Spread out the banana leaf in the center, glossy side up. Place the chicken mixture in the center of the leaf. Fold the bottom of the leaf toward the center to cover the fish; do the same with the top. Fold in the sides to create an envelope. Wrap with the foil just as you did with the banana leaf, folding in the bottom, top, and sides to form an envelope. Secure by crimping the top and bottom edges of the foil.

4. Add about 2 inches of water to a wok or other pan large enough to hold a metal or bamboo steamer. Set the steamer insert in place and bring the water to a boil over medium-high heat. Place the packet in the steamer and cook for 45 minutes. Transfer the packet to a serving platter; cool 10 minutes, still wrapped. Open the packet and serve. (Alternatively, cool completely and refrigerate. To serve, place the packet in the steamer and reheat for about 20 minutes.) Accompany with sticky rice.

STEAMED CATFISH IN BANANA LEAF WITH DILL AND LEMON BASIL MOK PLA DUK

The Lao dads in the 'hood would plan trips together to the San Francisco Bay Delta in Contra Costa County to catch catfish. It was a way to bond, simulating fishing in the Mekong River. The trips happened often, and even though it was rare that my father went, we always had plenty of catfish to eat from the haul that found its way back to Oakland. I love the dill in this dish, and steaming is one of my favorite ways to prepare fish, especially fish on the bone. You *could* use boneless catfish fillets for this recipe, but bones and skin provide essential moisture, flavor, and texture, a certain gelatinous succulence that makes this dish exceptional. To fully capture the aromas, make the marinade the day you plan to cook the catfish.

SERVES 4 TO 6

1 pound (454 grams) catfish steaks, ½ inch thick, skin on

½ cup (60 grams) thinly sliced lemongrass

3 peeled garlic cloves (20 grams)

9 whole makrut lime leaves (3 grams)

7 fresh Thai chiles (10 grams)

½ cup (80 grams) thinly sliced shallots

¼ cup (72 grams) raw sticky rice, soaked for 24 hours in cold water

2 tablespoons (24 grams) fish sauce

½ tablespoon (6 grams) kosher salt

½ teaspoon (2 grams) MSG (optional)

½ cup (30 grams) chopped fresh dill, stems included

½ cup (24 grams) lemon basil leaves

2 banana leaves, trimmed into 10-inch squares (see page 328)

1. Rinse the catfish with cold water and drain well. Transfer to a mixing bowl; set aside.

2. With a mortar and pestle, pound the aromatics (lemongrass, garlic, lime leaves, chiles, and shallots) to a coarse paste. Add the soaked and drained sticky rice and pound everything semifine. Mix in the fish sauce, salt, MSG, if using, dill, and half the lemon basil. Toss with the catfish steaks and set aside to marinate at room temperature at least 30 minutes. (If you plan to marinate them longer than 45 minutes, transfer to the refrigerator).

3. Clean the banana leaves by wiping with a damp towel. Place one 12-inch-square sheet of aluminum foil on your work surface. Spread out 1 banana leaf on the foil, glossy side up. Arrange half the marinated catfish steaks in the center of the banana leaf, side by side, in a single layer (it's okay if they touch). Fold the bottom of the banana leaf toward the center to cover the fish; do the same with the top. Fold in the sides to create an envelope. Wrap with the foil just as you did with the banana leaf, folding in the bottom, top, and sides to form an envelope. Secure by crimping the top and bottom edges of the foil. Repeat with a second sheet of foil, the second banana leaf, and the remaining catfish steaks.

4. Add about 2 inches of water to a wok or other pan large enough to hold a metal or bamboo steamer. Set the steamer insert in place and bring the water to a boil over medium-high heat. Place the packets, side by side, in the steamer and cook for 20 minutes. Transfer the packets to a serving platter; cool for 30 minutes, still wrapped.

5. Open the packets and sprinkle the catfish with the remaining lemon basil. Serve with sticky rice.

17

SAUCES AND CONDIMENTS

STICKY RICE KHAO NIAW

This is the one true thing that binds us as Lao family. In *A Short History of Laos*, Grant Evans writes that, in the nineteenth century, when the French were trying to consolidate the many ethnic groups of the Lan Xang Kingdom into a nation called Laos, the one cultural fact that bound everybody was a taste for sticky rice. *Khao niaw*, "sticky rice," is at the center of every Lao and Isan meal that doesn't include noodles. In my family, if we ate six times in a day, it meant we had sticky rice six times that day. A meal is never complete without sticky rice.

The thing about khao niaw is that, unlike jasmine rice, which starts the cooking process submerged in water, sticky rice is literally steamed: Rice kernels cook from start to finish in scalding vapor. (To be accurate, jasmine and other types of so-called steamed rice should really be called boiled, or simmered.)

Kernels of sticky rice are the same size and shape as jasmine, the only difference is the color. Compared to jasmine's sheen and slight translucency, sticky rice is opaque, a matte speckled white. Sticky rice is sometimes called glutinous rice, but it contains no gluten. The name comes from the texture—the cooked grains are sticky and chewy, like high-gluten breads. Sticky rice grains stick to each other in clumps—easy to shape into balls with the fingers of one hand—which is exactly how you should eat sticky rice.

No utensils are required to eat sticky rice, just your hands. Take a single bite-size clump of rice and mold it into a spoon shape by flattening. Use it to grab a bite of stew, a smear of chile dip, or a taste of laap. Whenever anyone at Hawker Fare asks me how to eat sticky rice, I tell them to think of it as a corn tortilla in a Mexican meal: something you tear into pieces, bite by bite, for dipping into salsas and scooping up beans and stews.

In our house sticky rice was always served in woven bamboo baskets with lids called *gatip khao*. Bamboo keeps in moisture and retains heat—our gatip were holding, traveling, and serving vessels all in one, and the centerpiece of our meals. Everyone sitting on *saats* (woven plastic-straw mats) would hover over the basket, anxiously waiting to grab a fistful of rice.

To cook sticky rice properly, you'll need to make a modest investment in the right equipment: a pot-bellied aluminum cooking vessel, a woven bamboo cone that sits on top of the pot, and a bamboo lid (the lid of a stockpot will also do). All are pretty inexpensive at Lao and Thai markets. And make only as much as you need for a single meal, since you should never throw out rice. When I was growing up, wasting rice was considered disrespectful, almost sinful. As my mother always preached, rice is life.

4 cups (1,152 grams) raw sticky rice (I use Three Ladies Brand)

1. Start by soaking the rice. Dump the rice into a large bowl and cover with enough room-temperature water to rise about 3 inches above the rice—it'll absorb most of it. Soak a minimum of 6 hours and no more than 24. (If you're in a hurry, use hot tap water and soak for 2 hours, but the results won't be as good—the longer the rice soaks, the better the hydration of the grains.)

2. Drain the soaked rice in a colander, then return it to the bowl and cover with fresh water. Move the rice around with your hands gently and drain it again. Repeat this two more times. The goal is to wash off excess starch. By the third rinse, the water should look pretty clear. Place the rice into the cone-shaped bamboo steaming basket and set aside.

3. Fill the cooking pot with enough water to come up 3 inches from the bottom. Bring the water to a boil over high heat, then lower the heat to achieve a gentle boil. Place the rice-filled steaming basket on the pot and cover. Steam the rice 15 to 20 minutes in total.

4. After about 7 minutes, lift the lid, remove the basket, and give it a shake to redistribute—the rice that was at the bottom should now be on the surface. Continue steaming the rice another 8 to 10 minutes. Taste the rice: If it's gummy, steam a few minutes more. When properly cooked, sticky rice should be slightly translucent and tender but not mushy.

5. You'll need a large, clean surface: a big wooden cutting board, baking sheet, shallow mixing bowl, or even the counter itself. Moisten the surface by smearing it with wet hands or misting with a spray bottle. Flip the hot rice onto the surface and, using a moistened wooden paddle or spoon, start fluffing—this is for releasing excess steam—an important step, since trapped steam eventually overcooks the rice and makes it mushy.

6. Transfer the rice to a gatip and wait 10 minutes before serving. It'll still be hot, but cool enough to dig into without scalding anyone's fingers. The rice will stay warm for about 45 minutes. To maintain the temperature longer than that, hold the rice-filled gatip in a small ice chest or enclose it in a plastic bag. If the rice gets cold, reheat in the microwave, but make sure it doesn't dry out.

7. Form leftover rice into patties. Dry them out in the sun or in a dehydrator. Fry the dried patties in hot oil (375°F) until they puff. Cool them and crumble on top of khao piak sen or khao soi. You can also drizzle the patties with melted palm sugar for a sweet snack.

FERMENTED FISH SAUCE PADAEK

If there's a mother sauce in Lao cuisine, it's padaek [pa-*dack*]: extremely fragrant and pungent, the funk of all funks. Regular fish sauce is clear and refined, but padaek is fierce: whole chunks of small fish mixed with salt and rice bran. It looks like mud. You know you've entered a Lao home if it smells like padaek and steamed sticky rice. That's a basic fact.

In the cuisine of Laos and Isan, padaek appears both raw and cooked in a lot of different dishes. Padaek's flavor is deep and rich. It has way more dimension than ordinary fish sauce. And the aroma is so intense that when you're muddling green papaya with padaek, people can smell it a room away, like smoke signals warning something big is happening, an explosion of umami and intense salinity.

Padaek has just three ingredients: fish, salt, and rice bran (you can add other things, but that's personal preference). In Laos, giant catfish from the Mekong River are a common source of padaek. Carp, another freshwater species, is good, especially if you're making padaek at home.

As padaek ages, it gets richer and more complex. The best-tasting ones have fermented a minimum of six months. Leaving them for a whole year yields mature, fully ripened flavors. I once tasted three-year-old padaek at my mom's and it was good, the stink equivalent of a ripe washed-rind cheese like Taleggio or Époisses.

Bottled Lao or Isan padaek and Thai *pla ra* can be found at Asian supermarkets (see The Lao and Isan Pantry, page 328). There's really no substitute for padaek in Lao and Isan recipes. Anchovy paste won't cut it, even if you try stewing tinned or bottled anchovy fillets in water and a bit of fish sauce until it becomes mush. It's just not the same.

Countries bordering Laos make decent substitutes, for example the Vietnamese fermented fish sauce called *mắm nêm* (I highly recommend the Super brand—the label calls it "Ground Preserved Fish Sauce"—which is consistently very good).

If you can't buy good padaek, or if you're ever curious, courageous, and have the time and patience, try making your own. You can find fresh carp (sometimes even live) at your Asian supermarket or seafood shop—you can even ask the fishmonger to do all the scaling, gutting, chopping, and washing. I suggest you age padaek in your garage or basement. Be warned: Flies love it.

MAKES 1 QUART

1 pound (454 grams) whole carp

6 ounces (170 grams) coarse sea salt

3 ounces (85 grams) rice bran (I've had good results with Bob's Red Mill brand)

1. Scale, gut, chop, and wash the fish, then drain it in a colander. Put the drained fish in a large mixing bowl and add the salt. Mix well, cover, and let sit for 12 hours at room temperature. When the 12 hours are up, add the rice bran and mix again. Transfer to a ceramic crock or large glass jar. Make sure there's at least 4 inches of space between the fish and the opening to allow for expansion once fermentation begins. Use your hand to press down the fish, expelling any air pockets, then lay a sheet of plastic wrap directly onto the fish. You'll need a weight to set on top of the plastic wrap—this keeps pressure on the fish, helping to extract its juices over the coming months. You can use a large rock or clay brick, first sanitized by boiling in water for a few minutes (cool before placing on the fish). Cover the fermenting vessel, and move it to a spot with a consistent temperature, away from sunlight. Then the waiting begins.

2. Don't touch it for a year, ideally, although you might be able to dip into it after only two months. Use your nose to determine ripeness. Padaek tells you when it's ready.

TOASTED RICE POWDER KHAO KUA

The presence of toasted rice powder is another way you can recognize if a dish is from Isan or Laos. It's a seasoning crucial to laap—without it, a salad is simply not laap. There are different degrees of "toastiness" in *khao kua*, from light to dark. It's a matter of personal preference, varying from cook to cook and from region to region. In our house we toast rice on the darker side, so it has the color of roasted coffee: not burnt, but walking that fine line. You have to toast the rice for khao kua in a pan or wok—toasting on a sheet tray in the oven, like nuts, will not do.

MAKES 2 CUPS

2 cups (445 grams) raw sticky rice

1. Start with a room-temperature pan or wok and add the sticky rice. Set over medium heat and begin toasting. Move the rice often by stirring with a spoon or giving the pan a good shake to ensure that all the kernels toast evenly. You'll begin to notice the slow but consistent darkening in the kernels with direct pan contact, so keeping everything moving is crucial. The pan will begin to smoke a bit but don't be alarmed, just keep moving the rice until it's a deep, even brown, the color of coffee. Don't try to rush the process by turning up the heat: Toasting over medium heat will result in a better product and leave less room for screwing up.

2. Transfer the toasted rice to a platter or baking sheet to cool. In a granite mortar, pound the rice to a semifine powder. Store in an airtight container at room temperature. Unground, the toasted rice will keep for 6 weeks. For the best aroma, grind just before using.

CHARRED CHILE DIP WITH BEEF BILE JAEW BHEE

Nothing is wasted in Lao cooking, not even beef bile, a dark, intensely bitter fluid that helps digestion. I loved bile even as a kid. My parents thought I was weird. Most kids love sweets, but I craved the complex bitterness of chocolate, even coffee: They made me feel like a grown-up. Bitterness magnifies strong flavors, and this dipping sauce is the perfect accompaniment for *seen ping* (page 232), grilled chewy beef brisket. Bile adds a bit of gaminess, and the mix of charred shallots, serrano chiles, and poblano peppers makes it smoky, making the brisket taste even beefier. Like they say, what grows together goes together! If you're squeamish, you can omit the bile and this sauce will still be good. *Jaew bhee* tastes best the day you make it, but will last two days.

MAKES ABOUT 4 CUPS

½ cup (120 grams) water

¼ cup (20 grams) sliced lemongrass, 1-inch bias cut

½ cup (84 grams) cherry tomatoes, stemmed

1 large fresh poblano pepper (120 grams)

¼ cup (45 grams) coarsely chopped roasted shallots (see page 334)

⅛ cup (25 grams) roasted garlic (see page 331)

¼ cup (50 grams) grilled serrano chiles (see page 329)

½ tablespoon (10 grams) finely minced fresh galangal

½ tablespoon (7 grams) pasteurized beef bile from the second stomach (see page 328)

¾ cup (144 grams) fish sauce

¼ cup (60 grams) fresh lime juice

½ tablespoon (3 grams) prik phong (ground toasted chile; see page 329)

Kosher salt, to taste

½ cup (24 grams) finely chopped cilantro, stems included

1. Bring the water and lemongrass to a boil in a small saucepan. Remove from the heat and set aside to cool and steep for 30 minutes. Strain, discarding the lemongrass. Set the infusion aside.

2. Meanwhile, enclose the cherry tomatoes in a tightly sealed aluminum foil packet. Place on the grill and cook for about 20 minutes until supersoft, flipping the packet often. Grill the poblano pepper directly on the grill until it's softened and blistered. Transfer to a zipper-top bag and seal; set aside to cool. Peel the poblano when cooled, remove and discard the seeds, and coarsely chop the flesh.

3. In a mortar, combine the roasted shallots, roasted garlic, grilled serrano chiles, chopped poblano, and galangal and pound to a paste. Add the cherry tomatoes and pound again. Add the lemongrass infusion, beef bile, fish sauce, lime juice, and prik phong and stir to combine. Transfer to a serving bowl. Season with salt. Just before serving, stir in the chopped cilantro.

CHARRED CHILE JAM NAAM PRIK PAO

A jam-like condiment with the fragrance of fried shallots, chiles, garlic, and dried shrimp, and the vivid flavor of tamarind. It's awesome as a dip for sticky rice, as a last-minute flavor boost to stir into soups, and to spread on toast—I've even seen it dabbed on pizza. At Hawker Fare we toss our fried chicken in *naam prik pao* and add it to our *dtom kha* mussels. If you want to make only one recipe from this book to keep on hand as an all-purpose condiment, this is it. I swear you'll end up smearing it on everything.

MAKES 2½ CUPS

¼ cup (23 grams) dried shrimp

½ cup (103 grams) canola oil

1 cup (35 grams) dried puya chiles

1 cup (160 grams) whole peeled shallots

½ cup (100 grams) peeled garlic cloves

¾ cup (150 grams) granulated sugar

½ cup (96 grams) fish sauce

½ cup (125 grams) Tamarind Water (page 299)

1. Toast the dried shrimp in a dry sauté pan over medium heat until fragrant but not browned. Set aside.

2. Line a plate with paper towels; set aside. Heat the oil in a wok or sauté pan over medium heat. Fry the chiles, one by one, until they turn a dark red hue and are brittle but not burnt, about 12 seconds each (be careful not to burn them). Using a slotted spoon, transfer the fried chiles to the paper towel–lined plate. Repeat with the shallots, frying them, one at a time, in the same oil until browned, then draining on paper towels. Repeat with the garlic cloves, and finally the dried shrimp. Let everything cool to room temperature. Strain the cooled oil and measure it; add additional oil to get ½ cup.

3. Add the fried chiles and dried shrimp to a large mortar and pound to a fine texture with the pestle. Add the fried garlic and shallots and pound again to produce a smooth, wet paste. Scrape the paste into a mixing bowl, stir in the sugar, fish sauce, and tamarind water and mix well. Add the reserved ½ cup of oil and mix again. Use right away, or cover tightly and store in the refrigerator for up to 4 weeks.

roasted green
CHILE RELISH
(PAGE 290)

CHARRED TOMATO AND
CHILE RELISH WITH
FERMENTED FISH (PAGE 289)

WATER BEETLE CHILE DIP
(PAGE 291)

LAO CARAMELIZED AROMATIC
CHILE DIP WITH COW'S SKIN
(PAGE 292)

DRY-FRIED FISH
CHILE RELISH
(PAGE 293)

CHARRED CHILE JAM
(PAGE 285)

LAO BBQ DIPPING SAUCE JAEW

The Lao equivalent of barbecue sauce, this goes with anything cooked on the grill, even vegetables (especially mushrooms). Keep for three days max—technically it lasts longer, but won't taste as fresh.

MAKES ABOUT 1½ CUPS

½ cup (96 grams) fish sauce

2 tablespoons (30 grams) dark brown sugar

2 tablespoons (10 grams) prik phong (ground toasted chile; see page 329)

½ cup (120 grams) fresh lime juice

1 tablespoon (12 grams) minced shallots

1 tablespoon (10 grams) Toasted Rice Powder (page 283)

1 tablespoon (6 grams) finely chopped cilantro, stems included

Combine the fish sauce, brown sugar, prik phong, and lime juice; stir well to dissolve the sugar. Just before serving, sprinkle with the shallots, toasted rice powder, and cilantro.

CHARRED TOMATO AND CHILE RELISH WITH FERMENTED FISH JAEW MAK LEN

A simple, delicious relish with a huge punch of umami from the combination of roasted cherry tomatoes and padaek and a kick of spice from dried chiles. Eat with sticky rice and beef jerky, any sort of grilled or fried fish or meat, or simply blanched vegetables. It's best to roast the cherry tomatoes nice and slow to concentrate the flavors and sugars, yielding a somewhat jammy relish.

MAKES 3 CUPS

- ⅓ cup (60 grams) whole shallots, unpeeled
- 8 peeled garlic cloves (28 grams)
- 12 ounces (340 grams) ripe red cherry tomatoes
- 1 tablespoon (12 grams) fish sauce
- 1 tablespoon (15 grams) padaek
- 1 tablespoon (15 grams) fresh lime juice
- 1 tablespoon (12 grams) granulated sugar
- 1 tablespoon (11 grams) kosher salt
- ¼ teaspoon (1 gram) MSG (optional)
- 2 tablespoons (10 grams) prik phong (ground toasted chile; see page 329)
- ½ cup (24 grams) finely chopped cilantro, stems included

1. Heat an outdoor grill to medium-hot. Place the unpeeled shallots on the grill. Cook slowly until the flesh is soft; check by giving each shallot a firm squeeze. When the shallots are done, set them aside to steam in their skins and cool. Peel when you're able to handle them comfortably; coarsely chop and set aside. Thread the garlic cloves onto a metal or bamboo skewer. Grill slowly over a medium flame until they're fragrant and tender (it's okay to end up with a bit of char). Remove from the skewer and set aside.

2. Meanwhile, place a heavy cast-iron skillet over high heat until it's very hot. Add the tomatoes to the skillet and swirl so they roast evenly; cook until they're soft and blistered. Set aside to cool to room temperature.

3. Combine the shallots and garlic in a mortar and pound to a paste. Add the tomatoes and pound to a cohesive paste. Stir in the fish sauce, padaek, lime juice, sugar, salt, MSG, if using, and prik phong. Fold in the chopped cilantro. The relish can be stored for up to a week in the refrigerator.

ROASTED GREEN CHILE RELISH

JAEW MAK PRIK (NAAM PRIK NOOM)

A chile pepper relish with warmth, not heat, from two types of green chile peppers. Since it doesn't contain any Thai chiles, it avoids that sharp burn. This is the jaew to serve alongside Lao sausage (*sai oua*). It's also a great snacking dip with pork rinds.

MAKES 2 CUPS

¼ cup (45 grams) whole unpeeled shallots

¼ cup (50 grams) fresh serrano chiles, stemmed

1 cup (200 grams) fresh Anaheim peppers

¼ cup (26 grams) canola oil

⅛ cup (20 grams) peeled garlic cloves

¼ cup (60 grams) padaek

¼ cup (12 grams) finely chopped cilantro, stems included

1. Place the unpeeled shallots on a medium-hot grill. Cook slowly until the flesh is soft; check by giving each shallot a firm squeeze. When the shallots are done set them aside to steam in their skins and cool. Peel when you're able to handle them comfortably; coarsely chop and set aside. Thread the serrano chiles onto a metal or bamboo skewer. Grill slowly over a medium flame until fragrant and tender (it's okay to end up with a bit of char). Grill the Anaheim peppers directly on the grill until they're softened and blistered; peel and seed them.

2. Warm the oil in a small sauté pan over medium heat. Add the garlic cloves and fry gently until they're browned and fragrant; drain on paper towels.

3. Combine the roasted shallots and fried garlic in a mortar and pound to a semismooth paste. Add the serranos and Anaheims and continue pounding away to achieve a paste with a smooth yet stringy texture. Add the padaek for seasoning; fold in the chopped cilantro right before serving. The relish can be stored (without the cilantro) for 1 week in the refrigerator.

WATER BEETLE CHILE DIP JAEW MANG-DA

If I were to blind-taste you on this dip you'd probably pause to decide whether ripe pears or cherimoya gave it such a fruity aroma. That was how I was introduced to this dip by my mother. She thought if she disclosed up front that she'd made it with richly fragrant bugs, there was a huge chance I wouldn't have even considered trying it. It took me years to find out the real secret behind *jaew mang-da*. When I did I was like, *So?* I thought it was even cooler that I'd been eating water beetles all this time.

MAKES 2½ CUPS

½ cup (51 grams) canola oil

1 cup (35 grams) whole dried puya chiles

1 cup (160 grams) whole peeled shallots

½ cup (100 grams) peeled garlic cloves

¼ cup (23 grams) dried shrimp

2 frozen mang-da (water beetles; 40 grams)

¾ cup (150 grams) granulated sugar

½ cup (96 grams) fish sauce

½ cup (125 grams) Tamarind Water (page 299)

1. Add the canola oil to a wok or large sauté pan and get it hot over medium heat. Fry the dried chiles until they're dark but not burnt; transfer to a plate lined with paper towels. Repeat with the shallots, garlic, dried shrimp, and mang-da in that order, transferring each to a paper towel–lined plate and setting them aside to cool. Strain the oil and let it cool; set aside.

2. In a granite mortar, pound the chiles, dried shrimp, and mang-da to a fine paste. Add the fried garlic and shallots and continue pounding until you have a smooth, wet paste. Transfer the paste to a mixing bowl and add the sugar, fish sauce, and tamarind water. Stir in the reserved frying oil and mix well. The dip will keep up to 4 weeks in the refrigerator.

LAO CARAMELIZED AROMATIC CHILE DIP WITH COW'S SKIN JAEW BONG

This is a staple in every Lao and Isan home, a natural partner for sticky rice, yet no two cooks make it exactly the same way. Traditionally it's made with fried beef jerky and water buffalo skin that's been dried, charred over an open flame or charcoal grill, pounded to tenderize it and flake off the carbon, then blanched and sliced. This recipe calls for a mix of easy-to-find Chinese pork floss and buffalo or cow skin to provide structure and meaty aroma. Of all the chile dips and relishes, *jaew bong* is my favorite. It's versatile and complex, with a secondary dimension of texture from dried meats, and has a great shelf life (it keeps in the refrigerator for 6 weeks). Serve with jasmine or sticky rice; in our house it was always surrounded by raw and blanched or steamed vegetables. In Luang Prabang, jaew bong comes with brittle squares of sun-dried river moss (they look like nori sheets speckled with sesame seeds and sometimes slices of tomato and shallot). It's one of the best snacks I've ever had.

MAKES ABOUT 2 CUPS

3 cups (615 grams) canola oil, for frying

Eight ⅛-inch slices fresh galangal (28 grams)

¼ cup (50 grams) peeled garlic cloves

¼ cup (40 grams) thinly sliced shallots

⅓ cup (40 grams) dried puya chiles

2 tablespoons (12 grams) dried shrimp

2 tablespoons (32 grams) Tamarind Water (page 299)

3 tablespoons (36 grams) fish sauce

½ cup (110 grams) dark brown sugar

1 ounce (28 grams) Chinese pork floss (see page 330)

3 tablespoons (33 grams) kosher salt

2 ounces (56 grams) buffalo or cow skin, charred, blanched, and sliced (see page 330)

1. Bring the canola oil to 375°F in a large, heavy saucepan over medium heat. Carefully slip the galangal slices into the oil and fry until they take on a dark caramelized color. Remove with a strainer and transfer to a mixing bowl. Repeat with the garlic, shallots, and chiles, adjusting the heat as necessary to maintain an even frying temperature. Set the fried aromatics aside. Cool and strain the oil to reuse for a future batch.

2. Place a sauté pan over low heat and add the dried shrimp. Cook, stirring constantly, until the shrimp are fragrant and brittle. Add them to the bowl of a food processor along with the fried galangal, garlic, shallots, and chiles. Add the tamarind water, fish sauce, brown sugar, and pork floss and blend to a chunky paste with the texture of marmalade. Stir in the salt and fold in the buffalo or cow skin. Transfer to a serving bowl and serve straightaway, or scrape into an airtight container and store for up to 6 weeks in the refrigerator.

DRY-FRIED FISH CHILE RELISH JAEW PLA HANK

Turning leftovers into gold. I love leftovers, especially when I can transform them into something extravagant. Whenever we found ourselves with fried fish on the table after a meal, it was time to make this relish (on its own, leftover fried fish wasn't as good as *jaew pla hank*). I like to sprinkle it over steamed jasmine rice. If I feel ambitious, I'll fry an egg to put on top of my rice, under the relish—such an easy meal, and a complete one. You can make this dip with *pla dat diew*, "sun-dried fish." To make it with leftover fried fish, just pick the flesh free of bones and scales, then sauté with minimal oil to cook out all the moisture.

MAKES 2½ CUPS

Canola oil, for frying

1 pound (454 grams) tilapia fillets, thinly sliced

½ cup (90 grams) whole unpeeled shallots

¼ cup (50 grams) peeled garlic cloves

¼ cup (50 grams) peeled and thinly sliced fresh ginger

2 tablespoons (30 grams) padaek

2 tablespoons (24 grams) granulated sugar

1 teaspoon (4 grams) MSG (optional)

1 tablespoon (11 grams) kosher salt

1. Add enough oil to come halfway up the sides of a large, heavy saucepan or Dutch oven. Set the pan over medium-high heat and bring the oil to 350°F, raising or lowering the heat as needed to maintain a steady temperature. Cut the fish into ½-inch pieces. Carefully drop into the hot oil and fry until the exterior of the fish is very crispy and dry. Transfer to a platter lined with paper towels to absorb any excess oil; cool to room temperature.

2. Place the unpeeled shallots on a medium-hot grill. Cook slowly until the flesh is soft; check by giving each shallot a firm squeeze. When the shallots are done, set them aside to steam in their skins and cool. Peel when you're able to handle them comfortably; coarsely chop and set aside. Meanwhile, thread the garlic cloves onto a metal or bamboo skewer and grill until soft and slightly charred. Remove from the skewer and set aside to cool.

3. In a mortar, combine the garlic, shallots, and ginger and pound to a paste. Add the fish and pound again to a paste. Add the seasonings (padaek, sugar, MSG, if using, and salt) and pound once more until they're absorbed. The relish will keep in the refrigerator for up to 6 weeks.

SPICY EGGPLANT RELISH JAEW MAK KHUA

Think of this as a Lao version of eggplant caviar. It's simple, delicious, and goes well with grilled fish. You can make it ahead of time and store in the fridge for up to one week.

MAKES 2 CUPS

½ cup (90 grams) whole shallots

⅛ cup (30 grams) peeled garlic cloves

1 pound (454 grams) green Thai eggplants

2 fresh green Thai chiles (3 grams)

6 tablespoons (90 grams) padaek

Chopped cilantro, for garnishing

1. Preheat a grill, preferably a charcoal one, though gas is fine; try to keep the heat medium-low. Skewer the shallots and garlic cloves, a separate skewer for each. Grill the shallot and garlic skewers slowly—you want them to end up soft and creamy without taking on too much color. Once they're done, slide them off the skewers; keep the grill going. Peel the shallots and place them in a mortar to cool along with the garlic.

2. Remove the stems from the eggplant and wrap them together in aluminum foil. Place the foil packet on the grill and cook over medium-low heat for about 20 minutes. Check after 15 minutes—the eggplants should be molten in the center, a soft pulp held together by the skins, like a ripe summer tomato. Remove the packets from the grill, open the foil, and let the eggplants cool to room temperature.

3. Add the stemmed chiles to the shallots and garlic in the mortar and pound to a paste. Add the cooled eggplant (including the skins) and pound everything to a smooth consistency. Stir in the padaek and transfer to a serving bowl. Sprinkle with chopped cilantro and serve.

HOT, SWEET, AND SOUR DIPPING SAUCE FOR BBQ CHICKEN NAAM JIM GAI YANG

You can buy this already made, but it's easy to assemble a version that tastes better—fresher and more vibrant—than the bottled. Like ketchup, it's a good thing to have on hand, a universal dipping sauce for fried and grilled things. My kids (ages four and six) are already addicted.

MAKES 6 CUPS

¼ cup (50 grams) peeled garlic cloves

1½ cups (240 grams) thinly sliced red Fresno chiles

3½ cups (700 grams) granulated sugar

1 cup (240 grams) fish sauce

½ cup (113 grams) distilled white vinegar

¼ cup (40 grams) tapioca starch

1 tablespoon (11 grams) kosher salt

Add the garlic and sliced Fresno chiles to a mortar and pound to a coarse paste. Transfer to a small nonreactive saucepan and add the sugar and fish sauce; set aside. Combine the vinegar and tapioca starch in a small bowl and stir to form a slurry; set aside. Bring the garlic and chile mixture to a boil over medium heat, then reduce to a simmer. Slowly pour the tapioca starch slurry into the simmering mixture in a gentle stream, whisking constantly. Bring back to a boil and season with salt. Remove from the heat and set aside to cool. Serve right away, or transfer to an airtight container and store for up to 4 weeks in the refrigerator.

HOT AND SOUR DIPPING SAUCE/SEAFOOD DIPPING SAUCE JAEW SOM/NAAM JIM SEAFOOD

Growing up, I heard my mother use two different names for this dipping sauce. *Jaew som* translates as "tart sauce condiment"; *Naam jim seafood* means "seafood sauce." No matter the name, it's a sauce that goes well with seafood of all kinds, grilled, poached, or steamed. It's especially good with barbecued oysters or shrimp, with mussels, boiled crab, and periwinkle snails, blood clams, and cockles. Freshly made is best, but it will hold for to up a week in the fridge.

MAKES ABOUT 1½ CUPS

⅛ cup (25 grams) peeled garlic cloves

1 tablespoon (20 grams) finely chopped cilantro root or stems

3 tablespoons (45 grams) fresh lime juice

3 tablespoons (45 grams) fresh lemon juice

¾ cup (145 grams) fish sauce

½ cup (100 grams) granulated sugar

10 fresh Thai chiles, thinly sliced (30 grams)

2 tablespoons (12 grams) finely chopped cilantro

Combine the garlic and cilantro root or stems in a mortar and pound to a paste. Add the citrus juices, fish sauce, and sugar; stir to dissolve and add the sliced chiles. Serve at once, or refrigerate in an airtight container for up to 1 week. Add the chopped cilantro just before serving.

SATAY PEANUT SAUCE NAAM JIM SATAY

You begin this simple, delicious satay sauce by deep-frying peanuts. Frying produces a deeper aroma than roasting in the oven (you'll need a deep-fry thermometer). If you have the homemade red curry paste on hand, it all comes together pretty fast. This will last five days, sealed tightly and refrigerated. Re-warm to slightly above room temperature before serving.

MAKES ABOUT 1 QUART

1 quart (820 grams) canola oil, for frying

1½ cups (336 grams) skinless peanuts

⅛ cup (18 grams) Red Curry Paste (page 301)

1¾ cups (455 grams) unsweetened coconut milk

1 tablespoon (11 grams) kosher salt, plus more as needed

½ cup (120 grams) water

1½ cups (180 grams) dark brown sugar

1. Heat the oil in a wok or heavy saucepan over medium-high heat. When the oil registers 350°F on a deep-fry thermometer, carefully lower in the peanuts and fry until they turn a rich caramel brown. Remove with a strainer and transfer to paper towels to drain and cool.

2. Transfer the cooled peanuts to a mortar and lightly crush them with a pestle to a coarse texture; set aside. Combine the red curry paste and ¼ cup (65 grams) of the coconut milk in a medium saucepan over medium heat. Cook, stirring occasionally, until the oil separates and the mixture becomes fragrant—be careful not to let it scorch. Add the remaining 1½ cups (325 grams) coconut milk, the measured salt, water, brown sugar, and crushed peanuts. Bring to a boil, then turn off the heat and let the mixture stand for 45 minutes to 1 hour to cool and allow the peanuts to hydrate.

3. Transfer to a blender and puree until the sauce is smooth. Taste and adjust the seasoning with more salt as needed.

CUCUMBER AJAT

A simple and refreshing relish for grilled meats. With Satay Peanut Sauce (page 297), it's the usual accompaniment for satay. You can make the vinegar and sugar dressing up to six weeks ahead of time (store it in the fridge), but assemble the relish the day you plan to serve it.

MAKES 2 CUPS

4 ounces (112 grams) medium pickling cucumbers, quartered lengthwise, sliced ¼ inch thick

¼ cup (40 grams) thinly sliced shallots

2 fresh Thai chiles, thinly sliced (3 grams)

¼ cup (56 grams) distilled white vinegar

¼ cup (50 grams) granulated sugar

1 teaspoon (4 grams) kosher salt

Combine the cucumbers, shallots, and chiles in a serving bowl. In a separate bowl whisk together the vinegar, sugar, and salt until the sugar has completely dissolved. Add the vinegar mixture to the cucumbers, making sure they're covered. Let the cucumbers pickle for at least 15 minutes before serving.

TAMARIND WATER NAHM MAKHAM

You can buy a premade version at Asian markets, but making your own lets you control the concentration of tamarind solids, yielding richer results. Tamarind paste comes in 14- to 16-ounce blocks (see page 334). You can use *nahm makham* in soups, naam jaew dipping sauces, dressings, and by adding simple syrup and lime juice, as a quick and easy beverage. It's another good staple to have on hand.

MAKES 3 CUPS

3 ounces (84 grams) tamarind paste
1½ cups (357 grams) water

1. Combine the tamarind paste and water in a medium saucepan and set over high heat. Bring the water to a boil and immediately turn off the heat. Pour into a nonreactive heatproof container and let the mixture cool to room temperature. Cover and refrigerate for 24 hours.

2. The next day, pour the mixture through a medium-mesh strainer into a bowl, using your hands to press through as much of the liquid as possible. Transfer to an airtight container and refrigerate for up to 1 week.

YANANG LEAF WATER NAAM BAI YANANG

Yanang leaves are harvested from a flowering plant (*Tiliacora triandra*) native to Southeast Asia and found mostly in Isan and Laos. Generally the leaves themselves aren't used, but the dark green vegetal juice they contain is extracted. You can buy canned or frozen yanang leaf water, but it's far better to make your own, using the whole frozen leaves from Asian markets. Just blend them up and pass through a chinois, like straining kale juice.

MAKES 5½ CUPS

4 ounces (112 grams) frozen yanang leaves, rinsed
6 cups (1,422 grams) water

Combine the leaves and water in a blender and puree smooth. Pass through a fine-mesh strainer or chinois. Store, refrigerated, for up to 1 week.

RED CURRY PASTE NAAM PRIK GAEND PHET

Since curry paste is versatile, it's a good idea to have some on hand at all times for making *khao poon* (page 160), *nam khao tod* (page 199), *mee katee* (page 171), and many other recipes. It lasts three months in the fridge. The measurements for this recipe are in grams alone, so you'll need a kitchen scale. The balance of the ingredients is crucial, so weigh everything carefully.

MAKES 2 CUPS

- 100 grams dried red chiles
- 30 grams shrimp paste
- 4 grams coriander seeds, toasted
- 4 grams cumin seeds, toasted
- 60 grams peeled garlic cloves
- 20 grams fresh galangal, thinly sliced
- 120 grams shallots, thinly sliced
- 40 grams lemongrass, thinly sliced
- 4 grams whole makrut lime leaves
- 30 grams krachai (*Boesenbergia rotunda*), also known as fingerroot or wild ginger (see page 335)
- 30 grams cilantro root or stems
- 20 grams kosher salt
- 115 grams water, more or less

Combine all the ingredients except the water in the blender. Turn the motor on, adding just enough water so that the blades catch the ingredients. (Add only as much water as you need—curry paste should be as dry as possible.) Puree until smooth. Transfer to an airtight container and keep in the refrigerator for up to 3 months.

FERMENTED CHINESE MUSTARD GREENS IN RICE BRINE SOM PAK GAAT

You see *som pak gaat* already prepared at Asian markets, packed in what look like hospital IV pouches filled with pickling brine. This is a very simple recipe, though, so do try making your own—the main thing you need is time. This is a great use for leftover cooked jasmine rice. And try to find Chinese mustard greens—they're less about the soft leaves than the common frizzled variety, more about stalks and ribs, plus they deliver more of a horseradish aromatic burn to the nostrils. It's crucial to submerge them completely in the brine. If any of the greens are exposed, they'll rot. Serve this pickle alongside *dtom khem* (page 257), or eat the chopped leaves on rice congee (page 178). With fried peanuts, it makes a great drinking snack.

MAKES 3 QUARTS

- 2 pounds (907 grams) Chinese mustard greens
- ¼ cup (50 grams) garlic cloves
- 8 fresh Thai chiles (12 grams)
- 7½ cups (1,799 grams) cold water
- 3 tablespoons (33 grams) kosher salt
- 3 tablespoons (45 grams) cooked jasmine rice
- 1 teaspoon (4 grams) MSG (optional)

1. Chop the mustard greens into large bite-size pieces, rinse under cold running water, and drain. Transfer to a large mixing bowl, add the garlic cloves and Thai chiles, and toss to mix. Pack everything into a large, clean glass jar or nonreactive bowl and press down to pack tightly. Set aside.

2. Pour the water into a separate mixing bowl, add the salt, and stir to dissolve. Add the cooked jasmine rice and let it soak for 30 minutes. Strain the water into a separate container, pressing the rice to remove as much liquid as possible; discard the rice.

3. Add the drained rice water to the mustard greens mixture, making sure everything is completely submerged. Lay a sheet of plastic wrap directly on the surface of the mixture; set a clean weight (a plate works fine) on top of the plastic to keep the greens submerged. Cover the jar or bowl with another sheet of plastic wrap.

4. Find a dark place to store the vessel at room temperature, away from sunlight. Allow it to ferment, undisturbed, for 3 days. On the third day, taste a piece of the greens—it should have a tart aroma and a sharp, tangy flavor. It may need to ferment an extra day, depending on the temperature of the room. When it's done, store in the refrigerator, covered, for 6 weeks.

RICE-FERMENTED CABBAGE
WITH PIG'S EAR AND SCALLIONS
(PAGE 304)

RICE-FERMENTED CABBAGE WITH PIG'S EAR AND SCALLIONS SOM PAK GALUM

I always forgot Moms had a batch of *som pak galum* going in a corner of the kitchen, hidden under the dining table and its beige vinyl cloth, until it really started to ferment. I'd chase the scent trail with my nose and find a treasure: soured cabbage in a Rubbermaid container covered with a yellow "Thank you!" bag recycled from our Chinatown shopping. I'd salivate and automatically reach for a crisp, gelatinous strip of pig's ear. It was so good! (More than once I got blamed for eating up all the pig's ear in a batch.) Som pak had a high value in the neighborhood food-barter circuit. Fortunately Moms made the best in the 'hood, so she had the ace.

MAKES 3 QUARTS

½ pound (226 grams) pig's ears, about 4 large	2 pounds (907 grams) green cabbage, cut into large dice	12 scallions, cut into 2-inch pieces (about 170 grams)	1 teaspoon (4 grams) MSG (optional)
2 tablespoons (36 grams) cooked sticky rice	9 tablespoons (112 grams) granulated sugar	3 tablespoons (33 grams) kosher salt	

1. Rinse the pig's ears under cold running water and place in a small saucepan. Cover with lightly salted cold water and bring to a boil. Reduce the heat to maintain a gentle simmer and cook for 1 hour. Drain and rinse under cold running water to cool. Slice the ears into ⅛-inch strips and place in a large mixing bowl. Set aside.

2. Place the cooked sticky rice in a small bowl, cover with cold water, and soak for 15 minutes. Drain, and add to the bowl with the pig's ear.

3. Meanwhile, soak the cabbage in cold water with 8 tablespoons of the sugar for 20 minutes. Drain, then transfer to the bowl with the ears and rice, along with the scallions, salt, the remaining 1 tablespoon sugar, and the MSG, if using. Knead the mixture gently for about 2 minutes to incorporate the salt and sugar. Transfer to a clean glass jar or nonreactive bowl and press down to pack it tightly. Lay a sheet of plastic wrap directly onto the surface of the cabbage mixture, and cover the jar or bowl with another sheet of plastic wrap.

4. Find a dark place to store the vessel at room temperature, away from sunlight. Let it ferment undisturbed for 3 days On the third day, taste a piece of cabbage—it should have a tart aroma and a sharp, tangy flavor. It may need to ferment an extra day, depending on the temperature of the room. When it's done, store in the refrigerator, covered, for as long as 4 to 6 weeks.

FERMENTED FISH AND TAMARIND CONDIMENT

JAEW PADAEK

There are a few different types of *jaew padaek*: This one, with tamarind, leans toward tartness. It's meant to go with Fried and Salt-Crusted Grilled Tilapia Lettuce Wraps (page 138), but feel free to serve it with pretty much anything (I like it with grilled meats). Again, the rules are not rigid.

MAKES 2 CUPS

½ cup (120 grams) tamarind paste

1½ cups (357 grams) water

3 tablespoons (36 grams) granulated sugar

6 tablespoons (90 grams) padaek

2 tablespoons (16 grams) peeled garlic cloves

4 fresh Thai chiles (6 grams)

1 teaspoon (2 grams) prik phong (ground toasted chile; see page 329)

1 teaspoon (4 grams) kosher salt

1. In a small saucepan, combine the tamarind paste, water, sugar, and padaek and bring to a rapid boil over high heat. Remove from the heat immediately; let the tamarind steep at room temperature.

2. After 30 minutes, strain the tamarind water through a sieve or chinois into a bowl. Use the bowl of a ladle to push on the pulp and extract as much of the juice as possible; set aside.

3. In a mortar, pound the garlic and chiles to a paste. Add the paste to the tamarind mixture, stir in the prik phong and salt, and serve. Stored airtight in the refrigerator, it has a shelf life of 3 weeks.

PICKLED SERRANO CHILES MAK PRIK DONG

A simple condiment for any brothy noodle dish.

MAKES 1½ CUPS

3 ounces (86 grams) fresh serrano chiles, thinly sliced
1 cup (226 grams) distilled white vinegar

Place the sliced chiles in a jar. Pour the vinegar over to cover and let stand at room temperature for at least 2 days. The chiles will continue to pickle over time—it's up to you if you like them fresher or more pickled.

FRIED SHALLOTS HUA HOM KROB

MAKES 1 CUP

6 whole peeled shallots
1 quart (820 grams) canola oil

With a mandoline or very sharp knife, slice the shallots as thinly as possible, starting from the root end and working backward. Heat the oil to 300°F. Carefully lower the shallots into the oil, being careful not to splash. You want the moisture in the shallots to cook and evaporate out before they become crisp. As the shallots start to become crisp, the bubbles in the oil will start to subside, and you'll notice some coloring. When the shallots are beige in color, using a spider or strainer, transfer them onto a paper towel–lined plate. The shallots will continue to brown and crisp while cooling. After they're cool, store them in an airtight container for 2 weeks. Strain and save the oil to fry a future batch of shallots.

FRIED CHILE OIL KIEW MAK PRIK

MAKES 2 CUPS

2 ounces (56 grams)
   dried red Thai chiles

2 ounces (56 grams)
   dried puya chiles

6 garlic cloves, finely
   minced (12 grams)

1½ cups (256 grams)
   canola oil

3 tablespoons
   (33 grams) kosher salt

In a coffee grinder reserved for spices, grind both kinds of dried chiles to a medium-fine powder. Combine the ground chiles with the remaining ingredients in a small saucepan set over medium heat. Slowly fry the chiles and garlic until fragrant. The chiles will start to turn dark red as the garlic toasts to a tan hue. At this point remove the pan from the heat and cool to room temperature. Store the chile oil in an airtight jar at room temperature. It lasts indefinitely.

FRIED GARLIC OIL KIEW KRA TIEM

Use this versatile oil (including the garlic bits) for *pho lao* (page 163), *khao piak sen* (tapioca noodles, page 175) and rice congee (page 178). Or strain out the fried garlic and use it as an additional seasoning for laap. The strained oil is a delicious cooking fat for *khao mun gai* rice (page 181).

MAKES JUST UNDER 1½ CUPS

½ cup (120 grams) minced garlic
1 cup (205 grams) canola oil

Combine the garlic and oil in a heavy-bottomed saucepan and stir to mix; have a mixing bowl within easy reach of your range. Set the saucepan over medium heat and cook, stirring constantly, until the garlic turns golden brown. Transfer immediately to the reserved mixing bowl to stop the cooking. Once the oil is cool, transfer to a jar or other airtight container. This oil keeps at room temperature for 3 weeks, and longer if you refrigerate it.

18

DESSERTS

BANANA AND COCONUT MILK RICE PUDDING STEAMED IN BANANA LEAVES

KHAO DTOM MAK GUAY

Whenever I knew there was a Buddhist holiday coming up the only thing I'd be able to think about was *khao dtom mak guay*. The delicious banana-leaf packets were always the thing Moms would make to offer the monks; I always made sure she made extra to offer my brother and me, a week's supply. All we had to do was pop them in the microwave whenever we wanted a snack. Look for frozen pandan leaves at Asian markets. It's important to soak the rice a minimum of 12 hours—a quick-soak cheat is not an option for good results, so plan accordingly. Since this recipe is a bit of a production, I suggest tripling it, especially because these make great gifts for friends and family. There's a history of offering behind each one.

MAKES 5 TO 6 DOUBLE PACKETS

15 banana leaves, cut into 8-inch squares

2½ cups (540 grams) unsweetened coconut cream

1 cup (200 grams) granulated sugar

2 teaspoons (8 grams) kosher salt

1 frozen pandan leaf, tied in a knot

2 cups (445 grams) raw sticky rice, soaked for 12 to 24 hours in cold water, drained well

4 Thai bananas, peeled, cut in quarters lengthwise

1. Cut the banana leaves into fifteen 8-inch squares with rounded sides (the top and bottom edges should be straight; the right and left sides should curve). Set aside.

2. In a shallow saucepan, combine the coconut cream, sugar, salt, and pandan leaf. Warm over medium heat for 10 minutes to infuse the pandan in the cream (keep the cream just below a boil—it scorches easily). Add the sticky rice and raise the heat to medium high, stirring continuously with a wooden spoon as if making risotto, 10 to 15 minutes, until the rice is fully cooked (be careful not to let the rice scorch). Transfer to a plate and cool, uncovered, at room temperature.

3. Arrange a banana leaf on your work surface with the rounded corners at the top and bottom. Place ¼ cup of the pudding in the center in the shape of an elongated rectangle, like a whole banana. Next place a quartered banana on top of the pudding with the cut side down. Fold the left side of the banana leaf toward the center to cover the banana and the pudding; repeat with the right side. Fold down the top edge, then up the bottom edge to create a parcel. Flip the parcel fold-side down to keep it closed and transfer to a platter. Repeat with the remaining banana leaf squares.

4. Add about 2 inches of water to a wok or other pan large enough to hold a metal or bamboo steamer. Set the steamer insert in place and bring the water to a boil over medium-high heat.

5. Place two banana-leaf parcels together, folded sides touching. Tie them together with a piece of butcher's twine wrapped around both parcels; repeat with a second piece of twine. Continue until all the parcels are paired into bundles. Place the bundles in the steamer, cover, and steam over medium-high heat for 30 minutes. Carefully remove the cooked bundles and cool, uncovered, at room temperature. Serve warm or at room temperature. You can also cool the bundles, put them in a zipper-top bag, and store them in the fridge up to 3 days. Resteam before serving.

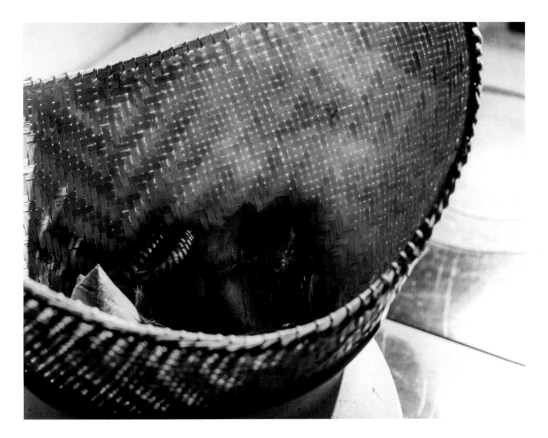

LOTUS BLOSSOM SUNDAE WITH BANANAS AND COCONUT ICE CREAM KANOM DOK BUA KLUP

We serve this dessert at Hawker Fare. I resisted putting fried bananas with ice cream on the menu since it's a Thai restaurant cliché. This sundae's a compromise, a rearrangement of familiar elements, same same but different. The cookies are a traditional delicacy made for Buddhist holidays and other ceremonies. To make them you'll need a brass lotus-pattern cookie mold (it looks like a brass stamp). Dip the mold in deep-fry oil to coat it, then dip it in the batter—the hot metal sears the batter and makes it adhere. Return to the hot oil to finish frying. When done, the cookie blossom releases from the mold. It's a fun process once you get into it.

MAKES 1 SUNDAE

3 tablespoons Palm Sugar Caramel (recipe follows)

1 Thai banana, sliced into coins

1 large scoop coconut ice cream or gelato

1 Sesame Lotus Blossom Cookie (recipe follows on page 316)

Warm the caramel in a small saucepan over medium heat. Add the banana slices and stir to coat; remove from heat. Place the banana caramel sauce in an individual serving bowl. Top with the scoop of ice cream or gelato. Set the cookie on top of the ice cream like a cap. Don't share.

PALM SUGAR CARAMEL

MAKES 1½ CUPS

½ cup (100 grams) granulated sugar

½ cup (120 grams) unsweetened coconut cream

1 teaspoon (4 grams) kosher salt

½ cup (120 grams) palm sugar

Place the granulated sugar in a small, heavy-bottomed saucepan and set over medium-high heat. Cook until the sugar melts and becomes a dark amber caramel. When it reaches the right color, slowly and carefully add the coconut cream to stop the sugar from browning further; give it a whisk off the heat. Once it stops boiling, add the salt and the palm sugar and cook on low heat until the palm sugar has dissolved. Remove from the heat and set aside to cool. Store the extra caramel in a sealed jar in the refrigerator.

SESAME LOTUS BLOSSOM COOKIES

MAKES 10 COOKIES

4 quarts (3,280 grams) canola oil, for frying

1 cup (135 grams) all-purpose flour

½ cup (100 grams) granulated sugar

¼ teaspoon (1 gram) kosher salt

1 tablespoon (13 grams) black sesame seeds

1 large egg (50 grams)

1¼ cups (325 grams) unsweetened coconut milk

1. Add enough oil to come halfway up the sides of a large, heavy saucepan or Dutch oven. Set the pan over medium-high heat and bring the oil to 350°F, raising or lowering the heat as needed to maintain a steady temperature.

2. Combine the flour, sugar, salt, and sesame seeds in a large mixing bowl and whisk to mix. Add the egg and coconut milk and mix thoroughly. Pass the cookie batter through a fine-mesh strainer into a small bowl. Line a baking sheet with paper towels. Take a small rice bowl no larger than 3 inches in diameter and place it, upside down, on the baking sheet (you'll need this to shape the hot cookies into cup-shaped blossoms). Place the brass lotus cookie mold in the oil for at least 30 seconds to get it hot. Carefully lift the mold out of the deep fryer and allow the excess oil to drip off. Slowly dip the mold into the batter, making sure not to have any of it touch the top of the face (if it touches, it'll be impossible to release the cookie). Let the mold sit in the batter for 5 seconds, lift, and let the excess batter drip back into the bowl. Carefully lower the mold into the oil, making sure all the batter is submerged. Move the mold in an up-and-down motion in the oil to start to shake the cookie free. Fry about 15 seconds on the first side, then flip with a slotted spoon and fry the second side for 10 seconds. Flip the cookie once more, then lift it out of the oil and let it drain a second or two. Immediately transfer the cookie to the inverted bowl and let it cool—it will harden in the shape of a lotus blossom. Once it's cool, remove the cookie. Repeat until all the batter is used. The cookies will keep for 3 days, stored airtight at room temperature.

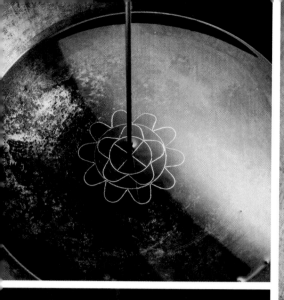

COCONUT AND SESAME FRIED BANANAS, YAMS, AND TARO ROOT WITH HONEY

This was the only dish I considered legit on the menu at Wat Phou and Manyda, my mother's two restaurants, since it was the only one unaltered to suit the mostly white customers' tastes. It was perfect the way it was: deep-fried Thai bananas, yams, and taro in a light, sesame-and-coconut-flavored batter. If you can't find Thai bananas, use regular ones, though the texture will be much different. Thai bananas have more starch—even ripe, their skins dark and speckled, they retain a firm, custardy texture. This dessert is best warm, when everything is crispy and the sweet, pleasant aromas of sesame seeds and coconut are still fresh. If you're pressed for time, feel free to fry only one or two of the elements, but a mix of all three is traditional.

SERVES 4 TO 6

- 2 quarts (1,040 grams) canola oil
- ¾ cup (105 grams) all-purpose flour
- ½ cup (60 grams) jasmine rice flour
- ¼ cup (50 grams) granulated sugar

- ½ teaspoon (5 grams) baking powder
- ½ teaspoon (2 grams) kosher salt
- 2 tablespoons (20 grams) white sesame seeds, untoasted

- 1 cup (100 grams) dried shredded coconut
- 1 cup (237 grams) water
- 3 ripe Thai bananas (170 grams)
- 4 ounces (113 grams) garnet yams, peeled and cut into ½-inch bâtons

- 4 ounces (113 grams) taro root, peeled and cut in matchsticks
- ¼ cup (65 grams) honey, for drizzling
- Coconut ice cream, for serving

1. Add the oil to a large, heavy saucepan or Dutch oven. Set the pan over medium-high heat and bring the oil to 350°F, regulating the heat as necessary to maintain a steady temperature. Line three plates with paper towels and set aside.

2. Into a medium mixing bowl, sift both flours, the sugar, baking powder, and salt. Stir in the sesame seeds and dried coconut. Using a whisk, mix the water into the flour to form a batter.

3. Peel and slice the bananas lengthwise. Dip the slices into the batter so they're completely submerged. Using chopsticks or your fingers, lift the bananas out of the batter, one by one, and carefully lower into the hot oil; fry for 2 to 3 minutes, carefully flipping the pieces and moving them around so they brown evenly. When they're a rich golden brown, remove from the oil and transfer them to a paper towel–lined plate. Set aside while you fry the other elements. Repeat this process to fry the yam bâtons, removing them from the oil to drain on a separate paper towel–lined plate.

4. Place all the sliced taro root in the batter. Using chopsticks or a fork, lift some of the taro slices out of the batter and carefully drop each portion in the hot oil to fry, in the shape of small free-form fritters. Move the taro fritters around as they fry; carefully flip to allow them to fry evenly. When the fritters are a rich golden brown, transfer them to a third paper towel–lined plate to drain.

5. Transfer the fried bananas, yams, and taro fritters to a serving platter while still warm. Drizzle with the honey and serve with coconut ice cream.

COCONUT MILK AND TAPIOCA SOUP WITH MELON AND CRUSHED ICE

On those rare scorching days in Oakland, my mother would make this refreshing, comforting dessert soup. Tapioca pearls are smaller than boba balls. They make this dish nicely sticky and viscous, while fat from the coconut milk helps keep each pearl separate. There are many variations of this dessert—Moms would freestyle it and add corn kernels or mung beans and diced taro root or gingko nuts. Saltiness is common in Lao and Thai desserts. It makes you salivate, tames the sugar, and makes sweets taste richer. The tapioca itself (without the melon balls) can be served warm. You can also serve it cold without the ice. Cook according to the recipe (you'll probably want to reduce the sugar a bit), cool to room temperature, then chill in the fridge. It's best with crushed ice, though: I love the dilution that happens as it melts, turning a dessert soup into a tasty beverage.

SERVES 8 TO 10

2½ cups (594 grams) water

½ cup (90 grams) uncooked small white tapioca pearls

1½ cups (250 grams) granulated sugar

2½ cups (650 grams) unsweetened coconut milk

1 tablespoon (11 grams) kosher salt

GARNISHES

24 to 30 medium-size cantaloupe balls, chilled

Crushed ice

1. Bring the water to a hard boil in a medium saucepan over high heat. Add the tapioca pearls and stir immediately to prevent clumping. Reduce the heat to maintain a slight simmer. Partially cover the pan and cook for 5 minutes. (Careful: Tapioca scorches easily.) Stir, then simmer 5 to 7 minutes more. The tapioca pearls should start to look translucent and the liquid should have a thick, gravy-like consistency. The pearls won't turn entirely crystal clear—some will remain opaque in the center even when cooked. Taste the pearls: They should have a soft yet chewy texture and no grittiness. Stir in the sugar, coconut milk, and salt and bring to a simmer to dissolve the sugar completely. Remove from the heat and cool to room temperature.

2. To serve, ladle the cooled tapioca into small bowls, no more than half full. Top with cantaloupe balls and crushed ice and serve immediately.

ACKNOWLEDGMENTS

Before this book was even an idea I knew it had to be a work of collaboration and support, involving many great, passionate, and talented people who, at times, believed in my story even more than I did.

John Birdsall, for his guidance and mentorship, who not only helped me write this book but also listened to me transforming my thoughts, ideas, and conversations into reality, for which I will always be grateful. Thank you for your true friendship.

Eric Wolfinger, the best photographer anyone could ever have, who understood from the get-go what needed to be accomplished in the storytelling, holding the team to the highest standard to get it done.

Kim Witherspoon, my agent at Inkwell Management, for being a true professional. Simply the best.

Anthony Bourdain: thank you, Chef, for giving a Laotian boy who grew up in Oakland a grand opportunity to be heard. Much respect and gratitude, always.

Daniel Halpern at HarperCollins Publishers, for giving us the freedom to be ourselves, and allowing us to put out a book we are truly proud of.

Roy Choi, for keeping it real from day one of our meeting in New York City and involuntarily putting me in check. Much love, brother.

David Kinch, chef and owner of Manresa, for your mentorship, showing me the highest level of cuisine and cookery I could only once dream about.

Chappy and Bix at Singha Beer, Bangkok, for treating our crew like family whenever we were in town. Let's do it again soon!

All of my managers, chefs, and team members at Commis, Hawker Fare Oakland, Hawker Fare San Francisco, and Old Kan Beer & Co. for your help holding it down at the shops so I could dedicate time to this personal project. I am especially thankful to Thomas Smith, Aaron Martinez, Keone Koki, Karen Cobb, Todd Stillman, Gray Nance, Israel Romero, Bilal Ali, Hoang Le, "A," Rebecca Nguyen, Manuel Bonilla, Christ Aivaliotis, "O" Supasit Puttikaew, Ray Hsieh, and Adam Lamoreaux.

My brothers David Syhabout, Mourad Lahlou, and Jeremy Fox for cheering me on.

Finally, Stacy Ly, my wife and my love, for her support. Without any doubts, she believed in me when I didn't.

THE LAO AND ISAN PANTRY
FRESH HERBS, BOTTLED MOTHER SAUCES, AND PURE FUNK

Shopping is a crucial part of learning any cuisine. Depending on where you live, sourcing Lao and Isan ingredients will take a little effort, although the Internet makes some things easier. Plan to spend some time at multiple Asian markets, walking down the aisles amid a matrix of herbs and sauces. Your local Whole Foods, or other fancy supermarket, should prove a handy source for common fresh ingredients such as lemongrass and turmeric.

For prepared sauces (soy, fish, oyster), brand recognition is key, since flavor profiles vary from brand to brand: some are sweeter, others saltier. The point of this glossary is to help you find the brands you'll need to cook the recipes in this book. If you remember nothing else, the crucial factor is where the product was made. If the label says Thailand or Vietnam, it's probably legit.

Fresh ingredients taste different from season to season, so taste first before adding to a dish. The perfect example is chiles. Since heat levels vary, always be cautious. Start with less, then add more until you achieve the desired kick.

BANANA LEAF

Hard to find fresh but always available in the frozen sections of Asian and some Latin markets. Wipe down the leaves with a damp cloth before use.

BEAN SPROUTS

Use mung bean sprouts for the recipes in this book. They're thinner than soybean sprouts, with yellow tops.

BEEF BILE, OR "BHEE"

Bile forms in the liver of the cow and functions as a digestive aid in the small intestines. It's a thin fluid with the consistency of water, ranging from dark green to yellowish brown in color. As a seasoning bile adds bitterness, gaminess, and complexity, and helps contain the heat of chiles in laaps, dips, and soups, such as the offal soup dtom keung nai kwuay (Beef Soup with Offal, Betel Leaves, and Bile, page 186). I have always found bile in the freezer section at Lao markets, packaged in small repurposed water bottles. (I once found it at a Mexican grocery, also in the freezer.) From animal to animal, bile has different strengths. Start with less than the recipe calls for and add more to taste.

BETEL LEAF

You can find fresh betel leaves in most Thai, Lao, and Vietnamese markets. If you don't see them in the produce aisle, ask.

BUFFALO SKIN

Honestly, even I have a hard time sourcing this stuff. Water buffalo skins are cleaned of hairs and boiled to retain a toothsome crunch totally different from pig's skin. In Laos you can buy buffalo skin fresh or dried, already sliced for your convenience. (If you're ever in Laos bring some dried skins back—be sure to bring enough for me, too.) Buffalo skin is always present in jaew bong (Lao Caramelized Aromatic Chile Dip with Cow's Skin, page 292). It shows up in laaps, soups, and the cassia leaf curry known as *gaeng kii lec*.

CHARCOAL

I like to cook over charcoal briquettes on an outdoor grill, squirted with lighter fluid to get them started. This is a personal preference—it gives off a nostalgic flavor of community backyard barbecues when I was growing up. Hardwood charcoal and straight-up hardwood are both great, of course, resulting in a different level of smokiness for grilled meats.

CHILES

The recipes in this book call for different kinds of chiles, both fresh and dried.

FRESH CHILES
ANAHEIM PEPPERS

These mild fresh green chiles are easy to find at supermarkets and in Mexican and Central American groceries.

SERRANO CHILES

These common fresh green chiles look like slender jalapeños. They combine warmth with fresh vegetal fragrance.

GRILLED SERRANO CHILES

Stem serrano chiles and thread them whole onto a bamboo skewer. Grill slowly over a medium flame until they're softened and blistered. Set aside until cool enough to handle. Peel the blistered skins.

THAI CHILES

Ripe red chiles and unripe green ones have different heat levels and aromas, so make sure you use whatever a recipe specifies (if none are specified, feel free to use a mix). If you can't find fresh red Thai chiles, look for frozen ones in Asian markets. The heat level is consistent with fresh.

DRIED CHILES
PRIK PHONG

The literal translation is "chile powder." In this book it refers to whole puya chiles toasted in a dry pan over low heat until they're dark and brittle (but not burned), tossing often to make sure they toast evenly. Cool and grind them. It's used for seasoning laaps, soups, jaews, and as a condiment for noodle dishes.

I find these Mexican chiles are the perfect substitute for *mak prik chii faa*, Thai dried chiles unavailable in the United States. Fresh, they look like red serrano chiles. The dried ones come from central Mexico. Find them in Mexican and Central American markets.

The name says it all: the dehydrated version of fresh Thai chiles. Make sure the package indicates Thailand as the place of origin.

CHINESE BROCCOLI

The Cantonese name is *gai lan*. Look for it at farmers' markets with Asian vendors, or at any Asian market. Buy the youngest, slenderest stalks you can find. If you can only get older, woodier Chinese broccoli, peel the lower ends of the stalks before cooking.

CHINESE CELERY

Like the Western variety only more fragrant, with long, slender stalks and many leaves. Available at Asian markets. You'll sometimes see it incorrectly labeled as lovage, though the two are botanically unrelated.

CHINESE PORK FLOSS

Called *moo yoong* in Thai, Chinese dried and shredded pork floss is as fine and wispy as steel wool. I use it for jaew bong (Lao Caramelized Aromatic Chile Dip with Cow's Skin, page 292). Look for the round plastic container with the label that reads Formosa Pork Fu. Choose the one with the blue label, which has a more neutral flavor.

CILANTRO

When a recipe in this book calls for chopped cilantro, it means the leaves and every inch of the stems, chopped together, nothing goes to waste. Look for extra-fragrant flowering cilantro, the plant when it starts to go to seed and develops lacy tops.

CILANTRO ROOT, A.K.A. CORIANDER ROOT

Cilantro almost always comes without the roots, but sometimes at the farmers' market you get lucky, finding bunches with the roots intact. The best way to get a regular supply is by befriending a farmer and asking a favor (growers typically discard the roots after trimming, so by offering to buy them you'll actually be doing the farmer a favor). Roots are the prize: The flavor is a little like parsnip but with the aroma of cilantro—earthy and sweet. Rinse well (you don't need to peel them). In a pinch, purchase packages of frozen cilantro roots from Thailand at markets specializing in Southeast Asian foods.

COCONUT MILK

Unsweetened is the only way to go. I recommend the Aroy-D brand from Thailand. It comes in asceptic boxes that indicate 100 percent coconut milk, no added stabilizers or emulsifiers. Read the package carefully to make sure you're buying coconut milk, not cream (one is not a substitute for the other). Aroy-D coconut milk also comes in cans, an acceptable substitute if you can't find the boxes. But boxed is superior all around. Coconut cream is thicker and richer.

DILL

Sometimes labeled dill weed, fresh dill at Asian markets tends to be from larger plants with intensified licorice flavors. Western dill will suffice. Do not substitute dried dill.

DRIED SHRIMP

Available in bulk or packaged, dried shrimp comes in different sizes. Choose medium-size shrimp, since they have the best texture. Large ones are overwhelmingly big, and the small ones tend to get lost in a dish. Whether in bulk or packaged, dried shrimp need to be picked through to remove small rocks and shells. Store in the freezer in zipper-top bags.

FISH SAUCE

Called *naam pla* in both Thai and Lao. Use only Thai brands (Vietnamese fish sauce tends to be too sweet for Lao dishes). I recommend the Tiparos brand; my second choice is Squid.

GALANGAL

A rhizome in the ginger family but definitely not a substitute for ginger (and vice versa). It has a spicy ginger aroma and flavor, but with an almost soapy finish. Dried galangal is available—use it only if you find yourself in a pinch, and only for soups, not curry pastes.

GARLIC

To roast garlic, thread whole garlic cloves onto a bamboo skewer. Grill slowly over a medium flame until they're fragrant, tender, and browned (it's okay to end up with a bit of char, but avoid burning them).

GREEN PAPAYA

Unripe papaya. When shopping, pick the firmest ones you can find, the firmer the better.

HOLY BASIL

Also called hot basil. It has woodier stems and the leaves are smaller and thin and a bit crinkled. The flavor has a hint of licorice with a subtle green chili spice.

JASMINE RICE

Use only jasmine rice from Thailand. I recommend Three Ladies brand. If it has a tag that says "new crop," buy it. New crop rice is from the harvest of the current year. It'll be more aromatic and require slightly less water for cooking.

LEMON BASIL

The leaves look like Thai basil but the stems and stalks are green, not purple. It smells like lemon verbena, with a hint of licorice in the taste. Lime basil is a worthy substitute.

LEMONGRASS

Extremely common in Lao and Thai cooking, fresh lemongrass stalks are easy to find these days at all Asian markets, Whole Foods and other grocery stores, and even farmers' markets. Look for firm, lively stalks that don't appear dried out. Examine the tops and bottoms and give it a whiff—fresh lemongrass has fragrance. In the kitchen, peel back any dried layers to get to the more fragrant layers in the middle. Slice from the root end and work your way to the top.

LIMES (ALSO SEE MAKRUT LIMES)

When a recipe in this book calls for lime juice, it means freshly squeezed. Limes with thinner skins contain more juice.

LONG BEANS

Also known as snake beans and yard-long beans. Sometimes Asian markets offer two types. Choose the thinner ones with darker skins. They have a better texture, a sweeter taste, and contain less starch than the fatter, pale-green ones.

MAKRUT LIMES (SEE ALSO LIMES)

Highly fragrant citrus native to Southeast Asia. A little goes a long way. Like the leaves, whole makrut limes freeze well, sealed in small zipper-top freezer bags. You can also buy frozen makrut limes.

MAKRUT LIME LEAVES

Fresh is best. Use frozen if you have to but never, ever use the dried leaves. Makrut lime leaves flavor soups, stews, and infusions for curries. They're pounded into curry pastes, sliced for some salads, and sometimes fried for garnishing. It's a good idea to buy a large amount of leaves in citrus season, store in zipper-top bags, and freeze. No need to thaw before using.

MSG

Monosodium glutamate, a white granular powder that works as a flavor enhancer. MSG is produced by the fermentation of starch and sugar beets, sugarcane, or molasses. In the food industry it's a taste enhancer with a level of umami that intensifies the meaty, savory flavors of food, just as naturally occurring glutamate does in stews and meat-based soups. For more on MSG, see page 66.

OYSTER SAUCE

Use only Thai brands, either Maekrua or Dragonfly. Avoid Chinese brands, which tend to be higher in salinity.

PADAEK OR PLA RAA

Fermented fish sauce, sometimes labeled pickled or salted gourami fish (gourami is a freshwater species from Southeast Asia). It's better to make your own padaek (read how on page 280), but the Pantainorasingh brand from Thailand is a decent substitute. Make sure the fish is whole or in fillets (avoid the creamy style). The Vietnamese fermented fish sauce called Mam Nem is another fine substitute and usually easier to find. I highly recommend the Super brand, which is consistently very good.

PALM SUGAR

For recipes in the book, use the one from Thailand marked 100 percent palm sugar. It comes as a disk, usually packaged in 1-pound bags at most Asian markets. The disks vary in size. I prefer smaller ones—they're easier to portion, and they dissolve faster. If only large disks are available, shave the block of sugar with a serrated bread knife and some elbow grease.

PANDAN LEAF

Sometimes called pandanus, these are the fresh, fragrant leaves of the screw pine plant. Pandan smells like fresh-cut green grass with hints of coconut and jasmine rice. Your best bet in the United States is to buy them frozen.

PEPPER WOOD, A.K.A. SAKAHN

A woody vine with a spicy aroma and a lingering tingly aftertaste that is used in northern Lao food. Like Sichuan peppercorns, pepper wood is slightly numbing to the tongue, though it lacks the citrus notes of the former. Pepper wood enhances the flavor of aw lam, the meaty stews of Luang Prabang. It's specifically available at Lao markets, though some Lao-owned Thai groceries might stock it. Pepper wood doesn't come in fancy packaging; look for unmarked zipper-top bags. The dried wood comes in many forms. The ones I see most often in the Bay Area are about 2 inches long and about ½ inch in diameter, split lengthwise. Because pepper wood is so dry you need to add it to the stock immediately when making aw lam to extract the maximum amount of flavor. If you cannot find pepper wood just omit it. (I've experimented using very tiny amounts of mixed black and Sichuan peppercorns as a substitute. The results were okay, but omitting it entirely is probably best.)

PORK BLOOD

When a recipe in this book calls for blood, it means raw pork blood. Blood comes in two forms, both required for specific recipes: liquid and cake. The butcher counters at Asian markets sell both kinds. Liquid blood comes in square, red, 3-quart-size buckets. Some markets sell blood cake in rectangular or square chunks already poached, but it's easy to cook it yourself. Cut the raw blood into squares about 2 inches by 2 inches, about 1 inch thick. Drop the squares in a saucepan of unsalted cold water, bring to a boil, and simmer for 15 minutes. Drain and rinse the cubes under cold water, and transfer to a bowl of ice water for about 20 minutes to make sure they cool all the way through.

RAU RAM

A fresh herb also known as Vietnamese cilantro, commonly used in laaps and as an accompaniment for the noodle soups called *khao poon*. The taste of the long, slender, pointed-arrow leaves has grassiness and a slight "egginess." (Unless very tender, the stems aren't edible.) Find rau ram at markets with Southeast Asian produce.

SALT

Use kosher salt for all of the recipes in this book that don't specifically call for iodized table salt.

SAW-TOOTH HERB

Also known as saw-leaf herb and, in Central American markets, culantro, this member of the coriander family has narrow leaves with serrated edges resembling saw blades. It's as fragrant as its cousin cilantro, but stronger and slightly more bitter. Common in Vietnamese cuisine.

SEASONING SAUCE

Seasoning sauce is a type of wheat-free soy, so it's gluten free (don't confuse it with Japanese tamari, also brewed without wheat; the two taste very different). Golden Mountain is the brand to buy. At first glance it looks like regular soy, but look for the words "seasoning sauce" on the label.

SHALLOTS

Small Asian shallots have better flavor and aroma, although Western shallots will do just fine for any of the recipes in this book. Thai shallots are small and bulbous—look for them at any Asian market.

ROASTED SHALLOTS

Place unpeeled shallots on a medium-hot grill. Cook slowly until the flesh is soft (check by giving each shallot a firm squeeze). When the shallots are done, set them aside to steam in their skins and cool. When they're cool enough to handle, slip off the skins.

SHRIMP PASTE

Twin Chicken and Pantainorasingh from Thailand are my go-to brands. Both are dark, very pungent semidry pastes packaged in plastic jars dry-covered with a wax layer to prevent drying out. Any good Asian market should carry at least one of these brands.

SOY SAUCE

BLACK SOY SAUCE

Molasses-like in color and very savory. Buy either Happy Boy brand (orange label) or Khong Hung Seng brand (brown cap), which I usually call dragonfly brand, after the one on the label.

SWEET SOY SAUCE

The sweetest of the soy sauces, high in sugar and thick like molasses. I recommend either Happy Boy brand (red label) or Kwong Hung Seng brand (blue cap—look for the dragonfly on the label).

THIN SOY SAUCE

Soy sauce with the lightest viscosity, high in salt content without the deep soy sauce flavor. I recommend either Happy Boy brand (yellow label) or Kwong Hung Seng brand (white cap), which has a dragonfly on the label.

STICKY RICE

Also called glutinous rice (although it's gluten free) and sweet rice. Only buy sticky rice from Thailand. I've found the Three Ladies brand to be the best and most consistent sticky rice available here.

TAMARIND PASTE

Comes in blocks of 14 or 16 ounces at Asian markets. Look for paste from Vietnam or Thailand with the seeds removed. It saves time and trouble.

THAI BASIL

An herb with a rich licorice fragrance. Look for Thai basil with purple stems and flower buds.

TOASTED RICE POWDER

Avoid purchasing the already toasted and ground stuff. It's easy to make your own and it tastes so much better—follow the instructions on page 281.

TOMATOES

When a recipe in this book calls for tomatoes (as opposed to cherry tomatoes), it means what packers call 5-by-6's, a grading that indicates a medium-small size. Don't be tempted to use soft, fully ripe tomatoes for the recipes in this book. Lao and Isan cooking calls for firm, underripe tomatoes, with less sweetness and juice than vine-ripened ones, more vegetable than fruit.

TURMERIC

Use dried turmeric powder. Do not substitute with fresh turmeric in the recipes.

WILD GINGER

Called *krachai*, it's available frozen from Southeast Asian markets. Don't waste your money on canned or jarred versions.

WOOD EAR MUSHROOMS

If you can't find fresh wood ear mushrooms use dried, soaked in warm water for at least 2 hours.

YANANG LEAF

The edible leaf of a flowering plant (*Tiliacora triandra*), yanang leaf is native to Southeast Asia, mostly in Isan and Laos. The taste is very green and deeply vegetal with an earthy nose, not unlike cooked black kale. I've never seen fresh yanang leaves for sale in U.S. markets. A puree called yanang water or extract is available canned or frozen in pouches, but I highly recommend buying frozen whole leaves from an Asian market and making your own puree (see Yanang Leaf Water, page 300).

YELLOW BEAN SAUCE

Yellow soybeans fermented using salt, available as a smooth puree or a chunky sauce with whole beans present. I prefer the one with whole beans—they provide a surprise savory saline bite. As for brands, buy either Happy Boy or Kwong Hung Seng (look for the dragonfly on the label).

CONVERSION SCALE

Weight, Mass: 1 ounce = 28 grams

Chiles, dried puya, whole: 1 cup = 45 grams

Cilantro, chopped: ¼ cup = 12 grams

Coconut Milk: ½ cup = 130 grams

Dried Shrimp: ½ cup = 45 grams

Fermented Yellow Beans: 1 cup = 233 grams; ½ cup = 117 grams

Fish Sauce: ½ cup = 96 grams; 1 tablespoon = 12 grams

Galangal, ¼-inch slice: 1 = 3 grams

Garlic, chopped: ⅛ cup = 40 grams

Garlic, finely minced: 1 tablespoon = 10 grams

Garlic, whole peeled: ⅛ cup = 25 grams; 1 tablespoon = 8 grams

Ginger, peeled and sliced: ¼ cup = 50 grams; 1 tablespoon = 13 grams

Ground Dried Chile: 1 tablespoon = 5 grams

Jasmine Rice Flour: 1 cup = 100 grams

Lemon Juice: 1 tablespoon = 15 grams; 1 cup = 240 grams; ½ cup = 120 grams

Lemongrass, bias cut: ½ cup = 40 grams

Lemongrass, thinly sliced: 1 cup = 120 grams

Lime Juice: 1 tablespoon = 15 grams; 1 cup = 240 grams; ½ cup = 120 grams

Makrut Lime Leaves, whole: 3 = 2 grams

Mint: ¼ cup = 8 grams

MSG: ¼ cup = 45 grams; 1 tablespoon = 11 grams; 1 teaspoon = 4 grams

Oil: 1 quart = 820 grams; 2 quarts = 1,640 grams; 1 cup = 205 grams; 1 tablespoon = 9 grams

Oyster Sauce: ¼ cup = 60 grams

Padaek: 1 tablespoon = 15 grams

Paddy Leaf Herb, chopped: ¼ cup = 8 grams

Peanuts: 1 cup = 224 grams; ¼ cup = 56 grams

Red Curry Paste: ½ cup = 140 grams

Salt, iodized: ¼ cup = 60 grams; 1 tablespoon = 15 grams; 1 teaspoon = 5 grams

Salt, kosher: ¼ cup = 45 grams; 1 teaspoon = 4 grams;

Salt, sea: ¼ cup = 40 grams; 1 tablespoon = 10 grams; 1 teaspoon = 3 grams

Saw-Tooth Herb: ⅛ cup = 6 grams

Scallions, sliced: ¼ cup = 12 grams

Seasoning Sauce: ¼ cup = 47 grams

Sesame Seeds: ⅛ cup = 20 grams; 1 tablespoon = 10 grams

Shallots, grilled and peeled: 1 cup = 180 grams

Shallots, thinly sliced: 1 cup = 160 grams

Shallots, whole: 1 cup = 90 grams

Shrimp Paste: ½ cup = 140 grams

Soy Sauce, sweet dark: ½ cup = 135 grams

Soy Sauce, thin: ½ cup = 130 grams

Sticky Rice, raw: 1 cup = 288 grams; ½ cup = 144 grams; 1 tablespoon = 18 grams

Sugar, brown: ½ cup = 105 grams; 1 tablespoon = 12 grams

Sugar, white granulated: ½ cup = 100 grams; 1 tablespoon = 12 grams

Tamarind Water: ½ cup = 125 grams

Thai Chiles, fresh: 1 = 1½ grams; 1 cup = 120 grams; ½ cup = 60 grams; ¼ cup = 30 grams; ⅛ cup = 15 grams

Toasted Rice Powder: 1 tablespoon = 10 grams

Water: 1 quart = 946 grams; 1 cup = 237 grams

INDEX

Note: Page references in *italics* indicate photographs.

A

Acacia-Leaf Omelet with Fried
    Eggplant and Mackerel,
    Grilled Shrimp Paste Dip,
    122, 123–24
Aw lam, 90

B

Bacon, Da's Blistered Green
    Beans with, 118–19
Bamboo (Shoots)
    Braised Shredded, Salad
        with Sesame Seeds, *204*,
        205
    Steamed, Casserole with
        Pork Belly and Coconut
        Milk Cooked in Banana
        Leaf, 259–60, *261*
    Stewed in Yanang Leaf
        Water with Fermented
        Fish Sauce, 262–63, *263*
Banana Blossom, Shaved,
    and Aromatics, Steamed
    Chicken Casserole with,
    268, 269–70
Banana leaves, about, 328
Banana(s)
    and Coconut Ice Cream,
        Lotus Blossom Sundae
        with, *314*, 315–16

and Coconut Milk Rice
    Pudding Steamed in
    Banana Leaves, *310*,
    311–13
Yams, and Taro Root,
    Coconut and Sesame
    Fried, with Honey, 318–19,
    319
Bean(s)
    Green, Blistered, with
        Bacon, 118–19
    long, about, 332
    Long, Muddled, Salad, *150*,
        151
Bean sprouts, for recipes, 328
Beef
    Bile, Charred Chile Dip with,
        284
    bile ("bhee"), about, 328
    Brisket, Chewy Flavorful
        Grilled, 232, *233*
    Fried Lemongrass-
        Marinated Beefsteak, 128,
        129
    Jerky, Sesame, A.K.A.
        "Heavenly Beef," *130*, 131
    Lao Beef Noodle Soup,
        A.K.A. Pho Lao, *162*,
        163–64
    Noodle Soup, Lao, A.K.A.
        Pho Lao, *162*, 163–64
    Raw, Laap, *216*, 217–18

Shank Stew, Earthy, with
    Bitter Pea Eggplants,
    Wood Ear Mushrooms,
    and Dill, 253–54, *255*
Short Ribs Satay, 236,
    237
Soup with Offal, Betel
    Leaves, and Bile, 186–87,
    187
Betel leaves, about, 329
Betelnut restaurant, 55
Bonilla, Manuel, 74
Buffalo skin, about, 329

C

Cabbage, Rice-Fermented,
    with Pig's Ear and
    Scallions, 304
Caramel, Palm Sugar, 315
Castro, Oriol, 59–60
Catfish, Steamed, in Banana
    Leaf with Dill and Lemon
    Basil, 271–72, *273*
Centeno, Joseph, 55
Charcoal, cooking over, 329
Chez Panisse, 52–53
Chicken
    Casserole, Steamed, with
        Aromatics and Shaved
        Banana Blossom, *268*,
        269–70

Chicken (continued)

-Coconut Curry Broth with Pork Blood, Rice Vermicelli in, 160–61, *161*

Fried, with Charred Chile Jam, *120*, 121

Isan BBQ, 240, *241*

Minced, Salad with Herbs and Toasted Rice Powder, 219

Poached, and Rice, *180*, 181–83

Shredded, Fried Garlic Oil, and Donuts, Fresh Rice and Tapioca Noodles with, *174*, 175–77

Shredded, Salad with Herbs, Fish Sauce, and Lime, 224, *225*

Wings, Gelatinous, Stewed with Pepper Wood, Morning Glory, and Lemon Basil, *248*, 249

Wings in Red Curry, *264*, 265

Chile(s)

adding to dishes, note about, 106

Anaheim peppers, 329

Charred, Dip with Beef Bile, 284

charred, for recipes, 106

Charred, Jam, 285, *287*

dried, types of, 329–30

fresh, types of, 329

Fried, Oil, 307

Green, Roasted, Relish, *286*, 290

Hot, Sweet, and Sour Dipping Sauce for BBQ Chicken, 295

Hot and Sour Dipping Sauce/Seafood Dipping Sauce, 296

Lao Caramelized Aromatic Chile Dip with Cow's Skin, *287*, 292

prik phong, 329

puya, 330

Red Curry Paste, 301

Serrano, 329

Serrano, grilled, 329

Serrano, Pickled, 306

and Shallot, Charred, Broth with Pork Offal, Rice Vermicelli in, 158–59, *159*

Thai, dried, 330

Thai, fresh, 329

Water Beetle Dip, *287*, 291

Chinese broccoli, about, 330

Chinese celery, about, 330

Chinese Mustard Greens, Fermented, in Rice Brine, 302, *303*

Chinese pork floss, about, 330

Cilantro, about, 330

Cilantro root (coriander), about, 330

Coconut

-Chicken Curry Broth with Pork Blood, Rice Vermicelli in, 160–61, *161*

Ice Cream and Bananas, Lotus Blossom Sundae with, *314*, 315–16

milk, for recipes, 330

Milk and Banana Rice Pudding Steamed in Banana Leaves, *310*, 311–13

Milk and Tapioca Soup with Melon and Crushed Ice, *320*, 321

Satay Peanut Sauce, 297

and Sesame Fried Bananas, Yams, and Taro Root with Honey, 318–19, *319*

Commis restaurant, 63–65, 69

Congee, Rice, with Pork Meatballs and Fried Garlic Oil, 178, *179*

Cookies, Sesame Lotus Blossom, *314*, 316

Crab, Dungeness, Salad, Lao, 201–2, *203*

Cucumber

Ajat, 298

Muddled, Salad with Rice Vermicelli and Dried Shrimp, 148, *149*

Curry

Prik Khing, Paste, 119

Red, Chicken Wings in, *264*, 265

Red, Paste, 301

Ubon Kassod-Leaf, with Water Buffalo Shank, *250*, 251–52

D

Desserts

Banana and Coconut Milk Rice Pudding Steamed in Banana Leaves, *310*, 311–13

Coconut and Sesame Fried Bananas, Yams, and Taro Root with Honey, 318–19, *319*

Coconut Milk and Tapioca Soup with Melon and Crushed Ice, *320*, 321

Lotus Blossom Sundae with Bananas and Coconut Ice Cream, *314*, 315–16

Dill, Asian, about, 331
Dips
    Caramelized Aromatic Chile, Lao, with Cow's Skin, *287*, 292
    for Tart, Unripe Fruit, 152, *153*
    Water Beetle Chile, *287*, 291
Donuts, Chinese, A.K.A. Pa Tong Go, *174*, 177
Duck Laap: Spicy, Herbaceous Minced Duck Salad, 214–15, *215*
Dumplings, Tapioca, Stuffed with Caramel-Cooked Pork, Salted Turnip, and Peanuts, *134*, 135–37

E

Eggplant
    and Mackerel, Fried, with Acacia-Leaf Omelet, Grilled Shrimp Paste Dip, *122*, 123–24
    Relish, Spicy, 294
Egg(s)
    Drop and Pork Curry Noodles, 171–72, *173*
    Dry-Fried Rice Noodles, A.K.A. Phat Lao, 165–66, *167*
    Fried, Salad, *226*, 227
    Fried Eggplant and Mackerel with Acacia-Leaf Omelet, Grilled Shrimp Paste Dip, *122*, 123–24
    hard-boiled, preparing, 258
    Poached, Mama Noodles with, 184, *185*
    for recipes, 106

and Tofu, Braised Pork Trotters and Belly in Caramel with, *256*, 257–58
El Bulli, 59–61

F

Fermented Yellow Bean Sauce
    about, 335
    recipe for, 183
Fish
    Bone, Dried and Grilled, Hot and Sour Soup, *192*, 193–94
    bones, to dry and grill, 194
    Dry-Fried, Chile Relish, *287*, 293
    Fermented, and Tamarind Condiment, 305
    Fried and Salt-Crusted Grilled Tilapia Lettuce Wrap with Padaek and Pineapple Jaew with Vermicelli Noodles, Herbs, and Garnishes, 138–43, *140–41*
    Fried Eggplant and Mackerel with Acacia-Leaf Omelet, Grilled Shrimp Paste Dip, *122*, 123–24
    "One Sunny Day Dried," 132, *133*
    Salad, Tart and Aromatic, *222*, 223
    Sauce, Fermented, 280–81
    Steamed Catfish in Banana Leaf with Dill and Lemon Basil, 271–72, *273*
Fermented Fish Sauce, 280–81
Fish sauce, about, 331

Fruit. *See also specific fruits*
    Tart, Unripe, Dip for, 152, *153*

G

Galangal, about, 331
Garlic
    charred, for recipes, 106
    deep-frying, 106
    Red Curry Paste, 301
    roasting, 331
Ginger, Pineapple, and Fish Sauce Dip, *141*, 143
Ginger, wild, about, 335
Green Papaya
    about, 331
    Salad, Lao, 147
Guinea Hen Soup, Simple Country-Style, 190, *191*

H

Hawker Fare, 67–71, 82, 87, 101–3
Herbs. *See also specific herbs*
    rinsing and draining, 106
Hill, Bruce, 55
Holy basil, about, 331

I

Ice Cream, Coconut, and Bananas, Lotus Blossom Sundae with, *314*, 315–16
Imperial Rolls, Lao, *116*, 116–17
Ingredients
    Lao and Isan, 328–35
    sourcing, 105–6
    standard and metric measurements, 106

J

Jam, Charred Chile, 285, *287*
Jerky, Sesame Beef, A.K.A.
    "Heavenly Beef," *130,*
    131

K

Kassod-Leaf Curry, Ubon, with
    Water Buffalo Shank, *250,*
    251–52
Kinch, David, 55, 56, 59

L

Laap
    description of, 207–8
    types of, 209
Lao food and culture
    communal eating, 18
    compared to Thai food, 5,
        6–7
    creating a Lao Isan meal,
        107
    description of, 5–9
    music, 79
Lemon basil, about, 331
Lemongrass, about, 331
Lime juice, for recipes, 332
Lotus Blossom Sundae with
    Bananas and Coconut Ice
    Cream, *314,* 315–16

M

Mackerel and Eggplant, Fried,
    with Acacia-Leaf Omelet,
    Grilled Shrimp Paste Dip,
    122, 123–24
Makrut lime leaves, about,
    332

Makrut limes, about, 332
Manresa restaurant, 55–59
Manyda restaurant, 53,
    64–65
Masa's restaurant, 55
Meatball(s)
    Fried Pork Laap, Lettuce
        Wraps, 210–11, *211*
    Pork, and Fried Garlic Oil,
        Rice Congee with, 178,
        179
Melon and Crushed Ice,
    Coconut Milk and Tapioca
    Soup with, *320,* 321
Mortar and pestle, working
    with, 42–43
MSG, about, 66, 332

N

Noodle(s)
    Bean Thread, Salad with
        Chile Jam, 228, *229*
    Beef Soup, Lao, A.K.A. Pho
        Lao, *162,* 163–64
    Dry-Fried Rice, A.K.A. Phat
        Lao, 165–66, *167*
    fermented rice vermicelli,
        about, 156–57
    Fresh Rice and Tapioca,
        with Shredded Chicken,
        Fried Garlic Oil, and
        Donuts, *174,* 175–77
    Lao Imperial Rolls, *116,*
        116–17
    Mama, with Poached Egg,
        184, *185*
    Muddled Cucumber Salad
        with Rice Vermicelli and
        Dried Shrimp, 148, *149*
    Pork and Egg Drop Curry,
        171–72, *173*

Rice, in Broth with Ground
    Pork Cooked in Lard, with
    Chiles, Tomatoes, and
    Stinky Yellow Beans, *168,*
    169–70
Rice Vermicelli in Charred
    Chile and Shallot Broth
    with Pork Offal, 158–59,
    159
Rice Vermicelli in Chicken-
    Coconut Curry Broth with
    Pork Blood, 160–61, *161*

O

Oils
    Fried Chile, 307
    Fried Garlic, 307
Ong, Alex, 54, 55
Oyster sauce, for recipes,
    332

P

Padaek
    about, 332
    recipe for, 280–81
    and Tamarind Jaew, *141,*
        143
Palm sugar, about, 332
Palm Sugar Caramel, 315
Pandan leaves, about, 333
Peanut(s)
    Fried Red, with Garlic,
        Lime Leaves, Chiles, and
        Iodized Salt, *112,* 113
    Sauce, Satay, 297
Pepper wood, about, 333
Pickled Serrano Chiles, 306
Pineapple, Ginger, and Fish
    Sauce Dip, *141,* 143
Pla raa, about, 332

Pork
    Bean Thread Noodle Salad
        with Chile Jam, 228, *229*
    Belly and Coconut Milk,
        Steamed Bamboo-Shoot
        Casserole with, Cooked
        in Banana Leaf, 259–60,
        261
    blood, for recipes, 333
    Caramel-Cooked, Salted
        Turnip, and Peanuts,
        Tapioca Dumplings
        Stuffed with, *134*, 135–37
    Chops, Grilled, *234*, 235
    Da's Blistered Green Beans
        with Bacon, 118–19
    and Egg Drop Curry
        Noodles, 171–72, *173*
    floss, Chinese, about, 330
    Ground, Cooked in Lard,
        with Chiles, Tomatoes,
        and Stinky Yellow Beans,
        Rice Noodles in Broth
        with, *168*, 169–70
    Jowl, Fried Fermented, *238*,
        239
    Laap Meatball, Fried,
        Lettuce Wraps, 210–11,
        211
    Lao Caramelized Aromatic
        Chile Dip with Cow's Skin,
        287, 292
    Lao Imperial Rolls, *116*,
        116–17
    Meatballs and Fried Garlic
        Oil, Rice Congee with,
        178, *179*
    Minced, Salad, Lao, *212*,
        213
    Offal, Rice Vermicelli in
        Charred Chile and Shallot
        Broth with, 158–59, *159*

    -Rib Cartilage, Hot and Sour
        Soup of, *188*, 189
    Riblets, Crispy Fried, *126*, 127
    -Rib Stew, Lao, with Pepper
        Wood, Dill, and Squash
        Vines, 266, *267*
    Rice-Fermented Cabbage
        with Pig's Ear and
        Scallions, 304
    Sausage, Sour Fermented,
        245
    Skin, Aromatic Lao Herb
        Sausage with, *242*,
        243–44
    Soured, 114, *115*
    Trotters and Belly, Braised,
        in Caramel with Tofu and
        Egg, *256*, 257–58
    Prik Khing Curry Paste, 119

R
Rau ram, about, 333
Relish
    Charred Tomato and Chile,
        with Fermented Fish, *286*,
        289
    Cucumber Ajat, 298
    Dry-Fried Fish Chile, *287*,
        293
    Eggplant, Spicy, 294
    Roasted Green Chile, *286*,
        290
Rice
    Ball, Crispy, Salad, *198*,
        199–200
    Congee with Pork Meatballs
        and Fried Garlic Oil, 178,
        179
    jasmine, about, 331
    Poached Chicken and, *180*,
        181–83

    Pudding, Banana and
        Coconut Milk, Steamed
        in Banana Leaves, *310*,
        311–13
    Sticky, 277–78, *279*
    sticky, buying, 334
    sticky, for Lao meals, 107
    Toasted, Powder, *282*, 283
    toasted, powder, about, 335

S
Salads
    Bean Thread Noodle, with
        Chile Jam, 228, *229*
    Braised Shredded Bamboo,
        with Sesame Seeds, *204*,
        205
    Crispy Rice Ball, *198*,
        199–200
    Dungeness Crab, Lao,
        201–2, *203*
    Fish, Tart and Aromatic,
        222, 223
    Fried Egg, *226*, 227
    Green Papaya, Lao, 147
    Minced Chicken, with Herbs
        and Toasted Rice Powder,
        219
    Minced Pork, Lao, *212*, 213
    Muddled Cucumber, with
        Rice Vermicelli and Dried
        Shrimp, 148, *149*
    Muddled Long Bean, *150*,
        151
    Shredded Chicken, with
        Herbs, Fish Sauce, and
        Lime, 224, *225*
    Spicy, Herbaceous Minced
        Duck: Duck Laap, 214–15,
        215
Salt, for recipes, 106, 333

Satay, Beef Short Ribs, 236, *237*

Satay Peanut Sauce, 297

Sauces

    Charred Chile Dip with Beef Bile, 284

    Fermented Yellow Bean, 183

    Hot, Sweet, and Sour Dipping, for BBQ Chicken, 295

    Hot and Sour Dipping, / Seafood Dipping Sauce, 296

    Lao BBQ Dipping, 288

    Padaek, 280–81

    Padaek and Tamarind Jaew, *141, 143*

    Pineapple, Ginger, and Fish Sauce Dip, *141, 143*

    Satay Peanut, 297

    Shrimp Paste Dip, 125

Sausage

    Aromatic Lao Herb, with Pork Skin, *242, 243–44*

    Pork, Sour Fermented, 245

Saw-tooth herb, about, 333

Scallions

    Dry-Fried Rice Noodles, A.K.A. Phat Lao, 165–66, *167*

    and Pig's Ear, Rice-Fermented Cabbage with, 304

Seasoning sauce, about, 334

Sesame (Seeds)

    Beef Jerky, A.K.A. "Heavenly Beef," *130,* 131

    Braised Shredded Bamboo Salad with, *204, 205*

    and Coconut Fried Bananas, Yams, and Taro Root with Honey, 318–19, *319*

Lotus Blossom Cookies, *314,* 316

Shallot(s)

    Asian, about, 334

    charred, for recipes, 106

    Fried, 306

    Red Curry Paste, 301

    roasted, 334

Shellfish. *See* Crab; Shrimp

Shrimp. *See also* Shrimp Paste

    Bean Thread Noodle Salad with Chile Jam, 228, *229*

    dried, about, 331

    Pounded Raw, Laap, 220–21, *221*

Shrimp Paste

    Dip, 125

    for recipes, 334

Siegal, Ron, 55

Snacks

    Crispy Fried Pork Riblets, *126,* 127

    Da's Blistered Green Beans with Bacon, 118–19

    Fried and Salt-Crusted Grilled Tilapia Lettuce Wrap with Padaek and Pineapple Jaew with Vermicelli Noodles, Herbs, and Garnishes, 138–43, *140–41*

    Fried Chicken with Charred Chile Jam, *120,* 121

    Fried Eggplant and Mackerel with Acacia-Leaf Omelet, Grilled Shrimp Paste Dip, *122,* 123–24

    Fried Lemongrass-Marinated Beefsteak, 128, *129*

Fried Red Peanuts with Garlic, Lime Leaves, Chiles, and Iodized Salt, *112,* 113

Lao Imperial Rolls, *116,* 116–17

"One Sunny Day Dried Fish," *132, 133*

Sesame Beef Jerky, A.K.A. "Heavenly Beef," *130,* 131

Shrimp Paste Dip, 125

Soured Pork, 114, *115*

Tapioca Dumplings Stuffed with Caramel-Cooked Pork, Salted Turnip, and Peanuts, *134,* 135–37

Soups

    Beef, with Offal, Betel Leaves, and Bile, 186–87, *187*

    Beef Noodle, Lao, A.K.A. Pho Lao, *162,* 163–64

    Coconut Milk and Tapioca, with Melon and Crushed Ice, *320, 321*

    Dried and Grilled Fish Bone, Hot and Sour, *192,* 193–94

    Guinea Hen, Simple Country-Style, 190, *191*

    Hot and Sour, of Pork-Rib Cartilage, *188,* 189

Soured Pork, 114, *115*

Soy sauce, types of, 334

Squash Vines, Pepper Wood, and Dill, Lao Pork-Rib Stew with, 266, *267*

Syhabout, James

    chooses culinary career, 47–49

closes Hawker Fare, 101–3
Concord, California, years, 27–33
creates Hawker Fare, 67–71
culinary school, 51–52
culinary *stages,* 52–61
European tour, 59–61
first visit to Thailand, 35–45
Oakland, California, years, 12–26
opens Commis, 63
second trip to Thailand, 73–85
third trip to Thailand, 87–99

T

Tamarind
  and Fermented Fish Condiment, 305
  and Padaek Jaew, *141,* 143
  paste, buying, 334
  Water, 299
Tapioca
  and Coconut Milk Soup with Melon and Crushed Ice, *320,* 321
  Dumplings Stuffed with Caramel-Cooked Pork, Salted Turnip, and Peanuts, *134,* 135–37

Taro Root, Bananas, and Yams, Coconut and Sesame Fried, with Honey, 318–19, *319*
Thai basil, about, 335
Thai food, compared to Lao food, 5, 6–7
Tilapia
  Dry-Fried Fish Chile Relish, *287,* 293
  "One Sunny Day Dried Fish," 132, *133*
  Whole, Fried, 139–40, *140–41*
  Whole, Grilled Salt-Crusted, 139–42, *140–41*
Tofu and Egg, Braised Pork Trotters and Belly in Caramel with, *256,* 257–58
Tomato(es)
  Charred, and Chile Relish with Fermented Fish, *286,* 289
  Chiles, and Stinky Yellow Beans, Rice Noodles in Broth with Ground Pork Cooked in Lard, with, *168,* 169–70
  Fried Egg Salad, *226,* 227
  Lao Green Papaya Salad, 147
  Muddled Long Bean Salad, *150,* 151
  for recipes, 335
Turmeric, for recipes, 335

V

Vegetables. *See also specific vegetables*
  leafy, rinsing and draining, 106

W

Water Beetle Chile Dip, *287,* 291
Water Buffalo Shank, Ubon Kassod-Leaf Curry with, *250,* 251–52
Water buffalo skin, about, 329
Wat Phou restaurant, 27–33, 53
Wild ginger, about, 335

X

Xanadu restaurant, 54–55

Y

Yams, Bananas, and Taro Root, Coconut and Sesame Fried, with Honey, 318–19, *319*
Yanang Leaf Water, 300
Yanang leaves, about, 335
Yellow bean sauce, about, 335
Yellow Bean Sauce, Fermented, 183
Yu, Justin, 70